*Vanishing Tribes*

# Vanishing Tribes

ROY PINNEY

Thomas Y. Crowell Company

ESTABLISHED 1834

NEW YORK

*Designed by Judith Woracek Barry*

MANUFACTURED IN THE UNITED STATES OF AMERICA

*L. C. Card: 68-13592*

ISBN 0-690-85943-0

3  4  5  6  7  8  9  10

*Photograph credits appear on page 266*

# *Introduction*

Since the nineteenth century, and especially during the twentieth, practically every human society on the planet has become accessible to study. Over most of the inhabited globe, customs, beliefs, and institutions have come under the scrutiny of anthropologists.

The tides of World War II swept into the most obscure corners of the earth—into the far north of America, into New Guinea, the hinterlands of Southeast Asia, and the islands of the Indonesian archipelago—thus exposing those lands where the last "savage" peoples had until then enjoyed a measure of safety in their isolation.

Today many names once charged with mystery and romance designate landing spots for long-distance jet liners. Swifter means of travel and the increasing world population have had the effect of shrinking the planet. There is no fraction of the human race, no matter how remote and retarded it may still appear, that is not directly or indirectly in contact with others; no people whose feelings, ambitions, desires, and fears do not affect the security and prosperity—indeed, the very existence—of those to whom material progress may once have given a feeling of ascendancy.

Civilized and primitive cultures are now part of the same world and before long will be part of the same civilization. For even societies with the most widely divergent patterns of thought, whose customs and mores took thousands of years to develop along isolated paths, must impregnate one another once contact is established. This occurs in many different ways: sometimes those ways are clear; more often they are not.

These problems of anthropology are no longer limited to scholars and explorers; they have become the direct and immediate concern of everyone.

Ironically, the very transformations that are spurring a growing theoretical interest in "primitives" are, in fact, hastening their extinction. This is not a new phenomenon. When Sir James Frazer, author of the monumental *Golden Bough*, inaugurated the chair of Social Anthropology at the University of Liverpool in 1908, he dramatically called the attention of governments and scholars to the problem.

More recently Dr. Claude Lévi-Strauss, noted professor of social anthropology at the Collège de France in Paris, whose findings constitute the basis of this introduction, has cited examples of the large-scale extinction of "primitive" peoples:

At the beginning of white settlement in Australia, the aborigines numbered 250,000; today no more than 40,000 are left. Official reports describe them as being herded onto reservations or clustered near mining centers, where, in place of their traditional food-gathering parties, they are reduced to sneak-scavenging in rubbish heaps outside the mining shacks. Other aborigines, who had retreated deep into the desert, have been uprooted by the installation of atomic-testing grounds and rocket-launching sites.

New Guinea, with its several million tribesmen, may well be the last sanctuary for primitive societies. But here too, despite the hostile environment, civilization is making such rapid inroads that the 600,000 inhabitants of the central mountains, unknown a mere twenty years ago, are now providing labor contingents for the building of roads. It is no rarity today to see road signs and milestones parachuted into the unexplored jungle.

With civilization have come alien diseases, such as tuberculosis, smallpox, gonorrhea, and syphilis, against which "primitives" have no natural defenses. In addition, the people are suffering from malaria, trachoma, leprosy, and the mysterious disease known as kuru. Kuru—a result of primitive man's contact with

LEANING AGAINST THE TRUNK OF A GNARLED KAPOK TREE, A BOY PLAYS HIS HARMONICA IN TOGOLAND, WEST AFRICA. THE TRIBAL COMPOUND IS IN THE BACKGROUND.

civilization, though not actually introduced by civilization—is a genetic deterioration for which no treatment is known and that inevitably ends in death.

In Brazil, one hundred tribes became extinct between 1900 and 1950. The Kaingang, from the state of São Paulo, numbered 1,200 in 1912, only 200 in 1916, and today have dwindled to 80. The Munduruku were 20,000 in 1925; in 1950 they numbered 1,200. Of the 10,000 Nambikuara in 1900, only 1,000 could be traced in 1940. The Kayapo of the River Araguaya were 2,500 in 1902 and 10 in 1950. The Timbira, who numbered 1,000 in 1900, were only 40 in 1950.

The Yahgan, Alacaluf, and Ona of Tierra del Fuego, who endured the world's worst climate for countless generations and are known to have numbered in the thousands, have almost totally disappeared. The few individuals who can still be traced are highly acculturated; they have became almost wholly detached from their native customs and traditions. Thus it becomes more and more difficult not only to study these primitive peoples, but even to define them satisfactorily.

In recent years a serious attempt has been made to revise existing thinking about protective legislation in the countries facing this problem.

Yet this is only half the picture. There are other parts of the world where tens and hundreds of millions of people live and whose numbers are increasing rapidly; for example, in Central America, the South American Andes, Southeast Asia, and Africa. These peoples are changing and their civilizations are gradually becoming Westernized.

It is the purpose of this book to examine the ingenious designs for living developed by a representative sampling of the primitive peoples throughout the world, and to present a record of their lives and achievements before they are lost forever in the mainstream of civilization.

# CONTENTS

# PHOTOGRAPHS

# Man and Culture

The mammoth, the sabre-tooth tiger, the passenger pigeon, and the whooping crane all share the fate of losers in the contest of evolution. Life is not a thing to be taken for granted: the life or death of a species depends on a delicate balance struck among a multitude of factors. A change in climate, a change in the food supply, the presence or absence of predators—not to mention the unpredictable interference of man—can quickly doom a thriving species.

Man represents what he likes to think is the ultimate in evolution. His specialization in the animal kingdom lies in not being specialized. In the Greek myth of creation, the shortsighted Epimetheus (literally, Afterthinker) distributed the gifts of animal nature with a prodigal hand; as a result, by the time he got to man his store was exhausted. But his wiser brother, Prometheus (Forethinker) took pity on the puny, hairless creature, and dared the wrath of Zeus to secure for man a unique gift: fire. Prometheus taught man to use fire, as well as his hands and mind.

Although the conception of man's place in evolution is ancient, the scientific theories of the process of evolution are not. To compensate for his physical mediocrity man had to use his intelligence. The resulting lack of reliance on specialized natural equipment

1

made it possible for him to adapt to great changes in his environment. However, culture, the special creation of man, has subjected him to another danger: the loss of the contest of cultural evolution, the loss of group identity.

Few groups of men have ever actually become physically extinct. The loss of culture, then, whether voluntary or involuntary, is the central problem of the vanishing tribes of the world.

What is "culture"? Anthropologists have devoted a great deal of serious study merely to secure good working definitions of this word. The first truly "anthropological" definition of culture was given in 1871 by Sir Edward Burnett Tylor, one of the founding fathers of the science, and though it has been greatly elaborated since then, Tylor's basic definition is still widely quoted and admired.

"Culture or Civilization," wrote Sir Edward Tylor in *Primitive Culture*, "taken in its wide ethnographic sense, is that complex whole which includes knowledge, belief, art, morals, law, custom, and any other capabilities and habits acquired by man as a member of society." It is this "wide ethnographic sense" of the word "culture" that will be intended in this book. In this sense, all men have culture; and they can be neither more "highly cultured" nor more "uncultured" than their fellows. These two terms generally refer in common usage to judgments of esthetic sensibilities made among members of one society.

Culture may be generally characterized as a set of ideas, including among other things law codes, attitudes toward one's parents, forms of gambling, designs of plows, songs and dances, sculpture, and quaint customs. A culture, then, ·is the system of ways of living typical of a group of people, which they transmit socially, rather than genetically, to their offspring. A society is a group of people who share a culture, and who live together in close and prolonged association.

What is "primitive culture"? As anthropology has gained in sophistication during the past century it has outgrown a series of terms regarding the development of culture. It was first thought, in the years of controversy that followed the publication of Darwin's *Origin of Species* and *The Descent of Man*, that just as some animals could be said to be higher or lower than others on the evolutionary scale, so could cultures (and races as well) be arranged hierarchically. Words such as "heathens," "barbarians," "savages," "primitives," were used innocently to describe non-Western and nonliterate cultures. Stages were set up, through which most cultures supposedly passed in their evolution. Living societies were identified with the various stages in the progression. Thus it was believed that the lower of the living peoples or "races" were, in the most important features of culture, virtually identical with the ancestors of civilized man.

Anthropology seemed a wonderful game, an adventure into the exotic and the mysterious in which one could recapture the childhood of the human race. But as the study of man left the armchair and moved out into the field, these naïve applications of evolutionary theory to culture fell away.

After a century of theorizing and field work, it is evident to us where the early writers went wrong—writers such as Lewis Henry Morgan, who postulated an orderly progression of culture in stages from "savagery" to "civilization"; Johann Bachofen, who traced the history of culture back to universal matriarchy; and Henry Maine, who saw the foundations of civilization in universal patriarchy. Their major error lay in their ethnocentrism: their failure to recognize the values of one's own culture for what they really are—arbitrary judgments and distinctions.

A language may seem simple if it does not recognize the grammatical distinctions that are made by familiar languages and are therefore thought to be absolutely indispensable. Certain types of languages may seem more simple than others. If, for example, some Australian languages have no words for numbers higher than three or four, we may call their mathematics quite primitive. On the other hand, Australian languages in general are very rich in kinship terms defining relationships that Westerners never think about. The Australian's sense for identifying many degrees of relatedness in a wide circle of kin makes most Westerners, by comparison, appear to be retarded children, pitiful creatures who can't recognize their own relatives.

In other respects, too, the languages of Australia are not simple. Anyone thinking so is invited to try learning them! Were he persistent enough, however, our student would find any one of these languages a workable vehicle for his thoughts. It may be said that languages differ not in what can or cannot be said with them, but in the relative ease with which particular concepts may be expressed through them.

3

The outstanding mistake of the ethnocentric outlook was—and still is—the tendency to take technological poverty as an indication of general cultural poverty, a notion that in turn prevents one from perceiving that primitive societies may be quite as complex as our own.

Thus it took many years for jurists to perceive law in societies lacking formal courts; for artists to see art in the primitive's "crude" distortions of nature and anatomy; for esthetes to find poetry in the vast range of oral literature of unlettered peoples; for moralists to find exotic legal and sexual practices tolerable. What these realizations have meant in anthropology is summarized by the expression, "the psychic unity of mankind." This expression ʰas undergone important changes in meaning since it first came ⁿto use in the nineteenth century, but as it is understood today, ₁t means simply that all men have the same basic potentials for developing culture, although all cultures are not necessarily equally developed.

Culture is seen as being subject to elaboration or restriction by a multitude of factors, of which two of the more important are climate and natural resources, and the least important are inherited racial characteristics. A Chinese baby born in the United States will probably not develop an Oriental way of thinking, and some English babies born in Kenya have done notably well living like the local inhabitants in the bush and speaking Kikuyu.

Culture spreads much more easily and rapidly than physical racial characteristics. If there are no "pure" races, there are surely no "pure" cultures. Any culture, particularly an advanced one, is built upon many layers of accumulated bits of culture, or traits, which are the smallest units in which culture can be analyzed. These bits of culture are of varying ages, and often of surprisingly varied origin.

The process of the movement of traits is known as diffusion, the study of which has been a prime concern of anthropology. One of the best demonstrations of the extent to which culture is an accumulation of traits from many sources was given by the late Ralph Linton, a great American anthropologist, in *The Study of Man*:

Our solid American citizen awakens in a bed built on a pattern which originated in the Near East but which was modified in Northern

4

Europe before it was transmitted to America. He throws back covers made from cotton, domesticated in India, or linen, domesticated in the Near East, or silk, the use of which was discovered in China. All of these materials have been spun and woven by processes invented in the Near East. He slips into his moccasins, invented by the Indians of the Eastern woodlands, and goes to the bathroom, whose fixtures are a mixture of European and American inventions, both of recent date. He takes off his pajamas, a garment invented in India, and washes with soap invented by the ancient Gauls. He then shaves, a masochistic rite which seems to have been derived from either Sumer or ancient Egypt.

After this adventure, Linton follows our solid American citizen as he dresses, buys a paper, has breakfast, smokes, and settles down to read the news: As he absorbs the accounts of foreign troubles he will, if he is a good, conservative citizen, thank a Hebrew deity in an Indo-European language that he is 100 percent American.

This amusing exercise serves as an excellent introduction to the idea of diffusion, which furnishes us with a useful perspective for considering vanishing cultures. Diffusion provides the means for the enrichment of culture. What we call modern or Western culture or civilization represents the intense and continuous ac-cumulation of bits and pieces of culture over a period of five or six thousand years. Many diverse peoples, from China to India to Scandinavia, have participated in and added to this cultural tradi-tion.

It is characteristic of the "vanishing" peoples that they have been isolated from centers of rapid cultural change and develop-ment, or have had only temporary and irregular contact with them. What are the reasons that these now-vanishing cultures have never nurtured a growing tradition, have never reached that degree of urban concentration we call civilization? Much of the attention of history and anthropology is devoted to this problem. The an-swer to this question is exceedingly complex; such factors as previous culture type, type of social organization, climate, and geography must be taken into account.

Any culture exists not only in the present; a culture is a tradi-tion above all. Like an iceberg, much of it is hidden from view, buried in the past. How rich it is, how complex is its technology, and how warlike or peaceful it is all depend largely on its history, on its cultural inventory of traits. People, individuals, are only as

5

civilized, as advanced, as the total structure of their cultures can make them.

Even a careful selection of, say, five hundred Europeans or Americans set down in the wilds of some undeveloped country would be set back culturally for many generations—perhaps forever. In any case, it is likely that if they ever succeeded in reaching anything like the levels of technological advancement and intellectual richness of their parent cultures, they would, in their isolation, have created an almost totally new and different culture.

Thus far in this chapter we have spoken of "vanishing peoples," "cultures," or "societies," and avoided using the word "tribe." The reason is that "tribe" is one of those popular, convenient, but often misused words that anthropologists find necessary to handle with care.

"Tribe" popularly has an exotic flavor. But why are the Navaho and the Tutsi called "tribes," and not the Irish, or the inhabitants of Brooklyn?

As it has come to be used in anthropology, a tribe is a group of individuals united by physical (geographic) ties, linguistic identity, cultural homogeneity, and some sort of over-all social organization. It may have a number of smaller groupings within it—villages; a variety of groups based on blood ties, real or imagined; marriage ties; and others. A "clan," for example, may be understood to mean a unilineal descent group: that is, a group united by real or assumed descent from a common ancestor, traced through one line, either the mother's maternal line or the father's paternal line. If descent is traced through the mother, the clan will be matrilineal; if through the father, the clan will be patrilineal.

Ideally, the members of a tribe have a clear knowledge of their distinct social identity, and are set off from neighboring tribes in speech by at least a difference in dialect; that is, they recognize regular linguistic differences between themselves and their neighbors. Often, they will have in their mythology a creation myth that sets them apart from all other men. Perhaps, like the Pueblo Indians, they will revere a particular spot, such as a hole in the ground where the tribal ancestors first came to live on Earth. In many primitive tribes the word for "man" or "people" is often the same as the name of the tribe.

The tribes described in this book show a great variety in size

6

and in degree of social integration or cohesion. Few of them have all the characteristics mentioned that serve to clearly demarcate tribal limits. But through various combinations of these characteristics, they do demonstrate a degree of cultural unity sufficient to give themselves—and the anthropologists who have studied them —the feeling that they are a limited group, apart and different from their neighbors.

The word "tribe" was developed for, and is best applicable to, societies with comparatively well-developed political systems, such as the more prominent African and American Indian tribes. Such tribes as the Ashanti and the Yoruba in Africa, the Iroquois, Cherokee, and Cheyenne in America, were important in early contacts with white men, and consequently much attention was paid to them and their political organization by colonial governments and later by anthropologists. But it was not until groups with "simpler," or smaller-scale, systems of political organization were adequately studied that it was possible to get a more general and more accurate view of how primitive societies are governed.

Although "tribe" is still a salient factor in their thinking, modern anthropologists have found it generally more useful to speak in terms of what are the functionally more important groups in almost all non-Western societies—kinship groups of various types. In order to really appreciate the ways in which primitive societies are held together and their cultures maintained, we must consider the more important types of these groups.

When primitive kinship groups were first studied, the most striking aspect was, at first, the terminology used for addressing or designating relatives. It was found that among some primitive peoples, one would call his brother's children "son" and "daughter," but would call his sister's children "nephew" and "niece." Among some peoples it was found that both the brother's and the sister's children were called "son" and "daughter." Further, societies were discovered that seemed to confuse the generations, that would, for example, call one's father's sister's daughter by the same term as one's sister's daughter.

Many hypotheses were advanced to account for these usages: some involve the operation of psychological identification; others deal with previous half-forgotten forms of marriage; still others argue the ignorance of biological paternity or a past history of sexual promiscuity.

7

The field of kinship is a rich anthropological field, but it has a tendency to turn muddy; too often the argument is not worth the effort necessary to follow it. Most of the concerns of kinship studies are far beyond the scope of this book. It is, however, necessary to define some concepts and terms that will be used later on in discussing primitive societies, and to try to whet the latent anthropological interests of the reader by raising a few provocative points.

Terminology is certainly provocative. It would seem strange to call your grandson by a certain term, and to have him call you by the same term; yet this takes place among some American Indian societies. This raises an interesting problem: How would you translate a term that meant both "grandfather," and "grandson?" The answer is you wouldn't, because it means neither. To understand this it is necessary to look not at the persons involved but at the *relationship*, at what the people involved share; and what they share in this case is a relationship through a third person, the son or daughter of one, the mother or father of the other. Similarly, if someone calls his father's brother "father," it doesn't necessarily mean that he is ignorant of who his real (biological) father is, or that he calls him "father" purely as an honor, as we call a Catholic priest "father," or as any old man may be called "father" in polite address in some cultures. "Father" is likely to be a class of relatives, men with whom one may have prescribed types of relationships—certain privileges, duties, and the like.

All of this points out the difference in function of kinship terminology and hence of kinship relations—the kinship system as a whole—in primitive cultures and in modern civilized cultures. We tend to think of our kinship system as simply a recognition of the basic facts of life: birth and marriage.

For the modern Westerner, for civilized man in general, a kinship system is little more than a set of social relationships that are accidents of his birth or the result of marriage and involve mostly ceremonial privileges and obligations. Ties of blood and, to a lesser degree, ties created by marriage entitle the civilized man to make greater demands upon the attention and hospitality of some of the people he comes to know than upon those of others.

Most of the time these duties and privileges are ceremonial. He knows he must visit Uncle Max and Aunt Samantha every so often, if only to keep peace in the family. If his is a large family, and he marries into an equally large family, the social burdens involved by custom may be exhausting, but will remain largely ceremonial. Of course, he may occasionally use blood or marriage ties for practical purposes. If his uncle is the sheriff he may have less trouble with fines for speeding. On the other hand, perhaps his wife will persuade him to give his brother-in-law a loan or take him into the business, although his shrewder instincts tell him his brother-in-law is a shiftless ne'er-do-well. Yet many people feel uneasy about having to either borrow from or lend money to relatives; and using kin ties to obtain favors from an arm of government is morally condemned as nepotism, though widely practiced, nevertheless.

Modern man is used to standing behind a mask of impersonality when dealing with money matters. If he, as a business man, has delinquent debtors he will lose little time in dunning them for payment; the less he knows them personally, the less he will hesitate. But the world of business, of modern economics, has rules that are incompatible with the rules of behavior we expect from our kinfolk. The story of the budding financier who loaned money to his grandmother at commercial rates of interest strikes us as very funny—unless it happened in our own family.

Primitive man has a different view of kinship. At first glance, studying primitive society, we see that the accidents of kinship count for much more than they do in our society. We find a young man, for example, bound by convention to work for his father, or his mother's brother, or his parent-in-law. We find that the accidents of birth prevent him from marrying certain classes of women, and induce or even compel him to choose a wife from among women of other classes.

We learn to see marriage in a primitive society as an important transaction, more of an economic union than a love match or a sexual convention. We are delighted by the hospitality of primitive man—or struck by the heavy burden of an economic system that appears to blunt individual initiative by demanding distribution of goods among a wide circle of kin. We tend to be revolted by the blood feud. The idea of a family taking revenge for murder by killing a kin of the murderer strikes us as anarchic, which of course it is.

9

Our systems of government are called civilized because they are based on multiples of the local group, a group organized into a body politic with regard only to place of residence, disregarding kin ties. It was the ancient city-state that first produced this type of government, and it is the Latin word *civitas*, city, that forms the root of the word "civilization."

The size and density of the city's population made the breakdown of kin-based politics necessary, and so formed the basis for all larger political aggregations. It is in the sense, then, that smaller, less complex groups of people—almost always, but not necessarily, kin-groups—had to come together before civilization could be achieved that we call uncivilized men "primitive."

But we must not make the mistake of taking primitive men as copies of what the forerunners of civilization were like. Eskimos, for example, depend more on the local group than on any definite kin group, and their "kinship system" is much like ours; yet their technology is quite primitive.

All societies, of course, do have some technology, however primitive, and it is usually (as in the case of the Eskimo) better adapted to the particular society's environment than machine-age technology. Having a nonscientific outlook on nature, however, the primitive attempts to supplement his technology with magic.

Magic quite often accomplishes things that would otherwise be impossible. He uses it as we might use a bulldozer, to perform tasks beyond our physical powers. He appeals to it in time of pain, as we might to heating pads, penicillin, or psychiatry. In addition, much magic is directed toward the production of effects that no technology in the world can achieve, and much magic is used in communication and interaction with supernatural forces and personalities.

To the Westerner looking at primitive society, "black" magic —witchcraft or sorcery—is no doubt the best known form of magic. This is, by definition, magic used for evil purposes, or for purposes condemned by the society at large. The principles behind the familiar voodoo doll are well-nigh universal in the black arts, and in "good," or "white," magic as well. A man's enemy fashions an effigy of him, then jabs the doll in a vital spot with a pin. Provided he accompanies this with the right incantation, the right prayer, or the right sacrifice, his victim will be mortally stricken in that area. He may also include in his effigy bits of material that have come into contact with his intended victim. Actual

MALARIA REMAINS THE MOST SERIOUS HEALTH PROBLEM IN THE WELL-WATERED CLIMATE SOUTH OF THE SAHARA. THIS VILLAGE NEAR YAOUNDE, IN CAMEROON, STANDS ON STILTS ABOVE A SWAMP—AN IDEAL BREEDING PLACE FOR MALARIAL MOSQUITOES.

castoffs of the person's body—fingernails, hair, spittle—are especially valuable and are often used to attack or to gain control over someone without making an effigy.

The two main acts involved here—jabbing an effigy and making magical use of material that has been in intimate contact with an intended victim—represent the two principal technical divisions of magic made by Frazer in *The Golden Bough*. The first is *sympathetic* magic, the bringing about of like effects by performing like actions. An example in white magic would be the ceremonial watering of the ground to bring rain, as practiced by some American Indians. The second, *contagious* magic, is based on association through contact. This is often associated with a belief in some sort of life force, or mana, a widely accepted anthropological term derived from a Polynesian word. It should be remembered that these classifications are nothing more than descriptive devices, useful for comparing techniques of magic. To associate them with the actual operation of the mind of primitive man, as some writers (including Frazer) have in the past, is to once again be guilty of ethnocentrism.

Naturally, the spectacular results some sorcerers achieve depend on the psychological state of the victim. He must be aware that his enemy is nearby, mumbling spells and concentrating on the victim's effigy. Sorcerers often take pains to make sure their victims know what is going on. It has been suggested that in some cases the actual dirty work is accomplished by hypnosis laid on a foundation of accumulated hysterical fear. Failing this, sorcerers —among the Dobu, for example—may slyly make use of real poison to achieve their immediate goal and protect their reputations as well.

Thus black magic is evil magic used for illicit, private purposes, for killing and maiming, for rendering people impotent or sterile, for destroying cattle, for making the land barren; whereas white magic combats black magic, defending against it, neutralizing it, building where black magic tears down. Because it is constructive and socially approved, white magic is much more common than black magic among primitive peoples. Black magic, for example, is almost never practiced against a member of one's own clan or other important kin group. On the other hand, the clan magician or shaman can provide protective magic only for his own clientele. That black magic serves a useful function

12

recognized by the societies which practice it, is illustrated in literature on Uganda where it was shown that the banning of black witchcraft (by the colonial administrators) led to social disintegration and violence.

An important distinction should be made here between magic and religion. For centuries "civilized" observers have been struck by the prevalence of magic in primitive societies and have often been unable to distinguish between the two. Much of the difficulty, no doubt, comes from the ethnocentric attitude already discussed. Western religions and the great religions of the East are basically otherworldly religions. They aim at a high degree of spiritual purity, are often more concerned with providing for a life beyond the grave than with material achievement. Westerners often tend to overlook the elements of magic or superstition in their own religions and can see them only in creeds foreign to them.

But the difficulty in distinguishing between magic and religion is not entirely a result of the Western observer's outlook. Religion and magic are interwoven to a much greater extent in primitive societies than in any modern society. Contrary to appearances, most religions of primitive peoples are more practical than those of modern societies. For one thing, life beyond the grave is not as a rule the great concern among primitives that it is among Christians and Moslems. For another, few primitive peoples worship an all-powerful distant God. They tend to worship a rich variety of gods limited in power; natural powers or cosmic principles; good and evil spirits; and often spirits of their own ancestors. In return for their devotion they usually reap, instead of metaphysical Christian "grace" or even the sensual paradise of Islamic afterlife, much more immediate advantages: protection from evil spirits, appeasement of good spirits, power over enemies, good crops, good hunting, rain.

The primitive often feels he must put pressure on his gods, spirits, or ancestors to get what he wants. In many cultures the supernatural world is a real part of the group's economy. The purpose of religion is usually to keep things in some sort of order, to maintain the sometimes precarious balance between man and man and between man and nature that permits life to go on. Religion in the sense of appeasement, in giving gods and spirits their due, is one way of maintaining this order. Magic techniques are another, and thus magic often becomes the right hand of religion. This sort of magic is, of course, white magic, often a priestly duty in primitive society. But in its association with religion magic is not confined to primitive society. To this day peasants, and even some city dwellers in parts of the Mediterranean area and in Latin America, will hang the statue of an unresponsive saint head down in a well, or fling him out the window in a fit of frustrated anger.

Westerners call black magic superstition—and acknowledge its power by knocking on wood, by walking around and not under a ladder, or by not hanging clothes in locker 13. Persons who are superstitious maintain that such customs are wise precautions—precisely the attitude of most primitives toward magic. Primitives who practice magic believe in it. In modern civilization, magic is no longer understood. Sawing a woman in two is not magic, but only a clever bit of trickery that no one, least of all the magician, believes in. A magician knowingly creates an illusion for his audience; but the primitive practitioner rarely means to deceive. Magic is an active part of the faith that gives meaning to his way of life.

If a religion is to be effective within a society, it must meet the needs of its people. These needs may be primarily spiritual, but the spiritual needs relate to the social, economic, and political well-being of the community. Therefore it is not surprising that within the last three hundred years, and especially within the last century, there have been many religious changes and upheavals among primitive societies around the world.

It is not simply because they have been reached by missionaries of the Christian faith and other great religions of the world that primitive peoples have changed their faith. Actually, few of the natives who have been converted to Christianity have completely espoused the new faith. Missionaries have been forced to realize that this is an impossibility because of a fundamental difference between Western civilization and most primitive societies: religion in primitive society has a much more pervasive impact on the culture than it does in the West. Life crises, economic activities, art, and in fact almost any aspect of a culture may have religious dimension, appropriate rituals, incantations, prohibitions. Removing or attempting to drastically change the nature of a primitive religion, if successful, may be likened to removing the string from the beads of a necklace; the necklace no longer exists as such. On the other hand, the old primitive

14

beliefs are not entirely acceptable either, because of the changes in attitudes and customs of the people through acculturation.

This state of change would in itself be enough to make one expect that many new religions, blends of new and old, would arise among the now-vanishing primitive peoples of the world. But the rise of new religious faiths has in many areas come about from even deeper needs in these primitive societies. The period of change for the majority of these people has been painful, confusing, and frequently disastrous because of the oppressive and overbearing policies of the civilizations, usually European, that have discovered them. These aboriginal peoples have had their lands taken away. Worse, they have been compelled, often by force, to abandon their old customs and means of livelihood.

New religious cults have arisen for the purpose of emancipating the natives from the oppression of their new rulers. Sometimes, as in Africa and Polynesia, these cults have had a militant and primarily political effect. Sometimes they preach a doctrine of acceptance—for example, the Peyote cult of North America—or advocate a doctrine of future deliverance—as the Cargo cult of Melanesia.

The desire for emancipation and an end to colonialism occurs even among societies that are not in any way primitive. For example, in Vietnam today there are two religions that started in the twentieth century largely as a protest against French colonialism. One of these, the Cao Dai sect, which made its first appearance in 1919, combines elements of Buddhism, Taoism, and Christianity. It is based on a spiritualistic concept of God, called Cao Dai, that is the newest sign of God's remittance of man's sins. Since previously God had remitted man's sins in the West by sending Moses and Jesus, and in the East by sending Buddha Sakyamuni and Lao-tse, this new manifestation becomes the "Third Pardon." The structure of the church is based largely on that of the Roman Catholic Church. It became a powerful force in Vietnam, with two million members. In its early years it was persecuted by the French; ultimately many of the members of one of its schisms turned to Communism.

The other religion, Noa Noa, was founded in 1939 by a peasant of the Mekong Delta area south of Saigon. A reformed Buddhism with great appeal to the peasant classes, the movement had at one time a million members, and it founded a political party, the

THE SURVIVAL OF PRIMITIVE MAN DEPENDS ON HIS ABILITY TO ASSIMILATE
THE WAYS OF THE MODERN WORLD. THIS WOMAN IS LEARNING TO READ AND
WRITE IN AN EVENING CLASS IN YAOUNDE.

A CHOCO INDIAN GIRL OF PANAMA SELLING BANANAS IN THE MARKET.

INDIAN RANCH HANDS ON THE RIO META IN COLOMBIA SLEEP OUT THE
MIDDAY HEAT OF THE TROPICS.

Social Democrats. Now it has lost its strength through schisms and dissensions.

The Cargo cult of the Melanesians is a strange manifestation of unrest among primitive peoples. The adherents of this movement believe that at a specified time (as with the millennium belief among some Christian groups) a Western ship, manned by white men, will arrive with riches for the natives. At this time slavery will be abolished, the natives will be the equals of the whites, and an era of great prosperity will begin. At the bottom of this lies the feeling of inferiority, as well as antagonism, of the dark-skinned natives in the face of the white man's civilization. The cult is based on an old belief among the islanders that a ship would one day arrive with their dead ancestors bearing riches and freedom from the cares and sorrows of life.

A later development of the Cargo cult among the people who live in inland New Guinea is the belief that the cargo will arrive in airplanes. The reaction of the New Guinea aborigines when the first plane landed in their midst in 1930 has been described by Ronald M. Berndt. They were terrified by the roar of the engines and threw themselves to the ground expecting to be killed at any moment. They thought that the plane had come from the Land of the Dead, and so they offered sacrifices to the spirits of the dead. The fat of a slain pig was spread over the ground for the dead to feed on.

In Africa the new religious cults have been influenced by the Moslem faith as well as by the Christian missionaries. These faiths are blended with the native religions. Many of the African cults have been militant, and it is significant that the Mau Mau uprisings in Kenya were sparked by a religious movement among the Kikuyu tribesmen.

The religious movements that started among the North American Indians offer good examples of how native elements and Christian ideas are blended to form spiritual beliefs in times of crisis. The two main movements are the Ghost Dance and the Peyote cults. In the Ghost Dance religion, a return to the ancestors' way of life would be followed by the leaving of the whites, the return of the dead, and the restoration of their lands and their old life.

To the Plains Indians such as the Sioux, among whom the Ghost Dance cult was strongest and led to the most tragic outcome,

18

the dance would also bring the bison back to the plains. It first appeared in 1870, among the Northern Paiute, or Paviotso tribe, of Walker Lake, Nevada. It was apparently the creation of a Paiute shaman named Wodziwob, who was the first prophet of the movement.

Followers of the cult came into contact with the Mormons, many of whom joined the Indian movement. The Mormons believed that the Indians were descendents of the twelve tribes of Israel. Significantly, many cults all over the world that have been introduced to the Bible through Christian missionaries tend to connect themselves with the Old Testament tribes of Israel, who, like them, were victims of persecution.

The Ghost Dance gained real strength as a religion in 1890 when Jack Wilson, better known by his Indian name Wovoka, ("the cutter"), became its leader. Wovoka was the son of a prophet who had been associated with Wodziwob in the earlier movement, and was also a Northern Paiute. The movement was peaceful at first. Wilson himself wore European-style clothing and recomended that the Indians follow white men's ways. Yet the return the dead would benefit only the Indian; the white man would ignored in the bright new world to come.

This paved the way for the great uprising of the Sioux nation. the cultists adopted the use of a shirt, called the ghost shirt, from the Mormons. Decorated with feathers, bones, arrows, birds, suns, and stars, the shirt was worn outside for religious occasions, and worn underneath other clothing by the warriors because of the supernatural strength it would impart to the wearer. The other articles used for the ghost dance, like bows, arrows, tomahawks, and spears, are all native to the Indians.

The dance itself lasts four or five days and takes place outside in a quadrangle, defined at its four points by bonfires. In the middle rises a decorated tree or pole covered with cloth streamers, feathers, and other items. The dancers paint their bodies to indicate the revelations they have received; then form a series of concentric circles with arms about one other's shoulders. The rhythm of the dance sways through the whole group, as if through a single body, while songs are sung by the priests. As the tension heightens the crowd falls into collective exaltation and trance. Members fall to the ground from exhaustion or in trance, but are soon on their feet again.

The Ghost Dance movement spread throughout the western part of the continent before it died out at the close of the nineteenth century. The only area where it met with little success was the Southwest. The movement made virtually no converts among the Hopi, Navaho, or Pueblos. The Hopi and particularly the Pueblos suffered little disorganization or impoverishment as a result of the influx of white men. The high degree of their integration of religion with the rest of their identification with the tribe enabled them to undergo some acculturation at the hands of the Spanish without becoming disorganized.

The Navaho were unaffected for a different reason. It is true that they, like the Hopi and Pueblos, were relatively well off. But more important, Navaho culture was characterized by a great fear of the dead and the ghosts of the dead. The Navaho, it was reported, were terrified at the thought that the dead might one day return.

The cult of peyote has been subjected to longstanding controversy in the United States because it involves the use of the mescal button, which contains drugs that produce hallucinations and giddiness.

Peyote is a small, carrot-shaped cactus native to the Rio Grande Valley and extending southward. Only the round top of the plant is seen above ground. Eating it produces a sensation of levitation, visions of brightly colored images, an inordinately acute perception of shapes and sounds, and visual and auditory hallucinations. Although peyote occasionally causes nausea the user suffers no aftereffects. The active properties in peyote are the more than ten alkaloids contained in the button, including anhaline, mescaline, and lophophorine.

The use of peyote in Mexico is pre-Columbian. During early Spanish times the custom spread northward. It was used to heal sickness and to alleviate spiritual and physical maladies. It was prized for its hallucinatory effects because of the belief, common among primitive peoples, that spiritual revelations come through visions. During the late nineteenth and the twentieth centuries Peyotism passed from a private cult to a pan-Indian one. It took on new moral precepts, many borrowed from Christianity, and sought to instill a new spiritual and moral strength in the Indians, who had been demoralized by the oppression of the white man. Contrary to the accusations of their enemies, the peyote cultists staged no wild orgies during their meetings, which were usually held at night, from sundown Saturday till sunup Sunday, and were meditative gatherings.

The function of peyote is to provide security to the Indian in his depressed state and to relieve the monotony and his personal feeling of impotence. Compared with the Ghost Dance, peyote-eating is a withdrawn activity. The user takes refuge in personal escape. His communion is not with others of his social unit, but with an entire cosmos of spirituality inside his own mind. An old Plains Indian once described the experience of taking peyote for an anthropologist. He described a feather fan and the color images that he saw appear on it. Then he spoke of his children and noted that because they would be able to read and write, they would not need peyote to see their dreams come true.

The Peyote cult has met with serious opposition. Morally and spiritually damned for its use of the drug, it has been politically feared because of its attempts to unify the Indian race. The Bureau of Indian Affairs has a history of early opposition to the cult. It influenced the passing of state laws against Peyotism, but could not bring about the passage of a federal law against the drug's use. In 1923–24, however, the bureau took it upon itself to ban the use of peyote and to forbid scientific research on the plant as well. When John Collier became Commissioner of Indian Affairs in 1933 he put an end to this ban and forbade the persecution of the Native American Church, which had been founded by the cult-ists in 1919. Now the church has split into two groups: the Native American Church, centered in Oklahoma; and the Native American Church of North America, covering the northern United States. There are in addition a number of smaller local bodies.

Religion, like society and man himself, is a dynamic thing, always growing and changing. This has never been more true than today, when widely differing groups engage in more and more intensive interaction.

If, through study of these groups of people, we can come to think of each group in its own terms as a different system toward which an individual has a complex of varying rights and responsi-bilities, then we shall have moved a long way toward the goal of humanistic anthropology: approaching the understanding of other cultures by taking that long hard first step—seeing one's own sun as just another star and one's culture as one among many.

21

# Africa

# THE TUAREG

The Tuareg are a white-skinned people whose home is the middle Sahara and its southern fringe. They are believed to be the descendents of Berber immigrants, who were forced to embrace a nomadic life in the Sahara when they were displaced by the Bedouin Arabs in the eleventh century. There are now about 300,000 Tuareg, and small numbers of them are scattered over all parts of the desert. Most of the Tuareg, however, no longer live in the Sahara proper, but have settled in the Sudan and Air regions on the outskirts of the desert.

Politically and socially the Tuareg are divided into many small and interconnected segments. They are split into several political confederations, each containing several tribes, which are further subdivided into clans and families. Families or clans often travel together in small migratory bands. The organization of the Tuareg divisions combines elements from both the Berber and Arab political systems. The Tuareg have tribal councils like those of the Berbers, and hereditary chiefs similar to Arab sheiks. The chief of the most noble clan within a particular tribe is normally chief of that tribe and also permanent chief, or Amenokal, of the entire confederation.

In Tuareg society, men govern each division of the political structure. Strangely, the inheritance of such things as social status, rights, and property goes to a man's eldest sister's eldest son through what anthropologists call a double descent system. Thus, some inheritance may be matrilineal—via the mother's line—and some patrilineal—via the father's line. The origin of this double descent system is not known. Some writers believe that the Tuareg were once matrilineal, and that descent through males is a recent development.* Others, notably G. D. Gibson, believe that the entire double descent system was present from the beginning. Whatever its origin, the cross-cutting aspect of the double descent system makes it possible for the politically fragmented society to maintain cultural uniformity and social cohesion.

Tuareg social organization contains five distinct classes or castes: (1) nobles or ruling Tuareg; (2) vassal Tuareg; (3) Negro serfs used for farming; (4) Negro slaves used for household and manual tasks; (5) Negro smiths and leatherworkers, who are outcastes. The social status of every Tuareg male is determined by the clan status of his wife or mother.

The Negro smiths represent an interesting enigma in Tuareg society. Unlike the main body of Tuareg, the smiths do not lead a nomadic life. On the contrary, they set up small camps consisting of two or three families, from which they make occasional trips to the scattered Tuareg camps to make repairs and sell new items. On the side, the smiths engage in spying and counterspying for the nobles and vassals in matters ranging from love affairs to intertribal warfare. Through all of this, however, the smiths retain their positions as outcastes.

The other four "in" castes show the combination of social and economic features that help to unite the Tuareg society. The caste system, ideally, is a unique division of labor in which each class has specific duties and responsibilities. The nobles scout for raiding possibilities and for pasture land for their herds of camels, goats, sheep, donkeys, and zebus; the vassals protect and care for the vast herds; and the Negro serfs and slaves help the Tuareg women in the home and take care of the small farm plots.

The economic system of the Tuareg has often been compared

* It has been suggested by J. P. Murdock that the matrilineal descent of status position is an adaptation by the controlling castes (i.e., the Tuareg themselves) to the inclusion of slave populations. That is, women's official mating could be more controlled than men's, and matrilineal descent made it less likely that offspring of subject peoples could enter Tuareg caste by marriage.

to the feudal system of medieval Europe. The main reason for the comparison is found in the status terms "nobles" and "vassals" and in their relationship to each other. As in medieval Europe, the vassals receive manpower services from their slaves, whom they have to protect from raiding parties. The vassals, in turn, must pay a tribute to the nobles in the form of produce and cattle, and rent for their plots of farmland. In addition, the vassals must give the nobles a portion of all booty they get from raids on caravans and native villages. Slaves are frequently a part of this booty.

Tuareg apparel consists of the poncholike robe, baggy pants, and sandals worn by all the desert dwellers. In addition, a head-dress called "teguelmoust" or "litham" is worn only by the men. The litham, a combination turban and veil, is made by winding a ten-foot-long cloth about the head and face so that only the eyes are visible through a narrow slit. No self-respecting male will ever let his mouth be seen, even when he is eating or drinking; he holds the cloth with his left hand and puts the food into his mouth with his right hand.

Though many theories exist regarding the origin of the Tuareg man's veil, no one really knows how the strange fashion evolved. If the Tuareg themselves know, they are not saying. Practically, the litham protects the head and face against desert sandstorms, which can have much the same effect on skin that sandblasting has on metal surfaces. But today its importance is largely one of status. Youths and women do not wear the veil; the more aristo-cratic the man, the more reluctant he is to remove it. One interest-ing theory suggests that the veil may be a way of creating "social distance" between upper and lower classes, just as high walls and hedges insulate the wealthy in Western society. This interpre-tation is reinforced by the sometimes-heard references to Black Tuareg and White Tuareg, which stem from the fact that the nobles usually wear black or indigo blue lithams, whereas the vassals wear white ones.

As in so many cases, initial contacts with Europeans increased the incidence of diseases that were formerly not common among the Tuareg. They had a detrimental effect upon Tuareg demog-raphy at first, but the availability of new medicines and the popula-tion's increasing tolerance to the various diseases have alleviated the situation.

Equally, much of the economic and political base of Tuareg

ABOUT 300,000 TUAREG, A WHITE RACE PROBABLY DESCENDED FROM THE BERBERS, ROAM THE DESERTS OF NORTHERN AFRICA. THE MALES DRAPE THEIR FACES WITH LONG TURBANS SO THAT ONLY THE EYES ARE REVEALED. AT LEFT IS A TRIBESMAN OF THE TASSILI PLATEAU IN SOUTHERN ALGERIA.

social organization was affected by colonial restraints placed against settlements and caravans. Nevertheless, colonial rule never became solid in many of the Tuareg areas; the central governments preferred to use forms of indirect rule, wherein much of the former local political organization was left intact and used as an arm of administration, so long as the most repugnant (to Westerners) traits and raiding were repressed. Indeed, in the last years of French rule in Algeria, and even after independence, many Tuareg groups were courted by the Algiers government, in order to maintain peace in the distant regions.

Although the Tuareg continue to acculturate to new ways and to adapt to take advantage of new opportunities, older ways have not died out. In 1962 the British Anti-Slavery League and UN special reports noted a recrudescence of slavery in many of the Saharan areas inhabited by the Tuareg, due in part to the decreasing control of such regions by the new central governments.

DESPITE THEIR WARLIKE APPEARANCE, THESE TUAREG WARRIORS ARE MERELY RACING THEIR HORSES IN A TRIBAL "FIELD DAY."

# THE HOTTENTOT

The Hottentot at one time occupied a territory covering more than 100,000 square miles of southwest Africa and roamed the plains with their flocks of sheep and horned cattle. They were discovered by the Dutch, who were the first to explore South Africa from the Cape of Good Hope.

Those early explorers' records tell us of seven tribes with an estimated population of 100,000. Today the Hottentot population is about 35,000. None of the Hottentot tribes have wholly avoided interbreeding with other racial groups. Furthermore, they have practically lost their cultural identity through the merger of their customs and beliefs with those of their neighbors, both white and black.

Though the name Hottentot is applied to this entire group, it was originally the name of only one of the tribes, which occupied the land bordering the Cape of Good Hope.

The physical features of the Hottentot are essentially Bushmanoid, although modified by early and more pervasive interbreeding with Bantu groups. Archeological finds indicate that around five thousand years ago peoples of approximately the same physical type as the Hottentot and the Bushmen were distributed all the way from the upper Nile throughout east and northeast Africa and over all of southern Africa.

[TOP] BAVENDA GIRLS PERFO
THE PYTHON DANCE IN KRUG
NATIONAL PARK, SOUTH AFRIC
[BOTTOM] A CLOSE-UP OF T
DANCE SHOWS THE GIRLS PRES
ING CLOSE TOGETHER TO FORM
SNAKE.

How these peoples came to be replaced by Negroid groups awaits further evidence, but the general view today is that the thinly spread Bushmanoid groups, which were composed of hunters and gatherers, were driven out of their former lands and biologically incorporated into the much larger new populations that could rely upon agriculture and domesticated animals.

Culturally and linguistically, as well as racially, the Hottentot are closely related to the Bushmen. Both peoples speak languages that use the click sounds, which have so intrigued and frustrated the foreigners attempting to imitate them. The name Hottentot itself is a Westernized phonetic imitation of two of the click sounds, "hot" and "tot." The click sounds, over twenty of which have been distinguished, are produced by putting the tongue against the teeth, the palate, and other parts inside the mouth, and then forcibly withdrawing it.

The Hottentot are short, the men averaging little more than five feet and the women less than that. They have pale-olive complexions, woolly hair, thick lips, flat noses. Their faces are triangular, with prominent cheekbones and narrow chins; the men have scanty beards.

The physical appearance of the Hottentot women has been much publicized. Early in the nineteenth century a Hottentot woman named Saartjie Baartman was brought to Europe by the enterprising surgeon of an African ship, to make her fortune—and his—by performing before French and English audiences. Billed as "The Hottentot Venus," she became such a hit that songs were written about her, political cartoons compared her to various public figures, and a Parisian play was inspired by her. Entitled *The Hottentot Venus; or, the Hatred of Frenchwomen*, the play is about a pretty French girl who can only win her boy friend's love by disguising herself as the Hottentot Venus. After Saartjie Baartman's death a plaster cast was made of her body and the skeleton was preserved. Both may be seen today in the Musée de l'Homme in the Palais du Chaillot in Paris.

A noticeable characteristic of the Hottentot woman, and of the Bushwoman as well, is steatopygia, a fatty development on the buttocks. The men also have steatopygia, but to a lesser extent. The buttocks are not rounded, as is the case with other fat Negro or Caucasian women. Instead the buttocks, seen in profile, look like a right triangle, with the top forming a sort of shelf, and the

EFT] A CENTRAL AFRICAN CHIEFTAIN WITH HIS WIFE, IN CEREMONIAL
ESS. [ABOVE] A YOUNG ZULU IN WARRIOR'S DRESS, WITH WIFE, IN NATAL,
UTH AFRICA.

mass sloping downward and inward, almost in a straight line, to meet the thigh.

One theory attributes steatopygia to a high intake of salt. However, the Hottentot do not have a particularly salty diet. Although the development may be due in part to sexual selection, there may be some functional as well as esthetic reason for it, especially as it is present in both men and women.

Some anthropologists believe a theory that steatopygia evolved as a result of the ancient hibernations, during which the person's body lived off the fatty tissue. Many travelers have observed that the Bushmen and the Hottentot gorge themselves in times of plenty, and then go for days without eating. If this theory is correct, the buttocks serve as a sort of camel's hump, well adapted for survival in an environment where food is scarce and periods of famine common.

Hottentot women and Bushwomen have in common another physical characteristic, which seems to have no functional purpose: an excessive enlargement of the labia minora, called Hottentot apron or *tablier*. The layers of skin and mucous membrane that make up the internal lips of the vulva and the covering of the clitoris are elongated so that they hang down, forming two lobes visible outside the labia majora. Early color drawings show these lobes to be purplish. Although travelers have told stories purporting to show that this condition is artificially induced, there seems to be no basis for this in fact; rather it is a natural, if unusual, development.

The breasts of both Hottentot women and Bushwomen have an unusually large aureola around the nipple, often measuring four inches in diameter.

Although the white man has taken an interest in the language and anatomy of the Hottentot, he has done little to help the culture. Europeans in Africa have generally looked upon the Hottentot as a troublesome breed—lazy and quarrelsome, and drunk on brandy made from the aromatic *buchu* plant.

When the Hottentot were still largely in possession of their cultural identity they wore loincloths and cloaks of skin. In addition, the women wore fringed girdles, skin caps, and ivory bracelets. The Hottentot practice of daubing the body with sooty fat for special occasions was regarded as repugnant by travelers.

34

Hottentot government was patriarchal. Each village, or kraal, had a captain who was a member of the chief's council. The captains were generally monogamous, but the chiefs often had several wives, as they could afford to pay the high marriage price of cattle to their wives' relatives. The chief was the tax collector, exacting a portion of the hunting catch. His council held court and tried cases. The punishments were generally harsh: Thieves were beaten, starved, or banished; murderers were beaten or stoned to death; women who committed adultery were often sentenced to death at the hands of the aggrieved husband.

The three tribal groups that survive to any extent today are scattered throughout the vast territory the Hottentot once possessed. One, the Griquas, intermarried extensively with the Dutch colonists. They adapted Dutch names and the Dutch language, so that by now they have completely lost their native language. They are called halfbreeds or *Bastaards* by the Europeans. A small number of halfbreeds with more Griqua blood do exist in Campbell and Boetsap in Griqualand, but they are steadily being replaced by more acculturated ones.

The Namas or Namaquas are the most unacculturated Hottentot group now in existence. As of the early 1920's, there were about three to five thousand of them left in Great Namaqualand, South-West Africa. Most of their traditions, however, have been lost, and many of them have adopted Christianity.

The Korana ("shoe wearers") still remain in some numbers in the far southern part of the Kalahari, although they have intermarried extensively with other tribes. They retained their ancient traditions and tribal solidarity longer than any of the other tribes; but now they too have capitulated, though not without a struggle. During the early nineteenth century they terrorized Bantu, Bushmen, other Hottentot tribes, and Europeans. Skilled warriors and plunderers, they soon became known as the Bedouin of South Africa. The prosperity they gained in this pursuit was not to last, as many of their number were destroyed in enemy reprisals. Their tribal identity was finally shattered when they took part in the unsuccessful revolt in British Bechuanaland in 1886. As punishment, the government took away their tribal rights, and they ceased to exist as an independent people. Racially and culturally very little remains of the Hottentot people today.

# THE BUSHMEN

Among the most primitive peoples in the world are the Bushmen of South-West Africa, who cling to their precarious existence in the unyielding Kalahari Desert. Their population has dwindled to some thirty thousand through illness, starvation, and assimilation in the taller, stronger Bantu tribes that surround them.

The Bushmen are not only a distinct group of tribes; they are also a distinct race. Not true Pygmies (they average five feet and will grow taller with proper nourishment), or true Negroes (their skin color is light yellowish brown), or even connected with the Mongoloids (despite their slight eye fold), they seem related only to themselves.

Bushmen's bodies are well adapted to the extraordinary hardships they must endure. Their wrinkled skins are tough and elastic. The women have the odd steatopygia, fleshy buttocks that store food.

Though the Bushman wears no clothing, the hot desert sun seldom burns his skin, and his deep-brown eyes often have remarkable acuity. Not least among the Bushman's equipment is an extraordinary degree of cunning, skill, and pride. Perhaps no other human group, with the possible exception of the Australian aborigines, has had to adapt to so harsh an environment with so few technological advantages.

36

The Bushman is a nomad and a hunter. He builds no permanent home, plants no seed, tends neither cattle nor sheep. His ornaments and handicrafts, compared with those of other African tribes, are few. If necessary, he sleeps out in the open, in a cleared area of sand warmed by a fire, or, when possible, beneath the protection of an overhanging rock. At times when the hunt is over he will return to an area near some permanent water supply, where he may have a hut fashioned of brush or skins.

But only the unknowing would mistake the simplicity of Bushman life for lack of intelligence. His hunting methods, for example, show an extraordinary degree of sophistication. Along with his skill with bow and arrow and spear, the Bushman possesses a remarkable knowledge of poisons. Unlike most primitive peoples, who, if they use poison at all use but a single kind, the Bushman has at his disposal a whole array of poisons, and he selects the appropriate one for the animal he is hunting.

When stalking fails, the Bushman constructs intricate traps to be placed in watering holes and along rivers. So delicate are these traps that at the slightest touch the animal is seized, hurtled into the air, and suspended like hung beef.

The Bushmen had elaborated the art of painting, although none of their masterpieces were produced in historical times. For thousands of years Bushmen have been leaving remnants of their genius on walls of stone, in caves, and on rocks. Although animals and hunters are naturally the favorite themes of these practical people, battle and religious scenes are also portrayed, all in a remarkably realistic manner. But the influx of the Bantu, and then of the white Afrikaner, has led to the destruction of much Bushman painting, just as it must ultimately lead to the destruction of the Bushmen themselves.

The terrible history of the Bushmen can be read in their paintings. Earliest paintings record only animals—antelope galloping across a small flat stone, or a herd of springbok fleeing over the panoramic walls of a cave at White Kei River. Then there are paintings of the Bushmen themselves, their families and their ceremonies, their wars and their joys. Then a new figure appears: the black Bantu; and finally a more threatening figure: a white man with a gun.

The severity of Bushman life, accentuated by his need to escape notice in the struggle against extermination during the

BY CLINGING TO TRADITIONAL WAYS, TRIBES WILL EVENTUALLY DIE OUT. THE BUSHMEN STILL BUILD NO HOMES AND HUNT BY BOW AND ARROW. ALTHOUGH THEY ARE FAST DISAPPEARING, SOME 30,000 REMAIN ON THE KALAHARI DESERT OF SOUTH-WEST AFRICA.

past century, does not allow for complex social structures and institutions. He travels in small hunting groups, a family or two, gathering in large numbers only in the rainy season when the land is gentler. A man need pay no bridal price, but simply prove he can hunt by bringing in game. His choice of a bride is less restricted by totems and taboos than in most other primitive societies. Lines of authority are also looser than in most other groups. The father is the head of the family, but there are no chiefs and no shamans—only elders, whose advice is sought when important decisions must be made. Polygamy is known among the Bushmen, but monogamy is more common. There is neither slavery nor class distinctions, although in the past some Bushmen have been forced into serfdom under the Bantu or white men.

But life, even for the Bushman, is not all work. The men may spend their leisure time playing an ancient version of checkers on squares marked in the sand, or a kind of badminton, with a shuttlecock made of a buzzard feather attached to a heavy *maravamma* nut. Bushmen also play at war—in pantomime, commemorating a real war involving the ravishing of a girl of one group by a dashing young Paris of another. Unlike other peoples who have ceremonies imitating wars, the Bushmen make it really a game.

Bushmen have their ceremonies, too, of course, and they make music with a variety of stringed instruments. Strangely, they have no drums, using their hands alone to make percussion sounds. They dance to worship the spirits they believe in—the spirit of the moon, which is at the center of Bushman mythology, and the related spirit of the mantis. The religion of these people is far simpler than that of other African tribes. In the former West Africa kingdoms of Ashanti and Dahomey, for example, the spirit world is rigidly organized into an empire or kingdom, just as mundane society is organized. In these relatively advanced societies we find separate pantheons of earth and sky gods, each with their own cults and their own devotees, admitted into divine service only after long and complicated initiation ceremonies.

The Bushman is secretive about his religion, and little is known of it, but it seems to be a simplified animism. Still, it is clear that the Bushmen are too naturalistic to let their religion dominate their lives, as it does the lives of other groups; their ceremonies and rites are reserved for the more lush seasons, when more food is available nearby.

The Bushmen are fast disappearing. Already many of their cultural traits are gone; for example, they no longer paint. From fifteen separate language groups they have been reduced to two or three, notably the Kung Bushmen, numbering some four thousand, who still follow the traditional way of life. The others have either disappeared, are in the process of disappearing, or are intermarrying and vanishing into the dominant Bantu culture of the region. It is a sad end for the Harmless People, as author E. M. Thomas, who lived among them, called them.

# THE PYGMIES

The dark, lush Ituri Forest of the Pygmies lies at the center of the African continent. Contrary to popular belief, most Africans, even the most primitive, do not live within the jungles; rather, they make their home on the edges of the jungle, and live in constant dread of what the jungle represents. The Pygmy, on the other hand, is a true child of the jungle. He is most at home beneath the thick roof of tropical treetops that block out the sunlight.

There are a number of similarities between the Bushmen and the Pygmies. Like the Bushman, the Pygmy is a hunter and a nomad, with no permanent villages, no fields, no cattle to care for; he has developed his hunting abilities to an art, knowing the animals of the region, their habits, homes, dangers, and vulnerabilities better than do other peoples; and he is an expert chemist when dealing with the herbaceous poisons with which he tips his crude arrows.

The Pygmy's nomadic way of life makes complex tribal structures, chieftains, and priests unnecessary; he lives in small family groups, relying for leadership upon both the most competent men in the hunting group and the elders of the clan. Like the Bushman, he is fearless where his taller neighbors are afraid; the spirits of the forest who keep the Babira and Balese close to their villages do not intimidate the little people. Indeed, the

Pygmies often invent spirit stories to tell to the Bantu as a means of keeping these tribesmen, who nominally hold the Pygmies in vassalage, under control.

In other respects the Pygmy is as different from the Bushman as the Ituri Forest, which is his home, differs from the barren wastes of the Bushman's Kalahari Desert. While the Bushman is clearly a race unto himself, the Pygmy's genealogy remains a mystery. On the one hand he seems closely related to the dominant Negro strain of Africa: his skin is dark; his hair is black and kinky; his nose is flat and broad; his lips are thick. But whether these characteristics are ancient or relatively modern, as a result of intermarriage, is not clear. One group of Pygmies, the Bambuti, who seem to have had less contact with the Negroes, have lighter skin, and their infants are often born with a downy body hair, lanugo, which ranges from blond to red. The Bambuti are the smallest of the Pygmies, averaging about four and a half feet tall and weighing less than ninety pounds. Other Pygmy groups, who seem to have intermarried more freely with the Bantu of the area, are taller, often topping five feet.

Intermarriage with the Bantu, as in the case of the Bushmen, is rapidly transforming the Pygmy race and way of life. Of the approximately 170,000 Pygmoid peoples in central Africa, about 30,000 relatively unchanged Pygmies remain in their ancient land —the central Ituri Forest in the northeast corner of the former Belgian Congo—but their numbers are rapidly dwindling. And their way of life is fast disappearing as the great social changes sweeping across the African continent lure the little people out of the forest.

Whether the Pygmies are direct descendents of prehistoric men of short stature, or the remnants of a population of larger men made small by their environment, is unknown. What is clear is that the Pygmies have been in central Africa far longer than the Bantu-speaking Negroes. In an Egyptian tomb of 2500 B.C. is a record showing that a Pygmy was ordered to be brought north by the Pharaoh Nefrikare.

The word "pygmy" is derived from the Greek *pygmaios,* for a measure of length called the cubit (about eighteen to twenty inches). Greek writers, among them Aristotle and Herodotus, mention the Pygmy. By the Middle Ages the Pygmies had become almost completely mythologized; the seventeenth-century English anatomist Edward Tyson, mistaking the skeleton of a chimpanzee for that of a Pygmy, wrote a learned treatise in which he concluded that the Pygmy was not human. Very little was known about the Pygmy until the nineteenth century, and even then little was known about how they actually lived until they were first seriously studied in the 1920's.

Our knowledge of the Pygmies must always be limited by the fact that the Bantu invasion changed their way of life. This movement of Bantu-speaking groups into what was formerly exclusively Pygmy territory began roughly two thousand years ago. It started from the Cameroon highlands and extended throughout all of the central rain-forest area in the succeeding centuries.

No Pygmy today speaks a Pygmy language. The ancient tongue has been completely lost, replaced by Bantu dialects. While learning the language of the Bantu the Pygmies were influenced by the culture of the Bantu, so that separating the traditional Pygmy practices from those acquired from the Bantu becomes one of the basic problems for the anthropologist.

The Bantu likes to think of the Pygmy as his serf. But the Bantu shuns the jungle and remains close to his village, where safety resides. The meat he needs he buys from the Pygmies, who emerge periodically from the jungle to sell the fruits of their hunts, often for shamefully small rewards. The Bantu treats the Pygmy like a child. For his part, the Pygmy looks on the Bantu's fear of the jungle with condescension and plays upon this fear to obtain a better deal in the trading.

When the Pygmy is in a Bantu village he will usually adopt Bantu customs, ceremonies, superstitions, and beliefs. Such calculated amiability led early white observers, who did their investigating in the comparative safety and comfort of Bantu villages, to think that the Pygmy had no culture of his own, but had adopted the "superior" one of the Bantu. Then anthropologist Colin Turnbull went into the forest to live with the Pygmies, was even initiated into one of their groups, and discovered that in the forest, away from the Bantu, the Pygmy reasserted his cultural heritage and became a different person altogether.

The temporary settlements thrown up by the Pygmies are as elaborate as those of the Bushmen. For protection against the frequent rains and the constant dripping from the jungle trees, they build hemispherical huts of mud and leaves. These are easily built and casually abandoned when the time comes to move to a new area of the forest for fresh game. Building the huts is woman's work; the men save their energies for hunting. Different tribes design different kinds of huts, from the simplest windbreaks to the complex structures with molded entrances built by the Binga group.

Polygamy is allowed among the Pygmies, although economics usually dictate monogamy. Unlike many other tribes that allow or even demand marriage between classificatory cousins, the Pygmies forbid it, and sexual intercourse between members of even the largest family groups is regarded as one of the worst crimes a Pygmy can commit and may lead to banishment in the forest. Marriage is often arranged on a complicated head-for-head basis; for example, a young man who wants to marry a girl of another clan may try to convince a relative of the girl to marry a woman from his own clan. Adultery is strictly forbidden by the Pygmies, most likely because of the difficulties it can cause between clans. Perhaps one of the most sensible customs the Pygmies have concerning marriage is that mothers-in-law are not allowed to interfere with newlyweds and sometimes not even to talk to them.

The Bushmen were great painters; the Pygmies are great musicians. Except when they are actually hunting, Pygmies moving through the forest will sing constantly and loudly. Besides expressing exuberance, this singing has its practical side; it warns away animals who may be waiting on the path ahead. A leopard or water buffalo, if come upon suddenly, will attack; given warning, it would prefer to retreat into the forest.

This is only one facet of the Pygmies' musical diamond. Weddings, funerals, births, successful hunting, initiations, and almost all other social occasions are commemorated with songs played on a large bamboo pipelike musical instrument, the molimo. This is the central ceremonial instrument of the Pygmies. It makes a mournful, almost humanlike singing sound, and is often used to intone a kind of answer to the song being sung. Usually it is taken into the jungle while the tribe sings; then from here, from there, from everywhere, the beautiful melancholy sound comes into the camp, like the voice of the jungle spirits, answering and encouraging the song, assuring the Pygmies that it is good.

Turnbull reports that the Pygmies are not particularly reverent about their molimo despite its importance to their culture. One group he stayed with stole a length of metal pipe from a road gang in the area and irreverently used that as their molimo. This follows from the general Pygmy lack of superstition.

When a Pygmy dies, for example, there is not the concern with the spirit of the deceased that there is among the Bantu; the death is accepted as final. The Bantu always seek a supernatural cause of death—a curse or evil spirit; the Pygmies never do, and they laugh at the Bantu's fears. This is not to say there is no Pygmy religion: Storms, thunder, and rainbows are all feared and kept away by "magic," whereas the sun is considered a benevolent spirit; but, like the Bushmen, the Pygmies have no time for complex religious juju and a class of priests who supply nothing to the tribal economy.

Fewer than sixty thousand Pygmies—mainly the thirty thousand members of the dwindling Bambuti clans of the Ituri—still live their traditional life, and every day many leave the forest, drawn from their ancient hunting grounds by a new understanding of money, which frees them from the Bantu; by white hunters who hire them to capture the rare okapi that live only in the Ituri; by the easier life of agriculture, which more and more of them are learning; or by the even easier life of begging.

As the modern world dissolves the culture, so intermarriage transforms and recombines older "racial" groupings. It will not be long before the little people of the Ituri Forest are only a memory.

[TOP] SPEARMEN ASSEMBLE FOR A TRIBAL HUNT IN NORTHERN UGANDA. LARGE GATHERINGS SUCH AS THIS ARE SELDOM SEEN, AS THE BIG-GAME ANIMALS ARE BECOMING INCREASINGLY RARE. [BOTTOM] THESE SMALL "VILLAGES" IN UGANDA ARE REALLY FAMILY COMPOUNDS. FIFTY YEARS AGO GAME WAS ABUNDANT IN THIS REGION. NOW DOMESTIC ANIMALS GRAZE IN THE SURROUNDING AREA.

# THE WATUSI

The story of the Watusi is a Greek tragedy played out on an African stage. No element is missing: A hero, larger than life, rises to power through his own skill, intelligence, and strength and becomes a mighty ruler; and then, through pride, is overthrown and destroyed.

It is destruction—not merely assimilation—that the proud tall warriors of the Watusi tribe face today. Their rigid way of life, unable to bend in the storm of change blowing through the African continent, has broken; their people peer into the future and see the grim-visaged specter of genocide.

We have until now been talking of little men who in one way or another adapted themselves to the harsh world of the jungle and desert. The Watusi are different. Their tall, lithe, athletic bodies are in marked contrast to the stunted, pot-bellied bodies of the Pygmies. Rather than succumb to nature, the Watusi fought against it. They disciplined themselves so they would not have to dig in the ground or hunt with stone weapons in order to have enough to eat. Instead, many centuries ago they acquired a hardy and beautiful strain of cattle and became herders. They organized their society so no man would go hungry, organized their army so they would be the masters rather than the slaves. They learned how to make poetry and how to dance and how to play—and how to hold their heads up—so that life could be glorious and beautiful. They learned self-control, and manners, and self-respect, so they could respect each other, and so other tribes would respect them. And they learned that power and skill, used with wisdom, could mean peace and tranquility.

Racially the Watusi are Negroes of Nilotic origin; their ancestors were born in the valleys of the Nile, and their cousins are the tall pastoral people of Somalia and Ethiopia, the Gallas, the Fulani, and the noble Masai. Perhaps, even, these same ancestors were allies of the ancient Egyptian pharaohs, and from the Egyptians learned the techniques of herding cattle.

About one thousand years ago the Nilotes began to expand southward into the African continent, following a line of least resistance and penetrating areas in East Africa and the Central Lakes regions, which offered good pasture for their herds and were not pre-empted by similar herding peoples. It is difficult to reconstruct the pressures behind this expansion; perhaps it was to escape war, drought, and disease, perhaps to find new pastures for a growing population. But one of the main factors that allowed the Nilotic groups to expand and penetrate areas held by already established agricultural people was the development of milking and dairy techniques. With these, the Nilotic groups could subsist completely on their herds. The resulting independence and mobility of the free-ranging pastoral groups proved to be a critical military advantage.

The Nilotes moved into Tanganyika and Kenya, into the Congo, and around the shores of Lake Victoria. About eight hundred years ago they moved into a small area on the northeast corner of the Congo that was to become the area of the kingdoms of Ruanda and Urundi—and the domain of the Watusi.

Ruanda–Urundi was originally the home of a Pygmy tribe whose descendents are now known as the Batwa. Years before the Watusi arrived the land was invaded by a Bantu-speaking group known as the Bahutu, who took the lands of the Pygmies, and drove the little people into the forest to hunt game for them. Then the agricultural Bahutu were themselves supplanted by an even taller group, the Watusi, who drove before them the crescent-horned cattle they herded, and protected themselves with disciplined armies armed with long spears.

Travelogues have firmly convinced many Westerners that all

Watusi warriors are at least seven feet tall. The truth is that the average height of the tribe is five feet nine inches—still making them the tallest people on earth—and that seven-footers, though not in the majority, are not rare. It is easy to see how the Watusi were able to subjugate the more primitive, more superstitious Bahutu. Within a short time the feudalistic Watusi social system was clamped upon the entire Ruanda–Urundi area, and would remain so for many centuries.

The Watusi brought with them from the north a complex social hierarchy, which they maintained in their new home. On top of the feudal pyramid was the king, or *Mwami*. To 1967 there had been forty-one Mwamis, and every Watusi schoolboy can tell you their names. The kingdom was divided into districts, each with two rulers—the *umunvabutaka*, in charge of cattle, and the *umunvamukenke*, in charge of land. Each district contained a number of local chiefs who nominally ruled over the several family heads who carried the lines of authority down to the individual level. The buttress of the entire system was the cattle, all nominally owned by the Mwami, but in practice distributed down the line so that each man had at least a few cows to care for and to supply him with the milk and spiced butter that make up the bulk of the Watusi diet.

Until their overthrow, even the lowest Watusi had a rank at least equivalent to that of knight in the European feudal system. The serf class was made up entirely of the Bahutu, who, in return for tributes and contributions to Watusi dowries, received protection from their overlords. Nor was protection an inconsiderable matter in those days when Arab slave traders were sweeping across the African continent in search of Negroes to be sold to Middle Eastern potentates or New World settlers. While the tribes of surrounding lands were being raided by the slavers the people of Ruanda–Urundi were safe behind the protective shield of the Watusi army, which was powerful enough to keep even the better armed Arabs at bay.

The Watusi army was made up of the young men of the tribe who had been trained not only as soldiers, but also as courtiers at the court of the Mwami. There they learned the precepts of Watusi gentility, the marks of the Watusi lord: how to dance and how to recite poetry; how to act with restraint and self-control; how to make conversation and how to sport; how to fight and how

A WATUSI WOMAN OF COLONIAL RUANDA–URUNDI. HER RACIAL CHARACTERISTICS ARE EVIDENT IN HER RELATIVELY NARROW NOSE AND HER SLENDER, GRACEFUL NECK. SHE CARRIES A SLEEPING BABY ON HER BACK, UNDER HER CLOAK.

A WATUSI PASTURE IN 1949. CATTLE WERE THE MOST IMPORTANT FORM OF WEALTH FOR THE WATUSI, AS THEY ARE FOR MANY PEOPLES IN THE EAST AFRICAN CATTLE BELT.

A LINE OF WATUSI DANCERS, SOME SEVEN FEET TALL, PHOTOGRAPHED IN 1956. SIX YEARS LATER, WITH THE INDEPENDENCE OF RUANDA–URUNDI (NOW THE SEPARATE NATIONS RWANDA AND BURUNDI), THE WATUSI LOST THEIR SUPREMACY OVER THEIR NEIGHBORING TRIBES. SINCE THEN THEY HAVE BEEN SLOWLY ANNIHILATED BY THE MORE NUMEROUS BAHUTU.

to be courteous. They learned how to treat the young women of the tribe, who were protected by a moral code as strict as any devised in medieval Europe—a code so strict that pre-marital intercourse was punished by death or total banishment. They learned also how to care for the sacred long-horned cattle of the tribe, and the various rituals and taboos that surrounded these cattle, so vital to Watusi welfare, so different in size and health from the bedraggled cows of lesser tribes.

Under the Watusi the Bahutu accepted their semibondage readily at first. Most of the concepts of democracy and political rights were, in those days, as distant as the far side of the moon. More important, the Watusi ruled with a velvet glove, sharing their cattle with the Bahutu while they protected them. Some Bahutu even prospered under the arrangement and married into the Watusi caste. But just as the new forces of mercantilism gutted medieval European political structures, so the forces of colonialism sweeping through Africa in the nineteenth century upset the delicately balanced relationship between Watusi over-lord and Bahutu serf. First the Germans, then the Belgians (who gained Ruanda–Urundi as a prize after the First World War) entered the area, and the applecart soon toppled.

Although conservative Belgian authorities made no calculated attempt to undo the feudal pattern, feeling that the innate stability could only be beneficial to them, their very presence eroded the foundation upon which the society was built. The mystique of Watusi supremacy was first to go; the Bahutu saw clearly enough that their traditional overlords were in turn overlorded by the colonial authorities. At the same time, the Belgians introduced coffee planting to the area and spread the idea of a money-based economy, thus effectively rendering the old cattle-based society an anachronism. Finally, through European-educated leaders, the ideas of liberty and democracy that had promoted revolution in nineteenth-century Europe trickled down to the Bahutu. Thus were the seeds of the conflict sown.

Tragedy might still have been avoided had the Watusi, as well as the Bahutu, bowed to the inevitable. In fact, in Urundi the Watusi hierarchy eventually decided to accommodate the more reasonable demands of the newly belligerent Bahutu, and allowed them to join the councils of the power structure. The Watusi leaders of Ruanda, on the other hand, kept their eyes fixed on their glorious past until the ferment around them boiled into open rebellion.

In 1959 the archbishop of Ruanda issued a pastoral letter calling for equality between the two tribes. It signaled a bloody assault upon the Watusi by the more numerous Bahutu; thousands died, and more thousands fled to the safety of refugee camps in nearby countries. An election held soon after, installed a Bahutu government; only intervention by the Belgian supervisors prevented immediate slaughter of the fallen Watusi.

In 1962 the Belgian trusteeship came to an end, and two new African nations—Burundi and Rwanda—emerged. In the Kingdom of Burundi, a slightly shaky peace has been maintained, with the Bahutu and Watusi sharing power. In Rwanda, however, the full storm broke in December 1963. The proud Watusi warriors staged an attack upon the Rwanda government, and outnumbered ten to one, fell before their former serfs. Since that battle the Bahutu have been systematically annihilating the Watusi.

Now the conscience of the world is slowly awakening to what has been going on in Rwanda, and some measures are being taken to stop the bloodshed. But clearly the power of the Watusi is on the wane, and—at least in Rwanda—the tribe is on the edge of extinction. Their choice now is either to submit to their old servants—and perhaps allow intermarriage and time to heal the wounds—or to die. In either case the Watusi way of life will disappear from the earth as surely as did the way of life of the medieval knights. The winds of change are too great for the sturdiest oak; only bending reeds can survive them.

# The Far East

# THE AINU

Two to three thousand years ago much of northeastern Asia was inhabited by Paleo–Siberian peoples dependent upon various methods of hunting, fishing, and food gathering. In the past, considerable controversy was generated as to whether these peoples were of the same genetic stock as Caucasians. In any case, they were not effectively a part of western Asian or European gene pools, and possessed distinctive physical characteristics of their own.

But these peoples were not to retain predominance in this part of the world. Most were exterminated, or intermarried with successive waves of Mongoloid peoples. Today these early peoples are believed to have vanished from the earth, except for one small group, the Ainu, who have managed to retain much of their distinctive physical features and ancient customs.

The Ainu allow us to take a fascinating look at a culture that is all but extinct in the world. Today they are settled mainly in northern Japan, on the island of Hokkaido, although some live on the Kuril Islands and on the southern part of the island of Sakhalin, which belong to the Soviet Union. The Ainu had a long history of war and defeat at the hands of the Japanese, who have constantly driven them northward until they reached their present location. There is evidence that they once occupied territory as far south as Kyoto, but were unable to resist the expansion of the more powerful and highly developed Japanese civilization. Many place names in Japan are Ainu terms, for example, the volcanic peak Fujiyama, which means fire goddess.

The constant attacks of a higher civilization are not over for the Ainu even today. The encroachments of civilization are making it increasingly difficult for them to survive by their old methods of hunting and fishing. Disease and poverty have taken their toll, and the Ainu have found it necessary to intermarry with the Japanese and other settlers. As of 1957 they totaled less than seventeen thousand, but the number of pure-blood Ainu may be no more than a few thousand. In addition to intermarriage, for the past few centuries women have made a practice of adopting Japanese babies and raising them as their own.

Because of this mixing, the Ainu often resemble the Japanese, but in their pure form they present quite a different appearance. They are a short stocky people, the men generally no taller than five feet five inches, the women a couple of inches shorter. Their skin is fair and rosy, but as their faces are usually tanned, they appear much darker; they do not have the Mongolian eye fold. Their hair, often long and wavy, is considered very handsome. Because travelers are astonished at the amount of hair the Ainu have, they are called the Hairy Ainu.

The men's most spectacular feature is their magnificent foot-long white beards, which give them a patriarchal appearance. Both men and women wear their hair about shoulder length. Their hairiness, however, has been exaggerated; they probably have no more body hair than the hairiest of Europeans. No doubt this erroneous reputation came about through the Ainu's being compared with their sparse-haired Mongoloid neighbors.

The Ainu value their hair highly, although today the more acculturated young people sport short foreign haircuts. In the past hair was regarded as a source of strength and longevity. The only time it was shaved was during mourning observances.

When beards were the fashion in the Western world, moustache cups were also popular. The Ainu long ago developed a similar device, which dignified the process of drinking and came to have a ritual significance: carved moustache lifters. These narrow strips of wood, about nine inches long, are carved in various geometric designs or in the likeness of a bear. At formal drinking

AFTER CENTURIES OF INTERMARRIAGE WITH THEIR JAPANESE NEIGHBORS, FEW PURE AINU REMAIN. ONE WOMAN IN THIS PICTURE HAS DISTINCTIVE MONGOLOID FEATURES.

AN AINU MAN AND WOMAN FROM THE ISLAND OF HOKKAIDO IN NORTHERN JAPAN. A CAUCASOID TRIBE IN ITS PURE FORM, THE AINU ARE PROUD OF THEIR ABUNDANT WAVY HAIR. THE WOMEN TATTOO THEIR WRISTS AND FACES.

ceremonies—funerals or housewarmings—specially carved moustache lifters are used, often with wood shavings attached ingeniously to the sides of the wooden strip. The men do not forget to offer a few drops of the liquor found on the end of the lifter to the gods. The Ainu drink a fermented beverage similar to sake, which they probably learned to make from the Japanese.

At first glance the foreigner may find the women disfigured by the elaborate tattoos around the mouth, and frequently on the forehead and hands. The tattoos are blue-black, and the mouth tattoo may extend from ear to ear, being elaborated upon from the time the girl is small to the time she marries.

Marriage generally takes place when the girl is from fifteen to seventeen and the boy about twenty, and the proceedings may be initiated by either the boy's or the girl's parents. In former times it was quite common for the girl to court the boy, but this is now

considered indecorous. The Ainu may frequently marry first cousins, and a man may often marry his niece; but a woman must never marry a man whose mother has the same design on her secret belt as she has. Every Ainu woman wears one of these belts, which she must never allow any man to see. Women even hesitate to speak to each other about their belts, whose designs indicate the line of matrilineal descent.

Betrothals are often arranged by the parents when the children are very young, and the boy and girl may have sexual intercourse as soon as they are able. If they decide not to marry when they come of age, they are free to break the engagement and seek other mates.

A romantic story is told by the Ainu of a beautiful young boy and girl who were paragons in every way. One day they met on a path, and the girl was so struck by the boy's appearance that she could not make herself step aside and let him pass, as the woman is supposed to do. They fell in love at first sight and wanted to marry, but each had been betrothed since childhood to remarkably ill-favored persons. The parents in each case considered the matches very politic and would not allow the young lovers to sever their previous commitments. So the handsome pair ran off to a wooded glen, twelve days' journey from their village, and led an idyllic life until the two who were jilted, accompanied by several cutthroats, finally found them and murdered the beautiful young man. The girl then committed suicide at her lover's side. The revenging pair also met violent deaths, as did the cutthroats, and got their just deserts for crossing true love. The lovers were assumed to be living a happy life together in the next world.

In this world, of course, marriage is not always so idyllic among the Ainu. Divorces, in such instances, are easy to obtain. The husband may send his wife back to her parents, or the wife may walk out on her husband. They may divorce on grounds of incompatibility, dislike, or adultery. The wife may leave a husband who does not adequately provide for her. The husband will frequently divorce his wife if she does not bear him a male child, since they believe that this is the woman's fault. Adultery is often punished by beating, in contrast to the considerable sexual freedom that is allowed before marriage. Male travelers have reported girls making open advances to them. The girls, despite their tattoos, are frequently attractive, and have charmed men with their sparkling

MOST AINU VILLAGES ARE CLOSE TO THE SEA, AND THE AINU ARE SKILLFUL FISHERMEN. UNTIL RECENTLY THEY WORE LONG COLORFUL ROBES WITH GEOMETRIC DESIGNS.

brown or hazel eyes and their playful nibbles, which is the Ainu form of kissing.

A man may have several wives, who live in separate houses. As a rule the wives do not get along well with each other.

When an Ainu woman learns she is pregnant, she gives a feast for her husband and family. At the time of birth she is assisted by the women. Meanwhile, her husband lies huddled in his house, feeling quite sick. It is believed that at this time the strength of the father is going out to the new child.

In a unique operation performed on the Ainu baby, an incision is made at the top of each thigh where it connects with the torso. The mother binds the wounds with strips of fungus taken from under the bark of certain dead trees. The operation is not a circumcision rite; according to the mother, it keeps the child from chafing between the legs.

The Ainu follow complex forms of etiquette. At mealtime the men eat first, and the women and children eat what is left. When the woman leaves the house she must go out backward; it is disrespectful for a woman to turn her back on a man. No one may enter another's house uninvited, and as it is very impolite to knock, a would-be visitor must stand outside, making noises and clearing his throat, in the hope that people inside will hear and invite him in. It is a marvelous sight to see two women greet each other who have not seen one another for a long time. Each puts her head on the other's shoulder and they begin to weep. Then in a weeping, sing-song chant both simultaneously relate what has happened to each since they last met. This ritualistic recitation can last up to a half hour. Whenever a woman meets a man, she steps aside, putting her hands over her mouth in a sign of respect.

Until fairly recently the Ainu wore long colorful cloth robes embroidered with elegant geometric designs. The cloth was woven of long strips of dyed thread that came from the soft inner bark of certain trees. During the winter the Ainu still wear robes made from animal skins.

At one time the Ainu lived in pit dwellings, but for some time now they have been making reed thatched huts. At night the sleeping occupants may be bothered by rats scampering over their bodies.

Most of the villages are close to the sea, but there are some scattered settlements farther inland. It is the inland hunters who have preserved more of the ancient way of life than have the seaside fishermen, who come into steady contact with other civilizations.

Besides hunting and fishing, the Ainu gather wild herbs, roots, and berries. They also do a little primitive gardening during the short growing season. Bows and arrows are used for hunting deer, although guns have been introduced.

Justice among the Ainu in former times was often decided through trial by ordeal. One method was to put the accused into a cauldron of water that was being heated over a fire and keep him there until he confessed. Fortunately this method was used only when the person's guilt was fairly certain. At times the accused would be dared to thrust his arm into a pot of boiling water. If he refused he was assumed guilty; if he put his arm in the pot and it came out scalded, this was also a sign of his guilt. He was declared innocent only if his arm emerged uninjured. A similar test was to have the accused hold a piece of heated iron or stone in his hand; if his hand blistered he was guilty.

The drinking ordeal, according to the Ainu, was very painful. The accused was forced to drink the contents of a large tub of water without taking his mouth from the tub. If he could do it, he was declared innocent. The favorite test for a woman was to force her to smoke several pipes of tobacco. The ashes were then put in a cup of water, which the woman had to drink. If she could do all this without getting sick, she was innocent.

The stake ordeal consisted of placing two stakes in the ground at the arm's length of the accused. He was attached, spread-eagled, to the stakes with rope and had to remain until he confessed. These ordeals were so painful that some Ainu committed suicide rather than submit to them.

The highlight of Ainu religious life is the Bear Sacrifice, a spectacular and gruesome ceremony in which the bear is killed so that he may go to the gods as an emissary of the people. As with most Arctic peoples, bears are regarded by the Ainu as a sacred animal. To prepare for this ceremony the men go out and catch a small bear cub, which they bring back to the village. It is given to a woman who nurses it with her own milk and treats it like a human baby. When it grows a little larger it is put into a cage. All the while it is fed generously and coddled. When the bear is large enough to break out of the wooden cage it is considered ready for the ceremony. Usually this is after about six months, but sometimes the bears are kept for two or three years.

The person in charge of the festival invites the villagers to the ceremonies. Various libations are made to the gods, who are supplicated to forgive the necessary sacrifice of the bear. A special cup of wine is offered to the bear. The woman who nursed the bear weeps in sorrow at his approaching fate. A series of dances follows. First the women and girls of the village dance around the cage, clapping and singing. Then, in contrast to this happy dance, comes a dance of sorrow and mourning performed by the bear's foster mother and all the other women of the village who have nursed previous bears. Finally the bear is brought out of the cage and tied up. He is paraded about, and the men shoot at him with specially decorated blunted arrows.

The excitement mounts, and the final moment arrives: A block of wood is forced into the bear's mouth; then wooden canes are placed in his throat and on his back. Several men lean on the cane on his back until the animal strangles. The bear is usually also shot or speared. The blood is carefully caught in a pot, as it would be sacrilegious if a single drop were to hit the ground. The men ceremoniously drink the blood, smearing it over their long beards. The bear is skinned, with his head attached to the skin, and several ceremonies are performed with the skin. The meat of the bear is cooked and then eaten, except for the liver, which is chopped up and eaten raw by the participants. Finally the bear's skull is hung on a fence, along with the other fetish skulls of the village.

Today, due to the influence of missionaries and the prohibitions of governments, this ceremony is practically a thing of the past. Soon the whole Ainu way of life will be gone,* and possibly the genetic distinctiveness of this group will be lost. It will be interesting to see if the origins and history of this unique people, who speak a language totally unrelated to any other known tongue, will be pieced together before they vanish.

* A few small Ainu villages in Hokkaido have maintained and even elaborated what they remember of their old customs because of contact with the Japanese. The villages have become tourist attractions, and the villagers are making a living from the Japanese visitors' interest in them.

# THE MURUNG

Few truly primitive, untouched peoples remain in the modern world, but a few such groups do exist in the hilly jungle region that lies between Eastern Pakistan and Burma. This border area, known as the Chittagong Hill Tracts, is five thousand square miles of dense tropical rain forest, periodically deluged by the monsoons and floods, and is inhabited by some 300,000 people belonging to at least twelve different groups. Some of the groups are comparatively civilized and follow the Buddhist or Hindu faiths. The more primitive groups are restricted to the less accessible Bandarban forest area; among these are the 16,000 Murung tribesmen.

Ethnically, the Murung people differ from the East Pakistani plainsmen; they appear to be racially connected with the primitive tribes who once stretched from Tibet to Thailand. Brownish or wheat-colored, with straight black hair, they are of medium height and strong build. They do not resemble the Mongoloid peoples in that their noses tend to be  straight, their cheekbones are not prominent, and their eyes have no epicanthic fold.

The Murung, despite the advances of modern transportation, are still effectively shut off from the outside world during the monsoon season. They live in scattered villages of five to fifteen families each, in houses built on bamboo stilts against the hillsides. Houses are constructed mainly of bamboo, with wooden poles to support the roof. There is a main central hall, an adjoining open courtyard, and a few attached rooms, which are ventilated by sliding windows. The main hall is used as a common sitting, working, and sleeping room by everyone except the young married couples; they live and sleep in the attached rooms, which are taboo to outsiders.

The young bride, who comes to live in her husband's family house, is assured of a private home. She has great responsibilities to shoulder; in fact, the women do much more work than the men. Under the Murung division of labor, the men do the cultivating, make bamboo fences for their fields, weave the baskets and mats, build the houses, gin the cotton, milk the cows and goats, go fishing, and do simple carpentry—mere relaxation in comparison with the women, who must tend the house, fetch water from the streams, collect fuel from the jungle brush, husk rice twice a day, spin and weave cloth and drapery, help harvest the grain, market the produce, and shop at the jungle bazaars.

Courtship is carried on in an orderly manner among the Murung, but elopement is allowed. However, if a couple is to be married, the village elders and the parents must give their consent. A young girl is visited in the evening by bachelors of her own and surrounding villages. The young people spend the evening chatting and singing romantic songs of love and yearning. The girl has ample opportunity to choose the young man she wants, and the courtship may go on for months before she finally decides to elope with her intended. After the elopement the girl's parents conduct a search and go to the boy's house to find out how much he has promised to pay for her. The price generally comes to the equivalent of about $70.

Although they do not have a currency of their own, the Murung obtain currency at the bazaars where they do their marketing. The girl's body is figured to be worth about $20, and $2.80 covers the cost of her mother's breast feeding. A portion goes to pay for the cost of the articles woven and prepared by the bride-to-be, which will be carried to the husband's home; the rest pays for the required wedding presents to the in-laws—a sword, an arrow, a pickax, a spear, and the daggerlike implement known as a "dao." The price is not due until after the wedding.

If the parents approve the price, and provided there is no

social barrier to the match, there will generally be an agreement to the marriage. The Murung have a kind of caste system, and if a girl elopes with a boy of inferior social status, there is sure to be trouble. The village elders meet to decide whether the boy or the girl was the instigator of the elopement. If it is the girl, she will get off with a fine of about $6. If the boy is responsible, he has to pay $15 and distribute newly slaughtered pig meat to all his fellow villagers. But there is hope for the ill-starred lovers. If they are able to stage four elopements, the boy may claim the girl as his legal wife, with no further fines, although he must pay the fines for the previous three elopments.

The wedding ceremony takes place in the groom's house. The bride arrives with red-painted palms, and is accompanied by her father and the village elders. No females may accompany her. The village priest conducts the ceremony, tying a black cotton thread that contains a bit of the right ear of a freshly slaughtered pig around the right wrists of bride and groom. A similar thread is tied around the wrists of all members of the groom's family who are present. Then a paste of turmeric and rice is applied to the forehead, breast, and spine of both bride and groom. After this they are declared man and wife. A feast follows the ceremony.

Much more is made of the ceremonies surrounding death, which is believed to be caused by evil spirits. The dead body is washed and wrapped in a white sheet with the face exposed. It is placed in the main hall for from one day to a week, depending on the family's wealth. During this time the family must provide the entire village with meals of buffalo, cow, pig, and goat meat, as well as chickens, boiled rice, and wine. The corpse will begin to smell, but this in no way deters the feasting taking place around it.

After the feasting period the body is carried outside the village for cremation. A dog is killed just before the cremation, so that it may lead the dead person to the great spirit Torai who lives high in the sky. It is believed that good people return from Torai and are reborn as human beings. For this reason the dead person's forehead is marked with a patch of red dye, and as soon as a child is born in the house, they examine the body for a birthmark in order to see if the same person has been reborn in their family.

If the deceased was a bad person, however, it is believed he will return to the world in animal form—as a pig or dog, or even as an insect or earthworm.

Each village has a priest, called a *sara,* who may invoke the aid of Torai, who controls all the evil spirits that bring misfortune and sickness to the lives of men. The sara conducts the ceremonies of the community and serves as the medicine man, offering sacrifices of animals to the evil spirits after first divining which spirit is responsible.

Music and dancing form an important part of Murung community life. Their musical instruments are a two-sided drum and assorted bamboo flutes, ranging from six inches to over eighteen feet, each attached to a gourd at its base. Only the unmarried girls may dance. They join hands to form a circle, moving slowly with a simple rhythmic step.

The main occasion for dancing is the Sachiya Kom, or "killing performance," when a cow is sacrificed to Torai. This ceremony takes place when an excellent harvest is gathered or when someone has vowed to thank the spirits for a recovery from illness. The cow is tied to a stake in an open space. The host serves a lavish feast to the village, and there is much drinking. The unmarried girls dance around the cow until the morning hours, and resume dancing the next day. In the afternoon of the second day the sara directs a young man to spear the cow, which he does with one tremendous thrust into the animal's heart. The cow's tongue is then pulled out and displayed as revenge against the cursed cow who, according to the myth, was guilty of eating the banana leaves on which their religious scriptures had been written.

The Murung need little clothing in their tropical climate: men wear loincloths; women wear aprons. Ornamentation takes the form of aluminum or other cheap metal bangles purchased at the bazaars. The faces of both men and women are stained with red and pink dyes. To enhance their beauty, women stain their teeth with black or deep-red dye, and men color their teeth coal black.

The Murung are self-sufficient in meeting their needs except for salt, oil, and metals. They have never learned to make pottery, using wood and fiber containers instead. These items are bought from other tribes at the bazaars in exchange for Murung products. The bazaar is the only contact they have with the outside world, and they are extremely wary of strangers.

The Murung practice a form of agriculture called *jhooming.*

66

A piece of land is cleared by burning off the jungle growth and removing the debris; then the sower deposits the seeds in small shallow holes, which he digs with his dao. Strangely, he is unconcerned about which crops get planted where. He just drops in at random any of the seeds that are all mixed together in the bag carried on his shoulder. Thus rice, cotton, corn, sesamum, pumpkins, melons, and tobacco come up in one common patch. The plants must be carefully weeded and protected from hungry wild animals. If the man has been faithful in his care, and if there have been no floods or severe storms, a bountiful harvest may be gathered that provides up to three or four times the annual needs of his family. The food is stored in large round bins kept in the attached rooms of the house. Each bin holds about a ton of food.

The simple self-sufficient life of these people provides us with a glance far back into the past. It is probable that even these inaccessible people will not remain for very long in their present state, threatened as they have been, first by the World War II army operations, then by the post-independence fighting in Burma and India and by the Indian pressure to Hinduize such areas, and now by the guerrilla war against the Indian army going on in the nearby Naga area.

# THE MOI

In the mountains of central Vietnam, Laos, and Cambodia live a number of primitive tribes whose total population is perhaps 500,000. They are called collectively by the Vietnamese word *Moi*, a generic term that means simply "savage." The Laotians call them the Kha and the Cambodians, Pnong. They live in the inaccessible jungle areas of the Indochina peninsula, but their isolation from the complex civilizations that have developed around them is also due in part to their suspicion of outsiders. Their more civilized neighbors have always regarded them as dangerous, savage people and have spread stories of their cannibalism, but these stories have not been verified.

The Moi live in a big-game hunter's paradise, although non-hunters might find it a bit harrowing. The elephant is an economic staple for them, and the tiger is their most feared and venerated enemy. A Moi village is often abandoned and a new site found merely to avoid the ravages of a man-eating tiger who has been preying on the villagers.

Comparatively little has been learned about the customs and beliefs of these peoples, some of whom live within one hundred miles of Saigon. It is possible that their culture, caught up in such a long period of war and strife, may be destroyed before much can ever be learned about them. Their jungles have been a complete mystery until quite recently. As late as the beginning of the twentieth century, the maps of Indochina left this area blank. One simply read: "Waste Land. Savages."

Many of the tribes live in villages fortified in a unique jungle style. The village must be approached through tunnels constructed of thorn bushes. When enemies approach, the villagers can quickly cut down the tunnels, and once collapsed, the thorns make the tunnels virtually impassable.

The Moi are descendents of aboriginal Indonesian peoples who later spread through much of the South Pacific. In addition, the Moi have been mixed with various Caucasian and Mongoloid peoples over the centuries. They are small, averaging around five feet five inches, with slim elegant bodies; a fat person is rarely seen. Their skin color ranges from reddish brown to dark yellow. Their coarse black hair is often wavy, and both men and women usually wear it rolled up in a knot at the back, fastened with a comb or band. The cheekbones are prominent, the nose broad, and the lips thick.

Travelers are intrigued by the ear plugs, which many of the Moi wear. In some areas only the women wear these decorations; in others they are worn by the men as well. When the Moi child is very young his ears are pierced, and bamboo sticks are inserted in the holes. Gradually the holes in the earlobes are stretched by inserting larger plugs. A greatly distended earlobe is a sign of beauty in a woman; occasionally a girl, by the time she reaches marriageable age, will have earlobes that reach to her shoulders.

Large ivory hoop earrings are an alternate to the ear plugs. Generally the most valued ear plugs are made of ivory as well, but one traveler tells of having delighted the tribesmen by giving them champagne corks, which they proudly wore in their ears.

Ear plugs are not solely decoration, however; sometimes a man will wear one hollow ear plug in which he carries the poison that he uses on his arrows when hunting. Back in the fiercer days when the Moi often engaged in intertribal war, or war with outsiders, the poison arrows were used on the enemy. As protection, the Moi warrior often carried an antidote to the poison in one of his hollow plugs so that he could treat himself if he were shot. Moi poisons are of the cardiac type and very lethal; they can kill a man in twenty minutes.

Many of the Moi tribes subject their men to a more painful

form of mutilation. In some tribes even the girls undergo the same painful process, which is performed in the name of beauty. At puberty, as part of the initiation rites, the boy's upper and lower front teeth are broken off close to the gum with a stone or knife. From then on, he will chew with only his back molars. Sometimes the broken stumps are filed to sharp points.

The only other body decorations are coiled bracelets. The copper needed for both these and the great copper gongs, which are the most highly prized musical instrument of the Moi, is obtained from shallow veins found just under the ground. Over the years it has been the custom of a group that discovers copper to immediately drive away all the other inhabitants of the area. This may have something to do with the legend that has grown up among the Moi about the smelting of copper. They say that the copper is obtained by a race of Amazon-like women, who visit their husbands only once a year and who kill all their male babies. The women are very vigorous and strong, have short tails, and are always accompanied by wild dogs.

Iron is also found in its natural state throughout Moi territory and is used for lances and knives. It is smelted by the so-called Catalan method. The iron ore is mixed with a great mass of charcoal and stirred for twenty-four hours in a large brick bin-like furnace. The iron produced is largely in the form of a "bloom," a stonelike mass of globules of iron, cinder, and fused minerals known as slag. Only a small percentage of the iron produced is free enough of these impurities to be hammered into wrought iron.

The Moi economy is based on hunting, fishing, food gathering, and primitive agriculture. They use the type of undeveloped rain-forest farming known as "slash and burn" to grow one crop of rice a year. At the end of the rainy season, in November, the villagers clear enough forest to supply an entire year's crop for the village. In April the fallen tree trunks, now dried by the sun, are burned. The fire lasts several days. The rice seed is then planted in hollow trenches made in the ashy soil, and left to be nourished by the rains and the soil. Although the Moi are not a nomadic people, they do change their villages from time to time when the forest lands about them have been exhausted by their agriculture. In addition to rice, the Moi grow corn—which attains an enormous size—tobacco, and cinnamon. If their food stores run low, they go out to gather bamboo shoots and forest roots.

The Moi are very fond of fish, and an abundant supply comes from their rivers. They fish with line, net, and spear. Wild pigs, goats, and deer are trapped with various cleverly devised snares, which make traveling through Moi territory perilous. Traps are also sometimes set for tigers and panthers, enemies of the jungle people.

The Moi have mercilessly slaughtered the elephants that once were abundant in this territory. They keep some of the ivory, but much of it is sold to outsiders. When an elephant has been killed the hunters greedily drink its blood. They cut off the tip of the trunk, for this section is considered a valuable amulet. The genitals are then cut off and served as the evening meal.

The Moi are a monogamous people. A man marries a girl within his own group rather than sending out envoys to distant villages. Thus, cousins often marry each other. Descent is traced through the mother's side of the family. The man changes his name when his first child and then his first grandchild are born, becoming "father of ———," and then "father's father of ———."

Premarital sex is common among the Moi. It is believed that sexual relations help the girl's breasts to develop, although the Moi concede that they do develop by themselves with age. Many believe that sexual intercourse is not the prime reason for pregnancy but that a spirit enters the girl's body and makes her pregnant. They do, however, concede that it is the sexual relations with a man that give the spirit an opening to approach the girl. Because these spirits of fertility are often found near water, unmarried girls do not stay bathing in the water for long periods.

Boys, once they reach puberty, sleep together in a separate hut, away from the rest of the village. Ostensibly, the reason for this isolation is to keep them away from the girls, but of course it is a small matter to arrange a rendezvous in the jungle. Sometimes the Moi girl kills her firstborn because no one comes forward to claim paternity. This is not regarded as a tragedy but serves as a proof of the girl's fertility.

Marriage arrangements are usually initiated by the parents of the boy, but this does not preclude an elaborate courtship period. The Moi have an abundant store of love songs that are to be sung in dialogue by a boy and girl. There is a story frequently told about a young tribesman who loved the most beautiful and

71

coquettish girl in his village. Because he was not handsome, the girl scorned him. One day he approached her and her girl friends at the village well, and in the presence of all, he begged the girl to marry him. She laughed and said that she would only marry him if he came to her with a nest of red ants in his mouth. To everyone's astonishment he complied with her request, and as soon as his mouth and throat were cured from the hideous ant bites, they were married. The girl said, "At least the father of my children shall be a brave man."

The parents of the man are expected to pay the girl's parents a purchase price. Frequently the young man serves a period of labor in the girl's household.

After marriage strict fidelity is expected. A husband has the right to beat his wife if he suspects her of infidelity. He may even kill a baby whose paternity he doubts.

At the time of childbirth the woman is put in a special hut, and only her closest relatives are allowed to be present when labor begins. She gives birth in a sitting position, leaning against the knees of one woman; the other women help along her labor by massaging her stomach with tiger gut. After delivery the mother rests on a low bed. A fire is kept constantly burning at her side, for the smoke is thought to act as an antiseptic. Her friends show their devotion by bringing wood for the fire. Within two weeks the mother is again doing her regular hard work.

Many of the Moi groups profess to be Buddhists, but their old religion, based on animism, prevails. Spirits are believed to inhabit certain stones, trees, and wild animals. Perhaps the most curious manifestation of this religion is among such groups as the Bahnar, who practice litholatry, or stone worship. Stones of immense size are set on high, bamboo-supported pedestals. These shrines are venerated by the natives, and at certain times sacrifices are made to the spirits dwelling in the stones.

Medicine men carry out ceremonies to extract the malevolent spirits, which can cause sickness. Often at the climax of the rites the medicine man holds up a handful of dirt that he has extracted from the sick one's body. The dirt contains the evil spirit.

Black magic is also practiced. A man will follow his enemy's tracks into the forest until he finds a place where the man has urinated; then he sticks a bamboo spear in the spot. This is supposed to make his enemy sick. The man will keep going back to the spot and thrusting the stick farther into the ground or pulling it out, according to whether he wishes to intensify or lessen the sickness of his enemy.

When someone dies the corpse is carefully brought out of the thatched bamboo hut through a hole cut in the roof or wall. This is so that the dead man's spirit will not know in what direction it has been removed; otherwise the spirit would surely return to haunt the house. The corpse is carried into the forest until the family burying ground is reached. The mourners choose a tree, cut it down, and hollow it out. The body is placed in the hollowed-out trunk, along with amulets, domestic tools, and food. A shallow grave is dug and then a palm-leaf roof is built over the grave, making a sort of shrine for the dead man.

In Moi government each village elects a chief. There is a slave class comprising debtors who have been forced to sell themselves into servitude. Blood revenge is an established form of justice, and justice is also frequently meted out by trial by ordeal. The accuser and the accused are both dunked in the river. He who stays under longer is in the right.

The Moi have been squeezed into an ever-shrinking territory during the twentieth century and have not escaped the influences of civilization. In their case these influences have far too often been those of war and destruction.

*Asia*

# THE BURYAT

The Buryat of southern Siberia provide a fascinating example of the manner in which a primitive clan society can be acculturated within a few centuries into a modern civilized nation.

The origins of the Buryat, who, according to their own legends, are descended from a great dark gray bull, are still not completely known. They probably are descended at least partly from the widespread hunters and gatherers who formerly inhabited Siberia, thus sharing a genetic and historical connection with many of the peoples of the eastern U.S.S.R.

During the first millennium of modern times the area was overrun with Turkic tribes with whom the Buryat were mixed. Then somewhere around the twelfth or thirteenth centuries, there were vast migrations of Mongols who overwhelmed these older inhabitants, impressing on them their culture, physical traits, and language. The result of this genetic and cultural blending created the beginnings of the present-day Buryat, primarily a Mongoloid people who speak a Mongol dialect.

The Buryat live in the mountainous area around Lake Baikal, one of the most magnificent scenic areas in Asia. More than three-quarters of their land is covered with dense forest, mostly coniferous, which is known as *taiga*. The two main divisions of the Buryat are eastern and western, according to which side of the lake they inhabit.

Marco Polo described the ancestors of the present Buryat as a wild people when he made his famous journey across Asia in the late thirteenth century. Between that time and the late seventeenth century the Buryat were left alone to develop on their own, except for the occasional influence of Chinese and Mongolian traders and religious men. During this time Buryat life remained essentially primitive while their neighbors and relatives, the Mongols to the south and east, were developing highly civilized cultures.

But the diversity that the Buryat have embraced during the last 250 years, since the arrival of the Russian Cossacks sent by the czar to subdue Siberia, has been astounding. The influx of Russian and Cossack traders and settlers not only created new pressures in general, but also provided new sources from which to acquire wealth and power for different Buryat groups.

In the early contact period the sociopolitical organization of Buryat society involved clan units—where rights to such strategic resources as grazing lands were more or less exclusively restricted to hereditary clan members—and wider federations of these clans, with tribute payment and directive powers reserved for certain units. Nevertheless, the power and wealth differences between and within clans were relatively fluid and comparatively minor.

With the arrival of new forms and sources of wealth and power, through trade and alliance with the Cossack colonists, greater internal differences within Buryat social and political units developed, with some taking a more stable ascendance over others. To a certain extent this was offset by later strategies by the Russian colonists, who saw the dangers inherent in a more united Buryat people. But later on, when the area was well integrated under the control of the Russian Empire, a more formal organization of Buryat groups again became desirable as an adjunct to effective administration.

Thus the Buryat developed from a society of isolated groups to a people with a typical nineteenth-century sense of national identity, much influenced by the teachings of outsiders, mostly political exiles. (Incidentally, most of the information we have on Siberian tribes has come from political exiles who found that studying the natives was the most interesting way to while away the long Siberian winters.)

The effects of acculturation and social modification were not limited to changes in political organization. By the twentieth century most of the Buryat had at least nominally accepted one of the two great foreign religions with which they came in contact—Buddhism and Christianity.

The eastern Buryat had been gradually converted to the northern form of the Buddhist faith, Lamaism, famous for its asceticism and its prayer wheels. Frequently Lamaism combined with old shamanistic practices to form a bizarre blend. In the western part of Siberia shamanism retained much of its old force, and when the Russian czars tried to convert the Buryat, the Buryat usually allowed themselves to be baptized while adhering to their old beliefs.

The indigenous Buryat religion contains two kinds of gods—the good, or "white," gods and the bad, or "black," gods. Both kinds must be invoked and placated, and the most usual method is by animal sacrifice. Sometimes these sacrifices are for private, individual reasons, and sometimes they involve an entire community. A private sacrifice may take place when a person is sick. He will call in the shaman, who will diagnose the cause of his illness by burning the shoulder blade of a sheep until it is white. He "reads" the resultant cracks in the bone to see what the man has done to anger which god. Often the god will demand the sacrifice of an animal, and the shaman knows from experience which god requires which animal—black ram, white ram, white goat, black goat, bull, or horse as the case may be.

The shaman kills the animal by making an incision in the breast and pulling out the heart. The body is disjointed at the neck and knees; the skin is removed, except from the legs and head; and the body is carried off to be boiled. The skin of the animal is hung on top of a long pole driven into the ground, the head facing the place where the responsible spirit dwells. The flesh is then eaten by the family, with some being offered to the gods. At other times the bones of the animal may be broken into small pieces and put into a bag along with the pleura. The bag is hung from a tall pole in the sick man's yard, where it remains until the bag rots and falls.

The most spectacular sacrifice is the annual horse ceremony, which has been performed since time immemorial. The ritual takes place on a hill where there are several stone altars, and involves the slaughter of a number of fine horses. Among a people so fond of horses, this sacrifice is a tribute to their veneration of the gods.

First the horse is purified by being led between a series of fires. Then it is taken to the officiating persons, who sprinkle milk on the horse's face and invoke all the gods in turn, as in a Christian litany. The horse's legs are tied with ropes and he is flipped on his back, helpless, held securely by several men. Another man, using a long sharp knife, makes a deep gash behind the breastbone, allowing him to pull out the horse's heart. If the man is skillful, the horse dies instantly. The horses are skinned, their bones burned on the altars, and their flesh boiled and eaten by the worshippers. With the meat, the people drink *tartasun,* a clear liquor distilled from sour milk.

The Buryat finally became a formally organized nation in 1923, the Buryat-Mongol Autonomous Soviet Socialist Republic (the name Mongol was dropped in 1958); but they were by this time only a minority of the population in the country that bore their name. Most of the population now consists of Russian settlers. This is not to say that the Buryat population declined; quite the opposite is true. When the Russians first met the Buryat they numbered around 25,000; by 1897 there were more than 285,000.

The Buryat culture is vanishing not through extinction of the Buryat people, but through their absorption into a larger and more highly developed group. In religion they have practiced simultaneously Christianity, Buddhism, and shamanism, or combinations of these. They have lived as primitive fishermen, nomadic herdsmen, sedentary farmers, and modern city dwellers employed in industry.

At the present day, most of the Buryat have become alienated from their old culture and way of life. This process, though perhaps inevitable everywhere, has been hastened in their case because of the official attitude, which has sought to stamp out or disregard cultural materials that the government does not regard as useful.

Despite the general acculturization of the Buryat, there are still some nomadic herdsmen who continue to practice the old religion and the old customs. These rapidly disappearing individuals live on the outskirts of the territory in the most remote areas of this mountainous country. Their homes are the ancient *yurtas,* large felt tents that have a hole at the top for smoke to escape, with a hole dug in the earth floor for the fire.

The rest of the Buryat who do not live in town (the principal city is Ulan-Ude, the capital) now live in simple wooden houses. They raise large herds of cattle and sheep and are fine horse breeders. As horsemen, the Buryat are among the world's best; but now, instead of fighting the Cossacks on horseback, they content themselves with engaging in relay races at their annual festivals.

The Soviets have encouraged agriculture among these people, and much of their land around the Selenga River Valley was put into cultivation during the Soviet "virgin lands" project of the 1950's. Most Buryat now receive some education, and they have a written language.

The name Buryat derives from a Russian word meaning "the brotherly people." The Buryat have had many new "brothers" settle in their country, and in the process have been obliged to change their way of life.

# THE CHUKCHI

In the northeasternmost part of Siberia, bordering on the Bering Strait, is the Chukchi Peninsula. On and around this peninsula live the Chukchi, one of the most ancient peoples of this section of the world. The Chukchi language is a member of the Paleo–Siberian language family. Though now restricted mainly to the northeast tip of Siberia, those who speak the various languages of this stock are thought to have once occupied large sections of Siberia and to have extended much farther west and south. Today they number about twelve thousand.

The Chukchi are the most prosperous people of the area. They make a livelihood either by fishing for sea mammals or by breeding reindeer. These two different occupations mark the distinction between the two groups—the Reindeer Chukchi and the Maritime Chukchi. The name Chukchi itself is derived from a word meaning "rich in reindeer," and was the term the Reindeer people used to distinguish themselves from other Maritime peoples. The Reindeer Chukchi have always been more prosperous than their Maritime brothers, especially since European and American fishing began depleting the waters. There is some evidence that all Chukchi were once a seagoing people, but then gradually turned to the forest as a more stable means of living.

Though there has been relatively little interbreeding with

recently arrived Caucasians and Mongolians, the Chukchi are undoubtedly part of the eastern Siberian gene pool. Their rather stocky heavy build has sometimes been suggested as evidence of close connection with Eskimo and Aleut peoples. However, much the same body structure is common to many primitive peoples who have resided in Arctic and sub-Arctic regions. There is, of course, considerable variation within the Chukchi population; although they all are generally black-haired and swarthy, the Maritime people are said to tend toward a darker complexion than the Reindeer people.

Because of their comparative economic wealth, the Chukchi are looked upon as attractive mates by the neighboring tribes, including their close relatives, the Koryaks. They have also intermarried to some extent with the Russian settlers.

The Reindeer Chukchi first started their great herds by raiding those of the Koryaks during the eighteenth century. Chukchi reindeer, squat, heavy, and half wild, are unsuitable for milking or riding, and less than ideal as harness animals. Their chief value is that they are hardy, and that they fatten quickly and make excellent food. The Chukchi often trade their food reindeer to the Lamuts in exchange for the Lamut reindeer, which make far better harness animals.

The presence of predators, coupled with the extremely harsh climatic conditions, has at times wreaked havoc upon the Chukchi herds. But certain favorable conditions help to build them up again rapidly: grazing lands, for example, though meager and broken, are extensive and unused by any other domestic animals. The isolation of the region decreases the incidence of epidemics among the scattered herds.

The Chukchi man wears two layers of reindeer fur—fur boots, trousers, and cap, and a loose-fitting fur shirt that can be tightened around the collar with a string. The women wear similar clothing, but the sleeves of the shirts are so unwieldy that they often keep one arm and breast bare in order to do their work without interference. They have a tremendous capacity to endure cold and frequently work outside in the snow, dressed in this way, the exertions of their labor keeping them warm. The Maritime people buy the cast-off clothing of their Reindeer relatives, since the latter wear new clothes each season.

The Chukchi live in large round tents, with an oblong inner

room serving as the main family room. The tent is always set to the same points of the compass, and the left side belongs traditionally to the master. The main meal is eaten in this inner room, which is lighted by a single lamp. At the meal, guests strip to the waist, and the members of the family are naked except for a belt about their waists. The heat becomes stifling and the stench considerable.

The social units among the Chukchi bind only loosely. The most important permanent unit is the family. The Maritime Chukchi live in villages organized on territorial contiguity rather than on family relationship. The family that has lived there the longest often occupies the front house and has a social superiority. In addition, each village—or camp, among the Reindeer people—has its "strong man," who is sometimes also regarded as the master of the camp. In former times, when the Chukchi were constantly warring with the Koryaks, Eskimos, and Cossacks, the strong man was considered the great warrior and hero of his people. In addition, among the Maritime people there is a social unit called the "boatful," consisting of eight oarsmen and a helmsman. The helmsman is the boat master and the owner of the boat. The crew is made up of his close relatives, and he distributes the products of the catch to them according to a set system.

Among the Reindeer Chukchi the main social unit is the *varat*, meaning "collection of those who are together." It consists of a group of related families. According to one authority, Waldemar Bogoras, the varat is what remains of a much stricter clan organization that existed in earlier times. Also there was at one time a slave class, although it has not existed since before the coming of Soviet rule.

Another name for the varat is *cin-yirin,* or "collection of those who take part in blood revenge." Until the consolidation of a state legal and administrative system in the area, during the early Soviet period, a prime function of the varat was to support its members during feuds.

If a murder is committed outside the family group or the varat, the members of the slain man's group will feud with the killer's group. In former times the revenge was frequently satisfied by replacing the murdered man with a man from the family of the murderer. The replacement had to perform all the work of the slain man and was treated like a slave. When a murder is committed within the family group it is handled by that group alone. Usually the murdered one is thought to be a "bad man" and is killed by his own family so that he cannot commit a crime and involve the family in a feud.

Although the family is the most stable social unit, it is not as firm an institution as among some other Siberian tribes. Indeed, there is no word for "family" in the Chukchi's language, only terms meaning "houseful" or "housemates." Among the Chukchi, unmarried persons are rare and generally have some sort of sexual deficiency. Virginity in a bride is neither expected nor required. There is no word for "girl" in the language, although there is an expression for a female: "not yet put in use." Frequently very young children are married; they then grow up together and are very much attached to each other when they become adults.

Families will often exchange children in marriage; and occasionally a family promises a child before it is born. Children reared together with a view to marriage sleep together. Bogoras tells of a boy of five married to a girl of twenty. In such a case the girl brings up the boy until he is old enough to be her husband. Sometimes the girl will be given a "marriage companion" in the meantime, and she may end up tending both a child of this union and her contracted husband at the same time. The man in most cases obtains his wife by working for her kinsmen. Marriage need not be permanent among the Chukchi, and the wife will frequently go home to her family. If there are children, those who require nursing go with the mother; the others go with the father.

Polygamy is rare among the less prosperous Maritime Chukchi, but it is fairly common among the Reindeer people. Many rich reindeer breeders who have several herds will keep a wife— and prospective bridegrooms of daughters—with each herd. There are also men with only one herd who will keep several wives in the same camp. In this case the man tries to keep them in separate tents, or at least in separate sleeping places under one tent.

An unusual custom that is practiced by the Chukchi is "group marriage," whereby a group of up to ten couples will hold one another's spouses in common. This union is usually sealed with a sort of marriage rite, and the participants become like relatives, helping and supporting each other. There are generally blood-revenge ties among them, too. Group marriages are contracted among members of different camps, since the wife exchange is an occasion thing and not a form of polygamy. People of other tribes are received into these unions, no doubt to further cement trade relations. The ties are also made with the Russians, who look on it as a form of prostitution.

There are reports of "hospitality prostitution," that is, the offering of the wife by her husband to a guest in exchange for a few presents, a custom also practiced by the Eskimos, but this seems to be a former custom no longer observed. After the death of a husband it is the duty of the next brother to succeed him, acting as husband to the widow, father to the children, and keeper of the dead man's reindeer herd. According to statistics, the Chukchi are the most prolific of the Siberian peoples, with from five to nine children per family.

Voluntary death is a Chukchi practice. When a person feels that he no longer wishes to live—perhaps because of the death of his wife, a quarrel in the family, chronic sickness, old age, or just a feeling of being tired of it all—he asks a close friend or a relative to kill him. The time is set, certain ceremonies are performed, and the person is duly stabbed or strangled to death. Sometimes young people commit suicide, but this is not considered a dignified way to die.

The extreme melancholy that leads to voluntary death is only one form of the nervous disorders to which these and other Siberian peoples seem to be susceptible. These disorders are often referred to as Arctic hysteria, and aside from syphilis, are the most frequent malady of the Siberians. One such disorder manifests itself in the patient's imitating all the gestures and words of bystanders, regardless of their nature or meaning. The afflicted one will even repeat the words of a language he does not know. During these attacks the patient may utter obscenities that he would not normally dream of saying.

It has been suggested that Arctic hysteria may be due in part to the psychological strains that develop among people in small groups living close together under extremely rigorous physical conditions. In many of the societies found throughout the Arctic and sub-Arctic, great emphasis is placed upon submerging and repressing all open forms of conflict with community members, since continual cooperation is the key to survival. Such repressed hostility sometimes breaks out in the form of hysteria, either in culturally acceptable forms like visions, or in purely individual psychotic acts. To what extent analogous situations arise among peoples of similar small groups in strikingly different environments, such as in desert or jungle regions, is not known.

Arctic hysteria when connected with religion is regarded as divine inspiration. As with other primitive peoples, this idea of inspiration is central to the shamanism practiced by the Chukchi. The Chukchi shaman may be either a man or a woman, but women are thought to be more naturally suited to the profession. A shaman must be someone who has shown his capacity for inspiration by being of a nervous and excitable disposition.

The shaman accepts one or more spirits of the supernatural world as his protectors or servants. By this means he enters into communication with the whole spirit world. The male Chukchi shaman must go through a long painful period of preparation for shamanism. The shaman is called upon to be a medicine man, driving out evil spirits that cause sickness; a priest, conducting ceremonies; and a prophet, reading the future in the shoulder blade of a sheep or the flight of arrows.

Among the Chukchi the shaman has no particular dress, but he does carry the drum of all shamans with which he communicates with the spirit world. His ceremonies are carried on within the inner room of the tent, late at night. During the ceremony the spirit, or *kelet*, descends on the shaman and expresses itself through the shaman's voice and drum. If the shaman is a ventriloquist, as the men frequently are, the kelet will speak in different voices from all over the room. The shaman also performs many dangerous tricks, such as stabbing himself and swallowing burning coals.

There have been frequent reports of shamans changing sexual status. There seems to be no physiological change involved; indeed the shaman may continue to have sexual relations with a member of the opposite sex while he officially takes a mate of the same sex.

In the Chukchi religion there are several kinds of spirits. There are the invisible spirits that bring disease and death, and the bloodthirsty cannibal spirits that are the particular enemies of warriors. There are also spirits that help the shaman. These take different forms and vary in temper. In addition, there is another class of spirits, the "monster," one of which occupies the body of the killer whale.

The Chukchi dead are not handled by the shaman but by a close relative, who rips open the dead body and exposes the vital organs from which he deduces the cause of death. In former times the flesh of the dead man was distributed among the mourners and was eaten, but now the mourners take pieces of his fur clothes instead.

Between 1919 and 1923 the control of eastern Siberia was heavily fought over. Civil war raged through the Chukchi Peninsula, involving Chukchi, Eskimos, and Russian settlers.

With the expulsion of the Japanese and "White Russian" troops, the Soviet government set about organizing collective reindeer herds, cooperative stores, and local and regional administrative and service organs.

These developments were slower in taking root among the Chukchi, especially among the scattered Chukchi reindeer herders of the interior, than among many other eastern Siberian groups. By the mid thirties reindeer-breeding cooperatives existed, but the animals themselves were owned mainly by individuals. Soviet accounts describe considerable disorganization and sabotage of the collectives by large herd owners during this period.

By the mid-fifties a large part of the reindeer were raised in collectives. The technical aid given by trained specialists in feeding, breeding, inoculation, and grazing seems to have attracted most owners.

In contrast to the inland herders, the coastal Chukchi economy and social life were much more rapidly collectivized, or at least modernized. Year-round residence in villages, now equipped with schools, health stations, and cooperative stores, was stabilized. Motorized tow boats and fishing boats were introduced, work in regional canning plants was developed, and small but less nomadic reindeer herds were re-established.

More or less traditional Chukchi bone carving has been fostered and has become fashionable throughout the cosmopolitan sectors of the Soviet Union, much as Eskimo stone carving has in Canada.

# The Middle East

# THE BEDOUIN

A nomadic people, the Bedouin inhabit the desert areas of north and central Saudi Arabia, part of Yemen, southwestern Iraq, and a crescent of wasteland from southern Israel, through Jordan, to eastern Syria. But even these accomplished desert dwellers have not been able to sustain themselves in the waterless wastes of the Empty Quarter, the great Arabian desert.

In an area of great cultural diversity, the different Bedouin groups, where their basic economic organization is the same, show considerable cultural homogeneity. All speak dialects of Arabic. Their religion is Islam. Allah is their God; the Koran is their bible, and they guide their lives according to it. Eating pork and drinking alcoholic beverages are forbidden.

The Bedouin breed and raise camel and sheep; having no agriculture, they depend on trading with their more sedentary neighbors.

In Saudi Arabia, the Bedouin are divided into four classifications. First in importance are the Badia, who live in black tents made of animal hair. Strictly camel breeders, they spend about nine months of the year in the desert. It is only during the driest months that they move their herds from the scorched backland to the slightly greener fringes of the farming areas. They consider other Bedouin inferior, and marriage takes place only within the confines of their social group.

Next on the social scale are the Arabdar. They live in towns during part of the year and are not regarded as real nomads. The Hukra care for the sheep of the more important tribes. They are looked down on by the other Bedouin because sheep do not travel as far as camels, and so the Hukra's nomadic wanderings are limited. The lowliest are the Hadbar who supply the true nomads with valuable merchandise and provide much of the town services. They live in mud houses the year round.

Of the true nomads, one of the leading tribes is the Anizah. The Ruála Bedouin, a division of the Anizah, are located in the north central section of Saudi Arabia. They are one of the better studied Bedouin groups and exemplify the camel nomads.

Though the Ruála camp group subsists mainly on the dairy foods and dates from its own herds and oases, it is dependent upon the non-Bedouin for a number of critical items. Cloth; iron and steel implements; additional food and condiments such as rice, coffee, and saffron—as well as weapons and ammunition—all must be obtained mostly from outside sources.

For these, the Ruála rely upon contacts with other groups of Bedouin near the towns and farming zones or, as was more usual in the past, upon traveling merchants and caravans. The required goods were—and to a considerable extent still are—obtained through the sale of camels and horses.

In addition, in the recent past many of the nomadic Bedouin groups of this area exacted tribute from caravans passing through their lands as protection payment. At times they were engaged in transport trade themselves.

The head of each Bedouin tribe is called sheik. He is generally selected from one or two outstanding patrilineal lineages, which form the aristocracy of the tribe. Above all, the sheik must have luck, or the tribe will not prosper.

The Bedouin family home is a thick cloth tent made of goat or sheep hair. About twenty-five feet long, it is partitioned into separate sections for men and women by beautifully decorated curtains. These curtains, as well as rugs, are handwoven by the Bedouin women.

The fireplace consists of a hole in the sand and is used for cooking and coffee making. Since the Koran prohibits liquor, coffee is the all-purpose drink. There are usually three coffee pots with long spouts and a coffee roaster that resembles a long spoon. Beans are ground with a mortar and pestle. The coffee is flavored

with cardamon seed, ginger, and saffron. The making of coffee is
almost a ceremony. Once the beans have been roasted and ground
to a powder, water is added and the coffee is poured into a second
pot, reboiled, and flavored. When the coffee is ready the coffee
boy hits the mortar with the pestle to assemble the guests. The
small handleless cups, which are about half full, are held in the
right hand, and it is an insult if at least three cups of coffee are not
consumed by each drinker.

All the foodstuffs, the drinking water, and the camel manure
fuel are stored in the women's section. The men's side contains
carpets and mattresses for sleeping, and camel saddles. Placed
at the west end of the tent, the women's quarters get the best
ventilation in hot weather and are sheltered from the sand storms
in cooler weather. The tents are moved every two weeks in order
to obtain new sanitary conditions for the Bedouin and grazing
facilities for the animals.

The Bedouin's staple foods are dates and camel milk, or the
butter made from it. Rice is an imported luxury. Because the

Bedouin have little water, much camel milk is drunk, either as is or after being hung in a leather bag to sour. The dates are eaten at every meal. Wheat is expensive, so bread is only for the rich Bedouin, though it is sometimes baked by the poor on special occasions. The bread, which is a flat round cake, can be used as both a napkin and a fork, and as a plate as well. As a starch substitute, water and salt are added to a flour made of maize or millet. A favorite porridge is made from bitter sesame seed flour mixed with ghee—a boiled butter that remains solid at high temperatures—and salt and water.

Sheep, camels, and goats are too expensive for the Bedouin to slaughter regularly. Locusts are considered a delicacy. When a swarm arrives, the whole tribe gathers a supply. The locusts are sun-dried, powdered for use in flour, or eaten raw. When roasted, the wings and legs are cut off, and the locusts are dipped in salt. Eaten this way, they taste something like pork.

Wolves, kangaroo mice, and rats are also eaten. The seaside Bedouin eat dried and salted fish. Because older men are revered, they eat first; then the younger men, and finally the women and children. The main meal is served on a large platter, and everyone scoops up the food with his right hand. Food is so savored that there is no time for dinner conversation. After a meal the hands

BEDOUIN HOSPITALITY CENTERS ON COFFEE, WHICH IS CEREMONIOUSLY PRE-PARED AND SERVED. THE GUESTS HOLD THE CUPS IN THEIR RIGHT HANDS AND MUST DRINK AT LEAST THREE CUPS TO BE POLITE.

are wiped on the tent, and the teeth are cleaned by chewing on sticks.

Most families live in one tent, and the small children live with the women. If a boy wishes a girl's hand in marriage, he helps her with her household chores and visits her at night in someone's vacant tent. Since family interests and policy are the deciding factor, elopement is a serious offense.

The Bedouin wedding ceremony is very simple. A female camel is sacrificed in front of the tent of the husband-to-be on the morning of the wedding. Toward evening a round tent, with the marriage bed inside, is set up by the women of the tribe. Then at sunset the bride is taken to the tent by her female relatives. The groom arrives later and closes up the tent. The meat of the sacrificed camel is shared among the married couple, relatives, and friends.

Although they hate people with easy lives, the Bedouin will not hire themselves out for work. *Sharaf* (pride) is the most outstanding quality a Bedouin can possess. Next is *arltr* (family honor), followed by hospitality and courtesy toward accepted friends. Outsiders are not readily accepted unless traveling with the tribe; but when they are accepted, they are treated well, served coffee, and given a resting place.

*Europe*

# THE LAPPS

The smallest people of Europe, only four to five feet tall, the Lapps have flat heads, high cheekbones, broad noses, and chestnut-colored hair. The shape of their skulls is their only Mongolian trait; in both language and racial background they resemble the Finns. The people refer to themselves as Samelats; Lapp is the Swedish word for nomad.

The Lapps have herds of domesticated reindeer and because reindeer feed on moss and lichen, their owners are necessarily nomadic in order to provide the herds with ample grazing lands.

The Norsemen invaded Lapland in the ninth century, and the Russian princes of Novgorod took over in the eleventh century. From the Russians, the Lapps adopted some Greek Orthodox beliefs and combined them with Swedish Lutheranism to form their religion.

The Lapps were settled for quite a while before history took notice of them. From the outset there have been a few different subdivisions of this people who inhabit the Arctic regions. The Scandinavian Lapps live on mountain plateaus; the Eastern Lapps dwell in parts of Sweden, Finland, and Russia, where the terrain is rocky and swampy. In the Swedish uplands, waterways are used as a means of transportation; in winter, sledges are used on the frozen lakes.

Lapp villages consist of an inn, a church, some wooden cottages, and a few windowless huts. Closed in the summer, they are opened in the winter for the Lapps who come to the midwinter fairs.

One group of Lapps lives in the mountains, and most of them live in tents in the nomadic style. The Lapps who live by the sea are fishermen only; forest- and river-dwelling groups set up villages. These last two hunt and fish for food and use domesticated reindeer as beasts of burden.

The general terrain of Lapland is uneven. Some parts are mountainous and snow-covered; the rest is mostly wasteland. More than half of Lapland is located above the Arctic Circle, and it is cold the year round. August, the warmest month, is only about fifty degrees Fahrenheit. In summer it is always light; in winter, always dark. Winter has totally set in by November, so the preparations for it begin early in September. And with the arrival of winter, the Lapps move southward, as food for their reindeer becomes scarce.

The Lapps are constantly moving their camps. They believe that whatever happens on the first days of a trip will continue; if misfortune befalls them on the first day, the entire journey will be unlucky. The Lapps are an extremely strong people and able to withstand great cold. The story is told of a pregnant woman who gave birth in the middle of such a journey. She placed the newborn baby in her tunic and kept going until a camp was reached. Next day, too weak to continue, she was left behind in a tent with someone to help her.

If a child is born under normal circumstances, it is wrapped in a reindeer skin, bathed in warm water, and placed in a cradle, where it remains the year round. The cradle is made of hollowed wood, with a hole carved to fit the baby's head. This tends to flatten the skull a bit. Infants are strapped to the reindeer while traveling. As they grow, they must learn to ride the reindeer, despite the extreme cold. When the children are old enough they must walk and keep up as best they can. This is also true for the old people, who sometimes die en route, and whose bodies are left out in the open. When a Lapp passes his prime, he ages quickly and grows thin.

Reindeer are the most important food source for the Lapps, and although they outnumber the Lapp population—some 400,000 reindeer to 30,000 Lapps—many die from infectious diseases, especially in summer. There are insects that lay maggots on the animal's back, and when these hatch they burrow into the skin. Wolves, too, are a constant threat to the herds.

The reindeer mating season begins the last week in September and lasts about two weeks. To prevent the young bulls from growing thin, and to produce a strong and healthy herd, most of the bulls are castrated; thus only the best bulls are used for breeding.

In some ways the Lapps and the reindeer resemble each other. Both are always on the move; both tend to be reticent and shy.

The Lapps have a ceremonial way of eating reindeer. When a deer is slaughtered, its stomach is used to catch the blood and then a sausage is made from it. The first parts to be eaten are the liver, back, and sausage. The brains are mixed with fat and tree bark and boiled to make a food, as well as a medicine for stomach ailments. The second meal consists of the legs, head, and bone marrow. The remainder may be eaten in any order.

In the winter the Lapps must protect their herds against their natural enemies—wolves. Wolf hunts are often conducted on skis; under some snow conditions this gives the hunters an advantage over the wolves, who break through the crust.

Bears also are hunted and are usually captured in snares. In order to disguise the odor of the rope, it is smeared with bark. The bear will try to free itself by biting through the rope, so the trap must be constantly watched.

When the Lapps change camps, they use plain wooden sleds about five feet long to carry their household supplies. Other sleds, used for general driving, have graceful shapes and are very ornate.

There is one large festival each year which is equivalent to the Westerners' celebration of Christmas. In preparation, reindeer are killed, clothes are made, and wood is cut. This wood is stacked up in a neat pile so that the spirit Stallo will not snag his sled on it; a stick is set up for Stallo to hitch his reindeer to. During the festivities no one works and there is much gaiety.

To bring good luck in hunting, the Lapps make offerings to the poor and malformed. This is an old custom; the Lapps say it started when they promised the animal spirit guardians they would give the gods a part of any large kill. It is said by Johan Turi, a middle-aged Lapp who learned to read and write in order to record his people's customs, that around the turn of the nineteenth century, the last human sacrifice was performed. It consisted of a husband and wife, a ten-year-old boy—and a reindeer.

*North America*

# INTRODUCTION
# TO THE INDIANS
# OF NORTH AMERICA

North America today is dominated by a complex, highly developed, and—thanks to modern communication—comparatively homogeneous civilization. It has developed rapidly and forcefully in only a few hundred years.

Although most people know that the continent was formerly inhabited exclusively by an aboriginal population, few are aware of the tremendous diversity of these peoples. Their different languages, customs, and even physical characteristics have been developing for at least ten thousand years, since their first ancestors came to this continent at the end of the last Ice Age. We still know only portions of their long history on this continent, but with the aid of modern science and scholarship, new facts are being gathered every day.

At the time the white man first came to North America there were some four hundred different aboriginal tribes, mainly of Mongoloid stock, inhabiting the land. These early migrators came to North America by way of the Bering Strait. Even today, Asia and America are separated by only fifty-six miles of open water, and this gulf is broken by the two Diomede Islands. Furthermore, during the peak of the last glacial advance, ten to twelve thousand years ago, a great deal of the ocean water was locked up in the ice, thus lowering the level of the sea. Since the gulf between Big and Little Diomede Islands, and the Bering Strait in general, is quite shallow, it is likely that a continuous land bridge existed between the continents for at least a few thousand years.

Some of the most notable animal species that are known to have spread to the New World from Asia at a late date are the mastodon and ancestral varieties of present-day caribou and bison. The early men who crossed the land bridge in pursuit of these animals found far different climatic conditions from those we know, for many of our deserts and grasslands were regions of dense forest.

Undoubtedly these people came in small bands over a long period of time. Arriving in Alaska, the newcomers found several routes open to them. First they wandered down the broad Mackenzie Valley in Alaska, where the ice had cleared early. They spread into the Plains region—east, to the Mississippi Valley, and west, to the foothills of the Rockies. Others worked their way south along the Pacific Coast, west of the Sierra Nevadas. Eventually they settled in what is now Mexico, Central America, and South America.

Much of the racial, linguistic, and cultural diversity of the American Indians is due to this vast expansion, which continued for more than ten thousand years. The bands of immigrants were originally of different Mongoloid racial strains. It is possible that some South Pacific islanders may have reached America in canoes, but not in great enough numbers to affect the racial characteristics of the North American population.

There are certain racial characteristics common to all North American Indians, such as dark brown eyes, coarse black hair, and broad faces with big features. Skin color ranges from yellow-brown to red-brown. The origin of the term "redskin" is uncertain, but it may refer to the widespread practice of painting the skin with red paint.

There is great diversity in other physical characteristics, from the tall, spare, longheaded, hook-nosed Plains Indian to the short, squat, broad-headed pueblo dwellers. The Eskimos, with their short stocky bodies, narrow skulls, broad square faces, yellow skin, and Mongoloid eyes, offer yet another striking racial contrast.

Linguistic diversity is even greater. In fact, there was more linguistic variety in the Western Hemisphere than in any other area of the world. At the time of the discovery of the New World there were at least fifty-five language families in North America alone. Most of these families seem to have been totally unrelated to each other, and even the languages within a language family were often not intelligible to other speakers within the same language family.

There is virtually no correlation between language and culture. Neighboring tribes, such as the Cheyenne and Crow of the western plains, live much the same way but speak totally unrelated languages. The Hopi farmers of the Southwest, on the other hand, speak a language closely related to the Paiute hunters and food gatherers of the Great Basin, although their cultures are vastly different. Some language families are widespread, like the Algonquin and Uto-Aztecan, while other minor linguistic stocks are spoken by only a few hundred people. Major John Wesley Powell made a comprehensive classification of North American Indian languages in 1891, and his system is still widely used. The most important of his listings north of the Mexican border are the following: Eskimo, Athabascan, Algonquin, Iroquoian, Muskogean, Siouan, and Uto-Aztecan. Linguistic diversity gives us clues to the waves of immigration that spread across North America. For example, the languages spoken by small, isolated tribes in California probably represent the speech of early inhabitants who were pushed aside by later migrating groups—the ancestors of tribes whose languages were widespread at the time of the discovery of the New World.

The cultures of the North American Indians are also widely diverse. Indeed, if we attempt to break them down to their lowest common denominator, the results are the generalized abilities and beliefs common to Stone Age men of the Old World as well. These factors include use of fire and utensils of stone and bone; magic; belief in spirits; the concept of the family group; knowledge of various types of songs, dances, and folktales; the ability to build some sort of shelter and to make clothing; the ability to make and use the bow and arrow, traps, and string. Beyond these minimal cultural implements, different groups specialized in different ways. This can be observed today both from archeological evidence and from the preservation of many of these cultures, which were until recently still intact.

The North American Indian population today is roughly 500,000, half the estimated population of the continent at the time of the discovery of the New World. Until the last few decades their numbers were decreasing at a fast rate, but now the Indians are a rapidly increasing population. The three largest tribes—Navaho, Sioux, and Cherokee—are now larger than when the white man first came.

Except for those who continue their old way of life in the Arctic or in the northern forests, most of today's Indians live on reservations concentrated in the western portion of the continent. Although some reservations coincide with the original territorial domains of their inhabitants, notably in the Southwest, most Indians live on lands far from their ancestral homes. They lead lives that are a curious mixture of the old and the new, but the trend toward the latter is inevitable.

# INDIANS OF THE
# NORTHEAST

The Algonquin tribes—or the Abnaki Indians, as they were collectively called by the colonists—were organized in small multi-family units. They were highly skilled in basketmaking and in the construction of canoes. During the first half of the eighteenth century large numbers of them, under the influence of French missionaries, migrated permanently to Canada. The Penobscot, Malecite, and Passamaquoddy remained, however, and in 1749 the Penobscot, as the principal tribe, made peace with the English and accepted fixed boundaries.

The Iroquois lived in palisaded villages, east and south of Lakes Erie and Ontario. Surrounded by hostile tribes, with whom they constantly warred before the arrival of the white man, they nevertheless controlled the vast region between the Hudson and Ohio rivers.

The Iroquois dwellings, representing the most advanced type of architecture achieved by the northeastern tribes, were rectangular lodges built of wooden poles and covered with elm bark, often one hundred feet or more in length. Partitions divided the interiors of these famous "long houses" at intervals of six, ten, or sometimes twenty feet, forming chambers or rooms that opened on a center hallway. Spaced along the passageway were fire pits, each shared by four of the "apartments." Thus, a long house with ten fire pits could accommodate forty families in separate apartments. Raised bunks around the sides of the apartments served as beds and benches for their occupants.

Each long house in an Iroquois village was the communal property of the women who resided in it. Their menfolk were regarded as belonging to the clan, and thus, by extension, to their mothers. As long as the men did their share in providing food, and otherwise behaved themselves, they were permitted to lodge with their wives and children, being treated something like honored guests. If, however, a warrior caused any trouble he was obliged to leave the long house. The women, for their part, built the houses and tilled the soil. The crops they raised were their common property.

Because the woman took care of the garden, in addition to her chores of cleaning, sewing, and cooking, outsiders thought Indian wives were chattels and virtual slaves of their husbands. This misconception undoubtedly arose when visitors saw the wife busily working while the husband lay about the long house, seemingly with nothing to do but be waited upon. Overlooked was the fact that the husband had been engaged while away from home in hunting, fishing, clearing the land, and making war against his tribal enemies.

Marriage involved mutual consent. So-called wife purchases are found, upon closer scrutiny, to have consisted of either compensation to the bride's family for loss of her services, or a mutual exchange of gifts by the families involved. The husband had no real authority over his wife's person; in most tribes the woman could leave her husband when she wished.

Among the Iroquois, women had an important voice in tribal councils and could nominate candidates for the chieftancy of the clan or tribe. An Iroquois mother even had the authority to forbid her son to go on the warpath.

It is not so surprising, then, that white women taken captive in Indian raids later often refused an opportunity to return to the pioneering life.

Among the Iroquois, hospitality was universal. When a man—any man, friend or stranger—entered a house it was the duty of the women to set food before him. Failure to do so was considered an unpardonable affront.

Indian etiquette forbade asking a visitor to state his business.

His hosts had to serve him with food and tobacco and maintain a respectful silence until, refreshed and rested, the visitor felt like speaking.

This law of hospitality helped to equalize the distribution of food, a necessity for people who live from day to day, largely dependent upon the uncertain fortunes of the hunt. So long as there was food in the community, no one need ever starve.

The domestic life of the Iroquois was on a remarkably high plane. Women were honored; parents were respected and indulged; children, though enjoying a good deal of liberty, were nevertheless brought up to be obedient and cooperative.

The Iroquois were an ingenious people who learned to hunt game despite winter's heavy snows, and to travel over the waterways of their homeland, a region of many lakes and rivers.

A wide variety of snowshoes were made, suitable for various snow conditions and stemming from local design preferences. Canoes were of the heavy dugout type or made with the lighter, more portable birchbark-covered frame. To the nomadic tribes of the northeast, the birchbark canoe was as necessary as is the automobile to modern man.

The Iroquois, like all the tribes of the northeastern woodlands, were simple but effective farmers. They planted their gardens in May, sowing corn and beans in rows at intervals of about three feet and heaping small hills of dirt over them. In open areas they planted pumpkin and squash.

Corn, or maize, was venerated by all the agricultural tribes of America because it was their principal means of subsistence. In fact, the Iroquois name for maize means "our life." Many varieties of beans and corn were cultivated, and there were numerous ways of preparing them as food. The New England dish of maize and beans still retains its Indian name—succotash.

When the fertility of the soil in their immediate vicinity became exhausted, or game became scarce, or firewood was in short supply the Indians simply moved.

The beliefs and customs of the Iroquois were typical to a great degree of the culture of the Indians of the Northeast. The religious beliefs of the Iroquois were a practical affair, designed to help him not only in a future life but also in the present one. Thus, when he thought himself plagued by an evil spirit he took steps to propitiate that spirit with offerings—an attitude unfortunately interpreted as a form of devil worship.

Underlying his preoccupation with good and evil spirits, the Indian had a mystic conception of an impersonal, supernatural force that permeated all nature, animated all phenomena, and controlled the destiny of man.

This force was conceived of as a sort of impersonal power source that men might draw upon in order to gain dominance over the natural world. It is akin to what anthropologists call mana, the Melanesian word for this force. It was part of the religious experience of many North American tribes and was found under a variety of names: the Algonquin called it *manitu;* the Ojibwa, *manito;* the Shoshone, *pokunt;* the Iroquois, *orenda.* The early white settlers, unable to comprehend the real nature of this concept, generally translated it as the "Great Spirit." In fact, it was under the guise of possessing a new, especially powerful manitu that the early missionaries often brought Christianity to the Indians.

The Iroquois peopled their world with strange beings and spirits. They had many secret societies and groups, typical of which was the Iroquois Society of False Faces. Donning carved wooden masks representing supernatural beings, members of the society would dance through the village, shaking huge turtle-shell rattles, a ritual that the cult members believed would drive out the demons of disease and misfortune.

In the spring and fall, when sickness was most prevalent, the Society of False Faces would proceed en masse through all the homes in an Indian community, uttering eerie cries, shaking their rattles, and addressing unseen spirits. False-face masks continue in use today.

Both the Iroquois and the Algonquin believed in a masked cannibal called Long Nose, who kidnapped bad children. Indian youngsters were never disciplined by corporal punishment; fear of Long Nose carrying them off in his huge basket usually was enough to assure their good behavior.

The fabric of the Indian's religion was woven about his intimate observations of nature's phenomena: The rising and setting of the sun; the waxing and waning of the moon; the regular migration of animals, birds and fish; lightning, wind, heat and cold—all were observed by the Indians and interpreted imaginatively in a rich mythology expressed largely in allegorical terms.

Unless a man belonged to one of the large family groups by birth or adoption, he was considered an alien. Kinship was traced solely through the mother's line. The family groups were known as *ohwachira*, and all members of an ohwachira were thought to be descended from the same female ancestor.

A woman's immediate household—her husband and children —belonged to the same "fireside," but the husband remained a member of his mother's ohwachira, never that of his wife, marriage between members of the same ohwachira being forbidden by law.

The younger members of the same ohwachira considered themselves brothers and sisters and so addressed each other. The older women were "sisters" to one another and "mothers" or "grandmothers" to the younger generation.

In like manner, just as all the women of a child's ohwachira were his mothers and grandmothers, so the brothers of the women were his uncles and granduncles. The nominal leadership of an ohwachira was always conferred upon a woman, although the senior active man in the unit dominated certain of the decision-making. Among the family groups, some would become closely allied with one another, and such ohwachira formed sisterhoods or clans. There were at least three and often more such clans in the tribes of the Five Nations. There were never more than eight clans, and their names were the same from nation to nation. They formed two groups of four clans each: Wolf, Bear, Beaver, and Turtle in the first; Deer, Snipe, Heron, and Hawk in the second. Marriage within these groups, which anthropologists call "moieties" (from the French *moitié*, meaning half) was ideally forbidden.

That the same clans were to be found in each nation accounts for the great strength and wide geographical spread of the League of the Iroquois. Members of the same clan in different nations felt bound by fraternal ties; war between the nations would thus have set clans against themselves, and brother fighting brother was unthinkable.

Although skilled as hunters and farmers, it was not these talents that gave the Iroquois their ascendancy over the other tribes in the East and compelled powerful European nations to treat them as equals. What made them stand out above all other Indian tribes was their genius for social organization, which reached its apex in a confederation that endured through two centuries, and which resembled in some respects the union of the colonies.

The League of the Iroquois was brought about chiefly through the vision of the great Indian statesman Deganawidah. This sixteenth-century leader, believed to have been a Huron, was assisted by Hiawatha, whose exploits have been immortalized by Longfellow.

Under the leadership of Deganawidah and Hiawatha, the Iroquois formed a confederation of the Seneca, Oneida, Mohawk, Onondaga, and Cayuga tribes. Known to the French as the "Long House" and to the English as the "Five Nations," the confederation was a unique reorganization among Northeast Indians of that time.

The Iroquois Confederacy was formed about 1570, after a number of earlier attempts had failed. At that time, several of the Algonquin tribes were reacting to the earlier expansion of the tribes that made up the confederacy. During the first decades of the Iroquoian confederacy strong Algonquin counterpressure, along with the muskets and fur trade goods and trade entry points —which lay mainly in non-Iroquois hands—put the confederated tribes at a considerable disadvantage. It was only their numbers and organization that allowed the Iroquois to maintain their position during this period. Though they were able to gain some arms and trade goods from Indian middlemen, they were faced with the close alliance of French colonists and various Algonquin groups. It was not until stable Dutch trading ports and settlements were established in the lower Hudson basin and shoreline that real access to European goods opened for them.

The underlying social structure of the Iroquois League of the Five Nations was remarkable in its character and complexity. Unlike modern society, in which an individual is the ultimate unit and groups of individuals form larger units, the Iroquois regarded the individual as nothing, the family as everything.

Each of the nations of the Iroquois was governed by a tribal council made up of sachems of the several clans. They voted not individually or by clans, but by phratries. The phratry was a sisterhood of clans, just as the clan was a sisterhood of ohwachira.

This complex system was the Indian way of conducting parliamentary procedure, during which all could speak until unanimity was reached.

The sachems of a clan, after agreeing upon a course of action, would consult with the representatives of the sister clans. After reaching agreement with them they would strive to come to a similar agreement with the sachems of the clans constituting the opposing phratry. A single sachem might at any time, by a dissenting voice, obstruct the progress of the council.

Each of the Five Nations was governed in this way, and it was but one more step to organize a Federal Council, which formed the ruling body of the League.

In founding the League, the Iroquois declared that it was being established for the promotion of universal peace among all the tribes of men, through the safeguarding of health, happiness, and human life. To that end the founders promulgated, as the proper basis of government, three great dual doctrines, or principles:

1. (a) Health of mind and body
   (b) Peace among individuals and groups of individuals
2. (a) Righteousness in conduct; its advocacy in thought and speech
   (b) Equity in thé adjustment of rights and obligations
3. (a) Maintenance of physical strength or power
   (b) Orenda, or magic power, of people and institutions

One reform instituted by the League was the substitution of legal tender, in blood feuds, as the price of the life of a man or woman. Twenty strings of wampum was fixed as the price of a man's life—ten strings for the dead man and ten for the forfeited life of his murderer. The legal tender for the life of a woman was thirty strings of wampum, because a woman's life was more valued by the community than that of a man.

At the zenith of the power of the Iroquois, the town of Onondaga, which had been established as the headquarters of the League, was the capital of a government whose dominion extended from the Hudson River on the east to the falls of the Ohio and Lake Michigan on the west, and from the Ottawa River and Lake Simcoe on the north to the Potomac River on the south.

Around the Great Council Fire of the League at Onondaga, the Federal senators of the Iroquois tribes initiated plans, formulated policies, and defined principles of government and political action that not only promoted their common welfare, but also greatly affected the contemporary history of the whites in North America.

Relentless enemies, the Iroquois intimidated the surrounding tribes so effectively that their mastery was acknowledged as far south as the Tennessee River. Many hostile tribes were practically exterminated, and their survivors were adopted, increasing the numbers and prestige of the Iroquois Confederacy. When the Tuscarora, a related people, were driven from their North Carolina homeland by the British settlers in 1711, they took refuge with the Iroquois, and about 1722 they became the sixth nation in the League.

At the time the first white settlers reached the shores of the New World the Iroquois were close to being exterminated by their tribal enemies. The French colonists, however, furnished the Iroquois with firearms, and they were then more than able to hold their own.

At this time, opinion was divided among the Indians of the Northeast as to what effect the coming of the white man would have on their lives. Many Indian leaders foresaw that the encroachment, if allowed to continue, would mean the end of their way of life and ultimately, their extermination.

Some, like the famous chief Cornplanter, held that the Indian should make friends with the white man and save himself by imitating them. Others, like the Wampanoag chief Metacom, known to the English as King Philip, contended that it was impossible for the Indian to change his basic nature to such a degree, and believed that the only hope of survival rested in resisting and repelling the invaders.

Canonchet was the chief of an Algonquin tribe in Rhode Island, the Narraganset. Although it was not a particularly important tribe initially, it was one of the few that had been relatively unaffected by the great 1617 epidemic that swept through southern New England, and this made it a rallying point for the remnants of other depleted tribes.

In the decade preceding King Philip's War, the English settlers, particularly those of the Plymouth colony, began to attack the Indian tribes in their area, sending many captives into slavery in the Caribbean. During this time Metacom had been secretly organizing the Indians of the New England region, and in 1675 declared war upon the whites. In a single year fifty-two English towns were attacked, and twelve of them were completely destroyed. When the uprising came almost all of the surviving Algonquin tribes from Massachusetts and lower Maine, including the bulk of the "mission" Indians and those living in servitude, rallied to the attack.

In the first few months of fighting nearly one thousand of the five thousand Narraganset were killed. Canonchet was killed in April of 1676. Metacom was betrayed; his hideout in Rhode Island was raided, and he was killed on August 12, 1676. Thus King Philip's War came to an end.

More than one hundred years later, a final desperate stand was made by the Indians, under the great Shawnee chief Tecumseh, to drive the white man from the northeastern United States. Tecumseh protested over the United States government's purchase of land from individual tribes, land that the Indian chief maintained belonged to all the tribes communally. When his contention was ignored, Tecumseh formed a great confederacy of virtually all the Indians east of the Mississippi River, with the hope of making the Ohio River the permanent boundary line between white men and Indians.

Before his plans were complete, Tecumseh's followers precipitated the battle of Tippecanoe in 1811, and the Indians' military movement collapsed. Tecumseh then allied himself with the British and was made a brigadier general in the British army, commanding 2,000 Indians in the War of 1812. He was killed in 1813 during the battle of the Thames near Chatham, Ontario, when a force of Americans, under General William H. Harrison, routed General Henry A. Proctor's British army regulars. With the death of Tecumseh, the last serious obstacle in the path of the white man's expansion was removed, and the doom of native Indian life in the Northeast was sealed.

Most Indian leaders owe their prominence in history books to their warlike activities, and this tends to produce an unbalanced picture of true Indian life. Warfare against the whites was largely forced upon them by the pressure of white expansion.

Infamous in history have been two practices connected with Indian warfare against the whites in the Northeast: the torture of prisoners and the taking of scalps. (Anthropologists say that the practice of scalping goes back to prehistory in America.) European rivals offered bounties to their Indian allies for enemy scalps, white or Indian. Sparked by this largesse, the practice of scalping spread rapidly and widely.

The most important reason for the hatred and bloodshed between white man and red man was, of course, their conflicting ideas about land ownership. The Indians regarded all land within tribal boundaries as belonging to the tribe; no Indian individual or family had a vested right in it. Each family might, however, appropriate or have assigned to it for cultivation what land it required for its own needs. Thus the Indians held that it was illegal for any chief, family, or section of a tribe to sell, trade, or give away any part of the tribal holdings.

Readjustment of individuals, families, and groups over the land was a common and continual process among all eastern tribes and bands. Sometimes this took the form of encroachment and military pressure between groups; more often *ad hoc* reciprocal arrangements were made that, in effect, leased the rights of land and resources to needy families and sections of other bands. These assignments of hunting and fishing tracts and agricultural plots were readjusted as required.

Formal treaties involving the transfer of land rights were therefore incomprehensible to the Indians, and the white settlers either were ignorant of this fact or found it expedient to ignore it. The Indian, for his part, felt that he had been tricked and robbed when the white man took possession of his lands.

Once the white man had entrenched himself in America, the breakdown of native Indian culture became inevitable. Diseases to which the Indians had developed no resistance—measles, smallpox, chicken pox—were introduced, and as a result whole tribes were badly depleted or exterminated. In addition, Indian health, pride, and spirit were often ruined by the white man's alcohol.

The basic occupations of tribal life also were obliterated by the white man's culture. When the encroachment of the white man destroyed game, fenced off hunting grounds, and forbade warfare, the Indian male was left with nothing to do. No longer was there any place for the weaponmaker, the warrior, the hunter.

The psychological effect of the white man's culture was also devastating to the Indian. Tribal organization was based on kinship and carried with it the obligation of mutual assistance and protection. One inherited rights, acquired basic social status, and came under the control and support of members of the entire matrilineage. Under the white man's system, children were put directly under parental authority, thus eliminating a feeling of oneness with a clan group.

The remnants of the once great Iroquois Confederacy are

113

now settled for the most part in seven state-administrated reservations—six of them in New York, and the seventh just over the boundary line in Pennsylvania.

Living close to large centers of population and white neighbors has brought about drastic changes in the Iroquois' mode of life, and few of them now live exclusively by Indian pursuits. Many devote part of their time to the manufacture of lacrosse sticks and snowshoes, or basketmaking and beadwork, but the chief occupations are dairying, farming, and to some extent poultry raising. Some find seasonal occupations in factories, shops, and canneries, and a few have gone into teaching, medicine, and the law.

One of the more interesting occupations of the descendents of the Iroquois is that of high-iron workers on the steel skeletons of skyscrapers under construction in our large eastern cities, particularly New York. More than five hundred Mohawk Indians, most of whom live in Brooklyn, are currently so employed.

After the American Revolution, the Mohawk, who had fought on the side of the British, were exiled to reservations in Canada, where for more than a century they managed to exist by farming and trapping. Sometime in the 1880's, a bridge company, erecting a span across the St. Lawrence River from the Indian reservation at Caughnawaga to Lachine, offered jobs as laborers to the Mohawk in return for the use of some of their land.

As the bridge went up, curious Mohawk coolly walked out on the beams to watch the hardened riveters working at dizzy heights. Impressed by their agility and fearlessness, an engineer taught some of them to rivet. When the bridge was finished the builders moved on to the next job—and so did the by now full-fledged Mohawk riveters, taking along their brothers, cousins, and friends.

After joining construction gangs all over Canada, the Mohawk followed jobs into the United States and soon found a happy working ground in the booming skyscraper construction business.

The Mohawk have been living in Brooklyn since the 1920's and form what is virtually their own small community. They have adapted themselves well. Nearly all are bilingual, and many of them have taken an active part in the various civic programs of their local neighborhood.

Services at Cuyler Presbyterian Church in the Clinton Hill section of Brooklyn are held once a month in the Mohawk language. Following the religious ceremony, the Mohawk conduct their own social gathering, usually featuring group singing of old Indian songs.

The principal modern settlement of the Penobscot is at Old Town, Maine. The Passamaquoddy have been joined by the Malecite. Many of the Old Town Indians, who are thrifty and progressive, are employed by the canoe factory that bears their name. At Passamaquoddy, fishing is the principal occupation.

The Maine Indians are generally regarded as good friends by their white neighbors, and there is little friction. The state of Maine administers the affairs of the Indians and provides an agent for each group. Old Indian ways have disappeared almost entirely, state marriage laws are observed, and divorce is practically unknown.

Health conditions are good. Physicians may be called in from nearby towns to attend the Indians, the state paying the bills. Schools are under state auspices; the teachers being supplied by the Roman Catholic Church but paid by the state. Most of the Indians belong to the Catholic Church, which has supervised their religious training since colonial days.

The Indians of Massachusetts include some at Gay Head, on the western end of Martha's Vineyard, who are probably the descendents of the Wampanoag, the tribe whose chief, Massasoit (father of Metacom), made a treaty of friendship with the Pilgrims soon after their landing at Plymouth. There are small groups of Indians at Mashpee, in Barnstable County; at New Bedford; and at various locations throughout Plymouth County.

A reservation at Mashpee was established in colonial days for the Indians who became Christianized, and a trust fund was left to Harvard College for the promotion of the Gospel among them. Later, proceeds of the fund were paid directly to the Baptist Church, which was the only church in Mashpee.

In modern times, there has been little or no distinction between Indians and whites in the area, and intermarriage has become fairly common. The people are all citizens, there are no separate schools for Indians, and government supervision is a thing of the past. The principal industry is fishing, and a few of the Indian men hold minor government positions. All speak, read, and write English, and nothing remains of old Indian customs or dress.

# THE PLAINS INDIANS

On movie and television screens, in pulp magazines and comic books, the Plains Indian lives on, as much a part of our American heritage as the cowboy.

But he is gone, vanished like the great herds of buffalo that were his life. His descendents are among us, but we have tamed them, put them on reservations, and taught them how to farm or assimilated them into our cities. And so the wheel has come full circle; for the Plains Indian way of life, which we have destroyed, was initially a creation of the white man.

It was the horses of Cortez and the Spanish conquistadors that produced the way of life of the Plains Indian as we know it. Before the Old World discovered the New, the Indians of the Plains lived much like their eastern neighbors, squeezing out a stark, sedentary existence from the earth. Buffalo herds were everywhere, but without the horse the Indian had no effective way of hunting them. The diet was maize, and crop failure spelled disaster for an entire tribe. The constant toll of disease also helped keep the Indian population small—at most in the tens of thousands.

The horse, first stolen or bought from the Spaniards and later caught wild from the great herds of mustangs engendered by the conquistadors' mounts, changed all that. It revolutionized

116

the Indians' way of life as completely as the automobile has revolutionized ours. It gave the Indian mobility, freeing him from dependence upon crops, and made him a seminomad, able to pack his household and move it across hundreds of miles to follow the buffalo herds.

This great social revolution took place largely unobserved, and we can only guess at its effect upon tribal life. We know, however, that the horse gave the Indian freedom, and that becoming a hunter placed new demands upon him. It brought forth the manly virtues—courage, strength, speed, ferocity—qualities that serve not only the hunter, but the warrior as well.

The life that typifies the Plains Indian in the popular mind came into being near the end of the seventeenth century and lasted two centuries before giving way to the movement of civilization and America's "manifest destiny." At its peak it spread over a third of the United States, from the Mississippi River to the Rockies, encompassing the Dakotas, Kansas, Nebraska, Oklahoma, most of Iowa, Missouri, Wisconsin, Texas, Utah, Montana, Wyoming, and Colorado, and stretching far up into the middle provinces of Canada. Among the tribes caught up in this way of life were the Blackfoot, Cheyenne, Arapaho, Cree, Crow, Sioux, Pawnee, Arikara, Wichita, Kiowa, Mandan, Dakota, Iowa, Omaha, Osage, Kansa, Comanche, Ute, Nez Percé, and Apache—names that echo in American geography as well as American history. The men produced by these tribes—Sitting Bull, Crazy Horse, Geronimo—warriors all, will never be forgotten.

It is no accident that the Plains Indians best remembered are warriors, for their contact with white men's civilization brought strife and bloodshed. But the hunt, rather than the battle, was what the young Plains Indian boy was trained for; the same skills happened to make him the fiercest of all American Indians.

Oddly enough, the proud self-reliant warrior began life as the most pampered of infants. He was suckled at his mother's breast whenever he desired, often not being weaned until his third or fourth year. Although Indians are often thought to be emotionally undemonstrative, they display great affection for their children.

Robert H. Lowie, in his excellent book *Indians of the Plains*, recalls a Blackfoot story about a scout who comes upon a tepee ". . . inhabited by a couple from the hostile tribe. Their baby, just able to walk, was dipping up soup from a kettle and detected the stranger peeping in by a hole. Toddling over, it fed the man again and again, unnoticed by the parents." The scout returned to his tribe to inform on the strangers, but found himself unwilling to cause the infant's death, and so said nothing; further, at the first opportunity he warned the parents to flee.

As the Plains Indian child grew to boyhood he began to learn the arts and crafts of hunting and warfare. He learned how to fashion a bow of wood or horn, and how to strengthen it with sinews glued along its back. He learned how to straighten wood shoots to make arrows, how to attach feathers to them to make them fly straight, and how to chip stone to make arrowheads. He practiced using a club—either the familiar tomahawk or a stone sewn in a leather bag, depending upon the tribe. Soon he owned a circular shield of buffalo hide, which he believed would protect him not only because of its thickness and toughness, but also because of the supernatural significance of its adornment. He carried a spear that, contrary to popular myth, was thrust at a target, never hurled.

As he neared manhood the young Indian had a best friend, the so-called blood brother, although the well-publicized ceremony of mixing blood was a white writer's fiction. The two friends shared dangers and preferred dying together to outliving one another.

The young Indian also became part of a group of warriors his own age, a group he would belong to—and go to war with—all his life. As the group grew older it would pass on its ceremonies, rituals, and responsibilities to a younger group and take on the new duties and medicines of an old-age group. Thus was continuity in Indian society assured.

Another step in the advance to manhood was accepting the responsibilities of religion. Indian religion was highly informal and individualistic, often revolving around a single Indian's relation with the spirits of the world. Most tribes had a shaman who supposedly was able to communicate with the spirits of the world and who demonstrated his powers by performing feats of magic and healing. Among the feats attributed to various shamans were the sudden maturing of cornstalks, walking on fire, and exorcising various objects from the bodies of sick people. Their methods of treating the sick included cupping and bleeding, as well as the

118

use of various herbs and spices, some of which had true medicinal value.

The shaman only occasionally had a priestly function, and in many tribes the medicine man and the priest were different individuals. The medicine man's function was to intervene directly with the gods and spirits to cure particular troubles, illness being the most common. The priest, on the other hand, claimed no special powers. His job was to lead the various ceremonies and rituals necessary to keep the spirits placated.

Tribal ceremonies were a relatively minor part of the individual Indian's life. Far more important was the securing of a vision, an essential duty of the young brave before he could claim a full role in the adult life of the tribe.

To seek his vision, the young Plains Indian left home and journeyed to some remote, desolate spot where he would spend many days praying, fasting, and generally preparing himself to receive the beneficence of the spirits. Sometimes it involved mortification or scarring the body to help bring on the vision.

Having a vision meant that some spirit had taken pity on the youth and had decided to accept him in guardianship. The spirit would then appear to the neophyte in the form of a bird or animal, or sometimes simply as a voice, and give him some symbol of the convenant. The spirit might, for example, teach the Indian a song, or give him a small object to keep as a charm —a feather, perhaps, or a section of animal skin. The vision made the young man brave; he could risk his life because he knew a spirit was protecting him.

Of course, the phenomenon of the vision can be explained scientifically: Experiments have shown that deprivation of sleep alone will cause hallucinations; to this add hunger, thirst, pain, and an open-minded readiness to believe. Even so, not every young warrior was able to have a vision. So the tribal code was forced to work out a system to assure the effectiveness of these presumably stolid-minded individuals. The system allowed young men to purchase a part of someone else's vision. Several parts of a particularly strong vision could be sold. Thus, in effect, the signs of a spirit's friendliness were often materially manifest at once.

Finally, a single vision was not always felt to be adequate to last a lifetime, and so a new vision was sought from time to time.

119

An Indian who felt his powers failing, or who was having bad luck in hunting or fighting, would repeat his ordeal, hoping for new strength from the gods.

Armed with the experience of his vision, the Indian was ready to take his part in the adult life of the community. He became part of the hunting parties that pursued the great herds of buffalo, and perhaps for the first time in his life came under strict discipline.

The buffalo hunt was a carefully planned collective enterprise, led by a chief and guarded by a formalized police contingent. It was the job of the police to ensure that no headstrong young brave, attempting to prove his valor, went ahead of the group to hunt on his own. Such an action would only scatter the buffalo herd, making the main task of killing enough buffalo for the entire village impossible. Punishment for such behavior was strict.

There were several ways of hunting buffalo. Before the advent of horses the most common method was to drive the buffalo herd over a cliff, the fall either killing them outright, or crippling them so that they were easily slaughtered. If there were no cliffs in the area, the buffalo were sometimes driven into corrals built of rock piles or brush. Fire was used on occasion: the brush would be set ablaze all around the buffalo, with one opening left where the hunters could slaughter the frenzied beasts as they sought to escape.

The arrival of the horse produced the buffalo hunts, which remain a permanent part of American lore. The braves on horseback would surround the herd, whooping and shouting, driving the herd in upon itself, thrusting lances and arrows into the seething mass. In this way a whole herd could be killed, providing not only meat but also the raw materials for clothes, houses, weapons, and ornaments for the entire tribe. So effective was this method that when the white man adapted it to his own use and employed his more efficient weapons he made the buffalo all but extinct within a decade.

War was far less important than the hunt in the life of the Indian. Until the coming of the white man, the only war the Plains Indians knew consisted of raids carried out by small groups of young braves. The purpose was usually to steal the horses of the enemy, as well as to prove courage in battle. Taking scalps was of little significance in proving the bravery of a warrior. More important was touching the enemy with the hand or a club; this personal contact was considered vital. A warrior who killed an enemy with an arrow gained less honor, Robert Lowie records, than another warrior who killed in a hand-to-hand encounter.

Marital customs differed widely from tribe to tribe within the Plains area. Sometimes marriage would be undertaken to ally two families, but just as often the marriage would spring from love. Some tribes allowed a man several wives; others demanded monogamy. In some tribes it was customary for the young couple to live with the groom's parents; in others they lived with the parents of the bride. Most often the groom would purchase his bride from her parents, usually paying a number of horses for her; but in some areas elopement was common, and accepted so long as the marriage proved stable. In other areas there was no payment as such, merely an exchange of gifts between families.

Marriage was considered a social rather than a sacramental bond, and thus an unsuccessful marriage was easily ended, often by pronouncing a few words. Nevertheless, Indian family life, on the whole, was remarkably stable; and great affection between husband and wife, and parents and children, was usual.

Primarily, the role of the man was to supply the family's meat; the woman was expected to supply the vegetables. Even at its peak, the buffalo-based Plains culture never forgot its agricultural heritage: maize, berries, and wild roots always supplemented the diet.

By no means was the woman considered the slave or servant of the man. Many tribes were matrilineal—descent and property being inherited through the mother. In regard to sex, however, there was a double standard: the girl was expected to remain chaste, whereas her brother sowed his wild oats.

The political life of the village was quite informal and democratic. There was usually not one but many chiefs, each playing a part in leading a particular activity—hunting, war, and rituals. The elders were respected and sought out to resolve disputes. Inevitably the son of a chief would have a better chance of becoming a chief himself than would the son of an insignificant man or an orphan, but direct inheritance of political power was by no means automatic. Each tribe had its own code of behavior, to which the individual was expected to adhere, and its own means of enforcing that code, relying often upon ridicule and loss of face rather than on direct punishment. The man who lived within the code and cooperated in such collective ventures as hunting and warfare had a great deal of individual freedom. The tribal organization itself was usually quite loose; individuals often roamed freely across the entire Plains area, as is shown by the development of a sign language that served as a lingua franca in every section of the Plains.

It would be wrong, however, to accept the romantic image of the Plains Indian as the "noble savage." Disease and malnutrition cut short his life span. His days were filled with superstitions and terror of the supernatural. Often unscrupulous shamans held him in their sway. Even his attachment to certain values we admire, such as courage and strength, came only at a price. The pressures of what some have called the ultramasculine role—the emphasizing of war, hunting, sexual adventure, and the quest for the personal vision—were not easily borne, and for many men an escape was needed. One escape was provided by becoming a berdache—that is, to don woman's clothing and do women's work. Sometimes berdaches were permitted to marry each other. By excelling at women's work, a berdache might even attain a certain level of esteem within his society.

The peculiar way of life of the Plains Indians was short-lived. When the American Civil War came to an end and the great rush to the West began, the Plains Indian was doomed. The railroad followed the prairie schooner across his lands, and the great herds of buffalo were destroyed to provide meat for the men who built the railroads. The Indians sometimes fought back—first with bows and arrows, and later with guns—but it was a hopeless battle; the victory of Sitting Bull at the Little Big Horn was nothing more than the dying gasp of a proud people.

Throughout the 1880's and into the 1890's there were sporadic uprisings, but they proved meaningless against the tide of westward expansion. On December 15, 1890, Sitting Bull was shot to death by Indian police who had been trained, clothed, and armed by the white men. The Indians who survived were assimilated or starved, or else dissipated their frustrations in such things as the Peyote cult.

# THE NAVAHO

The first experience of that portion of the Southwest where the Navaho Indians have lived for centuries fills one with awe—an awe created by the vastness, the desolateness, the beauty of the land. Traveling through this country, one feels swallowed up in an infinity of silent sky and earth; all that might be seen for hours is a series of endless stretches of sandy wastes dotted with lonely mesas, and mountains rising on faraway horizons. The heat is intense; the rainfall averages only eight inches a year; and agriculture, except of the most meager sort, is all but impossible.

There seems to be nothing here to attract any human life. Yet one will occasionally come across a wretched straggle of huts where a few Navaho are living. Perhaps only one hut will be standing alone against the sky, with an old man sitting before the doorway, in the sun. His life is a story of hunger, misery, and hardship, most of it written by the arid mercilessness of his environment. Yet nothing short of force could induce him to leave the land of his birth.

The Navaho Indian reservation, which covers nearly 16,000,-000 acres, stretches out over northeastern Arizona, northwestern New Mexico, and southeastern Utah. More than 1,000,000 acres of this land are barren and sandy, and another 100,000 are utterly inaccessible. The remainder, where the Navaho live, is hardly any better.

Because crops cannot be grown to any advantage, herding and tending flocks provide the primary livelihood of the Indians. Sheep are the main flock, and near the large villages these animals can be seen literally everywhere. Horses, which the Navaho esteem as much as their sheep, are also in abundance. Both animals are symbols of prestige.

In the case of the horse, this is illustrated by the Navaho language itself. In English one might say that "he owns one horse," or "she owned two horses," or "they own three horses." In the Navaho language, all the Indian need say is the word *bili*, whose total range of meaning includes his, her, its, or their horse or horses—that is, a verb state of horses being owned by some one or some unit, which may or may not be specified and elaborated as to the quality of ownership.

Navaho is a name applied by foreigners, never used by the Indians themselves. Then and now they still prefer their self-applied name Dine, "the People."

So far as history can be traced, it is believed that the Navahos have been living in their desert since the fifteenth century. Linguistically and culturally, they are related to Athabascan groups to the north of the present Navaho homeland. More precisely, it is likely that the ancestral Navaho groups moved into the Southwest from the Shoshonean plateau area of the central Rocky Mountains, bringing with them their hunting and food-gathering economy. As they penetrated the arid Southwest they modified some of their earlier techniques and acquired some rudiments of horticulture from the farming peoples they met and fought with there.

In the sixteenth century the Spaniards found the Navaho to be an insignificant tribe, based on hunting and gathering, with incipient horticulture. But because they were a people who could easily absorb the ideas of others and adapt their lives to their changing needs, they gradually increased in both number and importance.

They even improved on the ideas they borrowed from others. Take, for example, sand painting, an art that originated with the Pueblos. Today sand painting finds its finest and most elaborate expression with the Navaho.

There is little recorded of Navaho history until the beginning of the seventeenth century, at which time the Navaho became more active enemies of the surrounding sedentary tribes and of the Spanish colonists. Thus the Navaho began as a predatory people. Pueblo settlements and Spanish villages suffered continually from their raids up to the conquest of New Mexico by United States forces in 1846.

The establishment of military posts throughout the Southwest did not stop the Navaho completely. Because they had never made a sufficient living from their land, they still sought their livelihood at the expense of others. Although treaties were made with the tribe in 1846, 1848, and 1849, they failed to check the depredations, which continued until 1858. All during this time punitive expeditions were sent against the Indians, without much success. Although after 1858 most of the Indian raids ceased, conflicts continued to break out between the Navaho and the army. Finally, the tribe suffered so many losses that it agreed to an armistice in 1861.

Peace reigned for a while, but in the same year as the armistice a dozen Navaho were brutally killed while attending a horse race at an army fort. Emboldened by the withdrawal of troops at the onset of the Civil War, the Indians resumed their raids, which they continued without interruption until 1863. The famous Indian fighter Kit Carson took arms against the Navaho with the intention of moving them far away from their old homes into a remote part of New Mexico. By destroying their sheep, Carson finally subdued them; and as a result, almost 8,500 Navaho were forced into New Mexico by 1865.

The journey there was a terrible one for the Indians. One man who had endured it recalled the experience: "Many die. Always hungry, always thirsty. Women carry children. Men tired. Always we walked. We were very tired, very thirsty. Always we walked."

Imprisoned at Fort Sumner in New Mexico for four years, the Indians did not fare much better. Under close-packed and restrictive living conditions, scourged by new diseases, malnutrition, and even starvation, their ranks were badly depleted. The removal experiment turned out a failure. After the death of one thousand Indians, and the expenditure of $1,000,000, the remaining Navaho were returned to their old haunts in 1868. But so

125

INDIAN RUG-WEAVING AT MONUMENT VALLEY, ARIZONA.

traumatic was the episode that the scars remained for many years.

In recent times the Navaho's age-old customs and way of life have been disappearing under the impact of the white man's civilization and laws. Today they are maintained mainly for the sake of the once-great traditions and treasured memories they evoke.

One of the elements most strongly affected is their social organization. Family and clan ties were, until very recently, the most important factors in Navaho life, setting a strict and unbreakable pattern of living. For instance, a man belonged to the clan of his mother and could not marry a woman of his own clan or, in some cases, a woman from a clan related to his own. This is still followed to a certain extent in Navaho life. Certain rules made it taboo for a man to speak to or even look at his mother-in-law. But members of one clan always worked for one another to the point of sacrifice. Kinship was the basis of society, and there were specific obligations according to the kinship category in question. A woman's brothers, for instance, had standard responsibilities toward her children.

Even the elements of play and entertainment were regulated; for example, the permitted and expected forms of joking between two classes of relatives were prescribed in detail. So important was kinship that the Navaho's golden rule was formulated from it: "Behave toward everyone as you behave with your relatives."

Navaho religion, though it is being replaced by Christianity, has been the most intricate factor in Navaho life. Its main function is to ward off evil, and to persuade the holy ones to ensure success for the tribe's planting, building, wars, marriages, and so forth. Their dominant spirit, Changing Woman (in their religion, as in their society, the woman was the Navaho's guiding force), is the principal creator of man and could do only good; all the lesser spirits—Monster Slayer, Failed-to-Speak-People, Water-Sprinkler, Fringed-Mouth—are capable of doing both good and evil.

Because the Indians were always calling on the spirits to help them, they had a great many ceremonies, most of which were to cure illness. In these ceremonies, which are still practiced, the patient is given emetic and herbal medicines, sweated, sung and prayed over, and placed upon a sand painting.

Public dances and exhibitions, attended by thousands, are

part of the ceremonies. Many non-Indian spectators have vivid memories of the famous fire dance, in which the almost naked participants leap through flames and chase each other with burning brands. Some have reported seeing Navaho patients being cured by the medicinal herbs and therapeutic chants of the medicine men.

These were the customs of the people who were returned to their own lands after the New Mexico fiasco in 1868. But their problems were far from over. They were placed on a reservation that was much too small for them. The land was inferior, as much of the grass and water territory they had previously occupied lay outside the reservation boundaries.

Their difficulties mounted as their numbers and livestock increased. The insufficient and overgrazed lands became increasingly inadequate to sustain the Navaho economy. Even the continual expansion of the reservation to its present size was not enough to meet the problem.

These economic difficulties reached a critical point in 1930, and it was not until the outbreak of World War II that conditions became somewhat better. Some three thousand young Navaho men were drafted into the services. On their return they brought back new and expansive ideas for their closed tribal society. In addition, fifteen thousand Navaho had worked in wartime industries, thus earning money for their people.

After 1945 the Navaho way of life underwent vast changes. A shift from a pastoral to a wage economy was started. But to fire their ambitions they still had only new ideas, not the means. After the war another economically critical period began, culminating in 1950 when the United States government finally decided that it had a deeper responsibility to the Indian than it had previously demonstrated. It was then that the $88,570,000 Navaho–Hopi Long Range Rehabilitation Government Development Program was inaugurated to provide educational, health, and economic opportunities.

Economically, the rehabilitation program sought the development of irrigable lands on the reservation, eventually enabling the Indians to gain more of a livelihood from their hitherto inhospitable country. Additional development of reservation mineral resources was another goal, and as a result, the tribal income from oil and natural gas came to $1,500,000 in 1956.

THE NAVAHO BABY BOARD MAY BE ATTACHED TO A WALL, TREE, OR OTHER SUPPORT WHILE THE MOTHER WORKS.

Still another economic ambition of the program was the development of industries, located on or near the reservation, to employ Navaho, as well as financial aid and guidance for Navaho families wishing to relocate in industrial areas away from the reservation. The younger generation, not having the deep inherent love for their desert country that their fathers had had, have been taking advantage of this opportunity. As a consequence, about 2,500 Navaho Indians reside in greater Los Angeles at the present time.

Five federal and three mission hospitals have been built and are trying to cope with such problems as the high mortality rate among Navaho children under five years of age, and tuberculosis, which is ten times greater among the Navaho than for the rest of the nation. Slowly these problems are being overcome. Today the majority of Navaho people would rather go to a trained doctor than to their own medicine men. The medicine men themselves are inclined to seek out white doctors for advice and help in those cases where their own herbs and incantations will not effect a cure.

Perhaps the most significant advances are those being made in education. After the war the first developments on the Navaho reservation were accomplished in education. This got everything else started. All sorts of schools went up after the war: central boarding schools, community boarding schools, federal day schools, public schools, and mission schools. Finally came the trailer schools, with the idea that "if they can't come to you, you'd better go to them." The results were very successful. Today a majority of Navaho youngsters are receiving instruction. In 1957, 26,787 Navaho between the ages of six and eighteen were in school. This number represents 91 percent of their age group and the figures are getting better all the time. This is because the Indians are willing to help themselves and not relying solely on federal funds. In one year the tribal council appropriated $10,000,000 for Navaho students seeking an education beyond high school.

But in spite of these facts, many serious problems remain for the Navaho. He is a stranger in his own country, a man both poor and proud. Most Navaho live far removed from the small number of their own wealthy. Their homes are still the overcrowded mud and clay hogans they have always been. And the average Navaho earns less than $100 a year, usually tending sheep on deteriorating pasture land. Even the Navaho who has an education finds it difficult to acquire a salary commensurate with his abilities. Serious changes still need to be made, especially in administration.

The Navaho is the largest Indian tribe in the United States today. The Navaho people are a living example that the Indian is not the vanishing American. The population of the Navaho is increasing at the rate of 1,800 a year. In 1865 the Navaho tribe numbered 9,500; in 1935 it had grown to 45,000. At the last census, taken in 1960, the Navaho population was 90,000. This is one reason the Navaho has not been able to better his lot; he has grown so rapidly that no improvement program has been able to keep up with him.

But the Navaho Indian is becoming more and more a part of American society. He has shown himself willing to keep pace with his growth, and it is now up to society to have the same desire, to open up and receive one of its own.

# THE HOPI

In 1540 when Coronado traveled a thousand miles north of Mexico City to investigate rumors of the existence of seven fabulous cities of gold, he was disappointed to find only a few villages whose inhabitants lived in stone huts stacked on one another in block-line formations.

Having an appreciation for gold but not for anthropology, Coronado disparagingly called the Indian dwelling places "pueblos," the Spanish term for peasant villages. The name pueblo has stuck, but recent generations have appreciated the richness that exists there—not in gold, but in the elaborate customs and ceremonies and the remarkable means of subsistence that these people have developed, which can still be observed.

There are four distinct linguistic groups of Pueblo Indians who live in that section of the Colorado Plateau where the states of Utah, Colorado, New Mexico, and Arizona meet. Of these groups, the Hopi have managed to retain the least modified culture in the face of the white man's influence, and today they still refer to it as "the Hopi way." At present they form a community of approximately four thousand people, who live in nine villages on three spurs of the Black Mesa, northeast of Flagstaff, Arizona.

The heritage of the Hopi stretches back 1,500 years before the Spaniards came to the New World. The earliest known inhabitants of the area are now called the Basket Makers, due to their ability to weave beautiful baskets. The Basket Makers, who lived in crude huts similar to those used by the Plains Indians, were the first desert farmers, cultivating corn, which is still the main crop of the Hopi and other Pueblo Indians. They also initiated the peaceful, sober way of life that has been a hallmark of the civilization there ever since.

About A.D. 500 a number of new cultural traits began to appear in the area, partly because of newly available features among neighboring peoples, and partly because the Basket Makers were then at a level where such developments could be integrated into their culture.

This synthesis improved on the old methods of farming, and introduced the growing of cotton and weaving of cloth. They also introduced the bow and arrow and the making of pottery, as well as the practice of strapping their infants' heads to their cradle-boards, producing the flat-backed heads that are still considered a sign of beauty by the Hopi. But the most important innovation was the new kind of home that they built, which has come to be known as the pueblo.

The Hopi have developed from the Basket Maker culture, with archeological evidence showing an unbroken continuity of culture from the small settlements of the Basket Makers to the larger and more complex apartment-house type of village typical of today. They have lived continuously in one of their villages, Oraibi, for at least eight hundred years. Known as the Peaceful People, they nevertheless come from warlike stock unrelated to that of the other Pueblo peoples, the Tewa, Zuñi, and Taos. They are the only group of the Shoshonean Indians to adopt the non-nomadic, desert-farming existence of the Pueblo Indians. Closely related to them were the warlike Aztecs of Mexico, and the savage Utes, who were formerly frequent molesters of the Pueblo Indians.

The early pueblos were made of sandstone held together with mud, although later pueblos were often made of adobe. These structures, built entirely above ground except for the religious chamber, or kiva, were made up of a dozen or so small square rooms. Since they often had no doors or windows, they served as excellent fortresses against enemies, as the only entrance was through small holes in the roofs. Frequently the buildings were made in the form of a circle, an oval, or a U-shape, with doors and windows opening on a central patio. Although many of these structures were built on the valley floors, some Indians decided to build their homes on the tops or into the sides of steep mesas as further protection against marauders.

Today pueblos are still built on the tops of the mesas, requiring a long, laborious climb down the cliffs for the villagers to get to their fields. In recent years a few houses have been built on the valley floor, but for the most part custom is stronger than convenience. These first pueblo builders are popularly called Cliff Dwellers, and the remains of their houses, built into the sides of the cliffs, are still spectacular even in their ruined state.

The Hopi live a couple of hundred miles from the other Pueblo Indians, and this separation has allowed them to remain one of the few "full-blooded" tribes in existence today. They are a short (averaging five feet four inches), stocky people, with wide faces and slightly slanting eyes. The descriptions of them recorded by the Spaniards in the 1500's still fit perfectly today.

Their isolation has allowed the Hopi to escape much of the white man's influence, which has been keenly felt by the other Pueblo peoples. It is true that they felt sufficiently oppressed by the Spaniards to abandon their pacifism and join with their neighbors in the first American war of independence—the Pueblo Rebellion of 1680, in which the Spaniards were swept out of what is now New Mexico. In 1692 the Spanish again conquered the territory. But though the Spanish colonists, their expeditions, and their missionaries were able to subdue and reincorporate many of the surrounding areas and peoples, they never effectively reoccupied the western pueblos of the Hopi and Tewa.

The United States government, though less oppressive, has been more difficult to ignore. The present Hopi reservation was established by the government in 1882, and officials have attempted to dictate to the Indians various concepts of the American way of life that are alien to the Hopi—for example, the private ownership of land as opposed to clan ownership.

Around the turn of the century there was a great disagreement in the village of Oraibi caused by government attempts to send the children away to boarding schools. Two factions came into being in the village: those who agreed with the government, known as the Progressives or Friendlies, and those who were opposed, known as the Conservatives or Hostiles. The Hopi have no concept of majority rule, and so the argument was resolved in their traditional fashion. A solemn tug-of-war was held in the village plaza, and the Hostiles, who lost, left the village of Oraibi, and founded a new independent town named Hotavila. Thus Hopi arguments are settled and new villages are established. Incidentally, the government ultimately yielded, and day schools were set up at the foot of each mesa spur.

The tourist may get the impression that the beautiful pottery and basketry made by the women is the main commodity of the Hopi, but in reality their basic occupation is the cultivation of corn.

Seeing the arid land, the casual observer might not believe that anyone could obtain enough water to grow anything here, and yet the Hopi have devised two ingenious methods of irrigation. The first is similar to that of the farmers along the Nile Delta. Rain comes to the Colorado Plateau in occasional violent mountain storms that send great streams rushing down the mesa cliffs, carrying layers of soil with them. The farmer then plants his corn in the moist soil that collects at the foot of the mesa. This method, however, is precarious, since these showers are sporadic, and the corn may be either buried or left high and dry. For this reason the Hopi plants his corn in rotation on several different locations, which are reassigned each year.

The second method of obtaining water is more dependable. The mesa is made up of a thick layer of porous sandstone on top of a thicker layer of shale. These layers slope downward toward the south. After a rainfall some of the water seeps down through the sandstone and will emerge on the cliffs of the mesa two years later in the form of springs. The amount of water available for irrigation from this source can thus be calculated on a long-range basis.

Providing water for his crops is by no means the Hopi's only task in growing his food. He must plant his corn at least a foot deep in the hope that a few of the several seeds he puts in each hole will survive. Several seeds grow up from each hole, and are never weeded out. The result is a series of low bushes. The outer stalks serve as a windbreaker and sunshade for the inner stalks, which produce the ears of corn.

Although the men are in charge of the basic occupations of

HOPI CHILDREN WEARING INDIAN JEWELRY AND BEADED VESTS.

the society, the women have a prominent role, for theirs is a matrilineal society divided in clans descended from a clan mother. It is the clan mother who owns the home and the religious objects, and is responsible for distributing the clan's land and reassigning it each spring.

In marriage alliances it is also the woman who has the say. The Hopi maiden may propose to her young man by sending him a basket of *piki*, or corn wafers. He accepts her proposal by eating the wafers, and their engagement may then be made public by her combing his hair in the village plaza. It is also the woman who takes the initiative in divorce, by setting her spouse's goods outside the door. When he returns from the fields he must pick up his belongings and go home to mother.

It is the men, however, who have the ultimate ascendancy in the community as custodians of, and chief participators in, the religious activities that dominate Hopi society. There are about a dozen different religious societies among the Hopi, and they are all represented in each village. The society organization has sprung up out of the clan system, and the priest of each religious society is generally the eldest brother of the mother of the clan to which it is affiliated. However, any man may join whatever societies he wishes, regardless of his clan affiliation.

Each society claims certain powers, which it can exercise for the good of the community. It possesses these powers through the magic of its name and the fetish that it owns. Common to each society is the power to influence the weather and bring rain. The Snake society claims the power to bring August rains—and also to cure snakebite, through its brotherhood with the snakes gained long ago in the earliest beginnings of the Hopi people.

It has been estimated that the Hopi celebrate two hundred holidays during the course of a year, which calls for a careful system of scheduling. Each ceremonial holiday is carefully prepared for by the society in charge of it, with weeks of diligent practice and prayer taking place in the society's kiva. When the time for the holiday finally arrives the whole village is in a festive mood, and neighboring villages are often invited to attend.

The first important celebration of the year is that of the Soyala, or winter solstice, whose purpose is to ensure that the sun, now at its lowest point, will not fail to return and warm the land for another year. The culmination of this celebration takes place after several days of preparatory kiva rituals on the morning of the solstice, when the kachinas suddenly appear from the underground. The kachina dancers are actually village men, dressed to represent the numerous gods of the Hopi religion.

The kachinas exchange and distribute prayer sticks and go among the children, who are unaware of their real identity, giving out kachina dolls to the girls, bows and arrows to the boys. At the close of the ceremonies the kachinas vanish, since they are supposed to return to their home in the San Francisco mountains. They return, however, in February, for the Powamu, the ceremony of germination and growth. At this time the kachinas are bid to stay among the Hopi until the end of the corn-planting season in July, when the Home dance takes place to bid them farewell.

Among the numerous minor ceremonies, there is one that takes place every other August, which has awed generations of white visitors to the Black Mesa. The Snake dance takes place in order to bring on the late summer rains needed for the survival of the crops. The priest of the Snake Society observes the weather signs carefully, until the day comes when he announces that "the snakes want to dance," and then the sixteen-day ceremony begins. For over a week the members of the Snake Society scour the countryside for snakes, both harmless and poisonous. The live snakes are thrown into the kiva, where they are fed and cared for. The public dance takes place on the final day of the ceremony. The snakes are placed in a small brushwood shelter in the plaza, from which they are taken by the dancers who hold onto them with their teeth as they dance around the plaza.

Each man with a snake is accompanied by another man, who guides the dancer with one hand while seemingly pacifying the snake by brushing its head with a feather. Then all the snakes are dumped in the center of the plaza in a writhing mass. Finally the dancers rush in, grab armfuls of the snakes, bless them with cornmeal, and carry them down the mesa wall to the valley where they are released.

There has been much speculation and controversy as to how the dancers keep from being poisoned by the rattlers. Some have thought it useless to remove the snakes' fangs, since they grow back rapidly. Yet, according to Ruth Benedict, author of *Patterns of Culture*, "it has repeatedly been verified that the poison sacs of the rattlesnakes are removed for the dance." Whether or not this is absolutely effective in rendering the snakes harmless may be another matter. It seems likely that the Hopi's skillful handling of the snakes may have played an important part in preventing injury by averting snakebite in the first place.

The Hopi way continues today, to the delight of both tourists and serious students of anthropology, but its days are no doubt numbered. That it has survived this long must be attributed not only to an accident of geography, but also to its power to satisfy the deepest needs of its community.

# THE SEMINOLE

In the early part of the eighteenth century, the land held by the Seminole was rich both for cultivation and in food animals. William Bartram, a naturalist traveling through Florida in the 1770's, reported that no other part of the globe so abounded in wild game or creatures fit for the food of man. He found nothing to give the Seminole disquietude except the gradual encroachment of white people.

He also described Cuscowilla, the capital of the Alachua tribe. Early in the eighteenth century, the Alachua chief, Cowkeeper, led raids against the Spaniards in Florida. Cowkeeper's tribe had a prominent place in the Seminole nation; all head chiefs of the Seminole, until removal, were reckoned to be descended from this chief through the female line.

When visited by Bartram, Cuscowilla had thirty habitations, each family having two houses. One house, open on three sides, supported by cedar pillars, and roofed with thatch, was used for sleeping during the hot season. The other house contained a common hall and eating room in one half, a sleeping room in the other. There were small gardens in which corn, beans, tobacco, and citrus fruit were grown. The town itself was very clean, waste being deposited at a distance from the dwellings.

Two miles from the town was a plantation that provided the

major portion of the Indians' produce. Here each family had a part of the land, which was sectioned off at planting time. Cultivation was done by the village as a whole, but each family had a private granary in which its own produce was kept. There was also a public granary to which each family contributed and from which guests and indigents were fed. The system also allowed for an equitable sharing of produce in times of hardship.

For visitors, a hospitable banquet would be laid out, and the chief would slaughter some of his cattle for the occasion. Such a banquet might consist of venison stewed with bear oil, fresh corn cakes, milk, hominy, and honey mixed in water.

Another town visited in the late eighteenth century was Talahasochte, or White King's Town, on the Suwanee River in what is now Levy County, Florida. The houses of this town were constructed much like those at Cuscowilla. Using cypress canoes large enough to accomodate twenty or thirty people, the Indians carried on a lively trade along the coast with the Spanish, and made occasional trips to Cuba and the Bahamas. The Indians exported deerskins, honey, furs, and bear oil; they imported coffee, sugar, and liquor. Between 1812 and 1840 many Seminole and their Negro allies, feeling their struggle with the white man to be hopeless, left Florida in canoes and sailed to the Bahamas. In 1820 one such group, led by a man called Scipio Bowlegs, reached the Bahamas and settled there. Their descendents are thought to live there today.

Although the Seminole of Florida made war against their enemies, they were essentially a peace-loving people. Once, after several white settlers from Georgia had been killed, a white trader visited Talahasochte to see if the Indians were receptive to the re-establishment of a trading post, and whether they felt hostile toward all white people. After feasting, smoking, and drinking the Indian "black drink," the chief and elder statesmen announced that the men who had attacked the white settlers had been killed, and they entreated the trader to tell the white people of the tribe's desire to atone for the breach of peace and friendship.

The Seminole Indians living in Florida today are descendents of the several hundred unconquered people who refused to move westward after the Seminole war of the nineteenth century. They live in small isolated areas, as well as on the Big Cypress Reservation and along the Tamiami Trail, all in the Everglades.

In recent times the land held by most of these people has not been fit for farming or grazing. Small gardens are still tended, however, and some cattle, pigs, and chickens are raised. As most of this land is swamp, a man must take seasonal work in logging camps or on road gangs to eke out his meager income.

The Indians today, as in former times, live in houses of cypress logs and thatched roofs, built on hummocks, which are high dry islands in the swamp. Centrally located in each village is a community house in which the cooking is done. After the food is prepared it is brought back to the individual dwellings.

The Seminole are organized into matrilineal clans. Inheritance and descent are through the mother's side of the family. The mother is head of the household. When a man marries he lives with his wife's family. In clan functions, a boy receives instruction from his mother's brother, who is in his clan, rather than from his father. Marriage inside one's clan was once forbidden, but this rule is no longer strictly observed.

Although grouping into clans is still evident among the modern Seminole, more people are now separating from the clan to live on reservation land.

The Seminole have retained much of their former customs, folklore, and religion, and their myths have elements recognizable as common to the entire Southeast. There are origin myths for clans and for such everyday foods as corn and pumpkins. Generally the old people tell these stories in the evening around the campfire before the children fall asleep. Among the numerous myths that have been preserved are several versions of the origin of mankind. One of these holds that the Great Spirit fashioned men out of clay. He overbaked the first batch, which came out dark; these were the Negroes. The next batch was not baked enough and so came out pale; these were the white men. In his third attempt the Great Spirit created fresh models, baked them just enough, and they came out perfect. These were the Indians.

The Seminole still celebrate the Green Corn dance and the Autumnal Hunting dance, holdovers from their Greek ancestry. The Green Corn dance is a very old festival held on the first day of the new moon of the vernal equinox, which is the beginning of their new year. At this time houses are cleaned and discarded clothing, tools, and weapons are destroyed and replaced. Fires are extinguished and the hearths are sprinkled with clean white sand.

The most important part of this festival is the lighting of the

141

New Fire. In the town square, four large logs are placed so that they form a cross with its points facing in the four cardinal directions. At daybreak the Fire Maker faces the rising sun, lights a bundle of grass, and places it in the center of the four logs lighting the New Fire. The village people then sing and dance around the fire. At the end of the ceremony each woman is given an ember from this fire to rekindle her own.

All the clans of the Seminole then participate in a five-day meeting at which tribal problems are considered and marriages contracted. One of the rites is the drinking of an emetic brewed from the leaves of the yaupon tree. The Indians call it "asi"; outsiders call it the black drink. It is believed to purify the drinker and endow him with prowess in war, and is also used as a ritual expressing friendship.

The medicine man, who once played an important part in the religious life of the Seminole, is still in evidence. Curing power is acquired by a medicine man only after long hard study, and is measured in successive degrees of competence. An aspirant studies with a senior medicine man for years and learns to diagnose a patient's ills through interpreting his dreams. He may, for example, learn that the patient's soul has been detained while traveling outside the body, and will employ a specific chant to persuade the soul to return.

He concocts a special medicine to enable a woman to become pregnant. A root brew is made every new moon for four months; another one is made for the husband. If both take the medicine it is felt the woman will soon have a child. Love medicines, war medicines, and medicines for good luck in hunting are among the others employed. Medicine bundles—collections of feathers, stones, pieces of horn, and animal parts—are still in use, but now mainly as symbols.

Although missionaries are active among the Seminole, they have made relatively few converts. However, elements of Christianity have become intermingled with traditional Seminole ideas. As an example, the Indians speak of a great spirit who lives in the sky and who never comes down to Earth. The general resistance of these people to Christianity has been attributed to their resistance to, and suspicion of, the white man.

The attitude of the Seminole toward the help of the United States government differs from that of many other tribes in the

SEMINOLE WOMAN AND CHILD. THE WOMAN'S NEGROID FEATURES ARE A RESULT OF THE TRIBE'S INTERBREEDING WITH RUNAWAY SLAVES WHO FLED TO FLORIDA IN THE NINETEENTH CENTURY.

country. The government has given funds to western tribes for land they once held, but the Seminoles were never compensated for the loss of their land.

On the Tamiami Trail most Indians are legally squatters and subject to eviction at any time, but this is seldom enforced because the land is poor. The Seminole would like land better suited to grazing and cultivation.

In 1938 Seminole leaders met with United States government agents for the first time since the Seminole uprising ninety years before. They were led by Richard Osceola, who spoke of the needs of the Seminole, among them schools, hospitals, horses, better land, and better beef stock. They had been forced to accept the help of the white man, which they are now getting.

Because the Seminole live in scattered, isolated pockets in the Everglades, they present a problem to the Indian agency in Florida, which is trying to help them. But the agency does offer advice and help in cattle raising, encourages school attendance, and helps the Seminole to find employment.

Weaving, a long-neglected art, is being revived. The distinctive Seminole style of brightly colored, appliquéd clothing is now being made for the tourist trade. Seminole are now permitted to buy land they have developed. The Seminole Indian Association of Florida and the Friends of the Seminole, along with missionaries, work with the government agency to help bring the living standard of the Indians abreast of modern times.

# MISSION INDIANS
# OF CALIFORNIA

When the Spaniards came to Southern California they found a generally friendly native population, who readily adopted Christianity and lived in or around the Spanish missions. For this reason they are often collectively called the Mission Indians. Although they belong to many different tribes, all but one belong to the same linguistic family, the Shoshonean. The sole exception, the Diegueño, belong to the Yuman family.

Most of these tribes did not have names for themselves, and so today they are called by names adapted from Spanish. For example, the Luiseño are named after the Spanish mission of San Luis Rey de Francia. Today, many of these tribes are extinct, including the Chumash, the Gabrielino, the Fernandeño, and the Juaneño. The populations of the tribes that still remain, retaining portions of their original customs and institutions, are greatly reduced.

Although the techniques of dry horticulture had probably spread to some of the Indian groups in Southern California from related peoples in the Colorado basin, it was the influence of the missions that effectively introduced agriculture to the Mission Indians.

By the early 1800's most of the bands associated with mission stations had become basically agricultural, growing the classical American complement of crops—maize, squash, cotton, and some introduced plants. Hunting game, collecting wild produce, and —for some groups—fishing still retained a subsidiary importance, or acquired primary importance in years of disaster or bad harvest.

One of the primary functions of the missions was to act as protectors of the Indian groups against the ravages of white settlers and miners, who descended in a flood tide after 1849. This protection allowed the Mission Indians to retain their style of life, which they had developed in their early adaptation to "reservation" living, until the beginning of the twentieth century, when they began to approximate more and more the patterns of other neighboring groups settled on government reserves.

The original territory of the Luiseño was mostly inland, hilly country extending west of the divide that stretches south from Mount San Jacinto. Like the other Mission Indians, they were food gatherers and hunters. In order to be near the best foods, the Luiseño changed their homes with the season. The women went out each day with baskets on their backs, which were held in place by a net hanging from their foreheads and slung around the basket.

A few fruits, berries, and roots were gathered, but the staple food was acorns. To be made edible, acorns were first dried out; then the meat was picked out and ground into flour. Next, the poisonous tannic acid had to be removed from the acorn flour. The Indians long ago discovered that the poison could be extracted by pouring large amounts of water over the flour. This leaching process was hastened with boiling water. The flour was placed in a basket or a hole in the sand and the water was allowed to seep through. The prepared flour was then boiled in a pot with water until the mush thickened to the consistency of oatmeal. When cool it could be sliced. This pink mush is still considered a delicacy by the Indians.

The Luiseño did not have much large game to eat, although deer were occasionally shot or snared. Besides shooting game with bows and arrows, the Indians used a number of devices for catching their prey. Rabbits were frequently knocked over with a curved rabbit stick similar to a boomerang, or were driven into long nets stretched across their feeding patches. Wood rats, ground squirrels, and mice were trapped, or were burned out

146

of their nests. Quail were frequently run down by the young boys, or were lured at night by the blaze of burning cactus and struck down with sticks. Ducks, too, were brought down with sticks, or shot with arrows. Meat was broiled on coals or roasted in earthen ovens, and whatever flesh and bone was not immediately eaten was pounded, dried, and stored for future use.

The Luiseño house, about the size of a small room, was built over a hole a couple of feet deep in the ground. Brush and earth covered a simple frame of poles. There was a smoke hole at the top, and a door cut into the side. Cooking was done outside whenever possible. In addition to the family houses, each campground had a sweat house where the men gathered in the evening for steam baths heated by wood fires. The other main structure of the village was the *wamkish*, or temple, consisting of a circular brush fence in which the religious ceremonies of the community were conducted.

The balmy California climate made clothes unnecessary for much of the year. Generally the men went about naked, although they sometimes wore a skin loincloth. The women wore the so-called California double apron—a skirt consisting of two fringes, one in front and a longer one in back, made of shredded bark or Indian hemp. In addition they frequently wore caps, which kept their foreheads from being chafed by the basket straps. During the winter both men and women wore long capes of woven rabbit fur, deerskins, or sea otter furs, obtained in barter with their coastal neighbors. The only ornaments of the Indians were shell necklaces and the heavy tattooing of the men.

The important deity of the Luiseño was Chungichnish, or Changichnish, who was worshipped by many different tribes, having been brought to the Luiseño from the Juaneño. Chungichnish is a sort of Jehovah, a living, all-present god who watches and punishes his people. Many authorities feel that the rise of his cult has close connections with Christianity; its spread coincided with that of the Spanish missions.

The two important religious ceremonies were the girls' and boys' initiation ceremonies, and the mourning rites. The boys' initiation ceremony began with the drinking of the toloache, or Jimson-weed potion, within the ceremonial enclosure. The effects of the narcotic were strong and sometimes fatal; it took from one to four days for the drug to wear off. At first the drugged boys would dance, but soon they would stagger and fall unconscious.

147

The drug produced visions, usually of animals, while the boy was in a deep sleep. This dream vision retained an intimate sanctity for the individual throughout his life; the Indian would never kill the animal that appeared to him in his toloache dream. Thus the narcotic weed achieved much the same end as did fasting, lack of sleep, and torture in the vision quest of the Plains Indian. After the drug had worn off, the boys observed several periods of fasting and ceremonial dancing.

The prominent part of the girls' initiation ceremony, which was conducted by all the Southern California Shoshonean, was the "roasting." After a preliminary ordeal in which the girl's virtue was evaluated by her ability to keep down swallowed tobacco balls, she was placed in a pit lined with heated stones and carpeted with sedge and grass. The girl had to lie in this pit for three days, with only a short respite every twenty-four hours when she got up and ate, at which time the stones were reheated. Two heated stones were placed on her belly, and her head was covered with a basket. During this time she had to lie very still and not scratch herself with her fingernails. If she did have to scratch herself, special ceremonial sticks were provided. The roasting was supposed to increase her fertility and was repeated in modified form after the first few times she gave birth.

Another important part of both initiation ceremonies was the instruction the boys and girls received from the ground paintings. This institution was connected with the sand paintings of the Navaho and the Pueblos, but it had gone through an independent and distinct local development among the Shoshonean and the Diegueño of Southern California. The painting was executed inside the wamkish and represented the universe. The drawings were circular, and within them were depicted the encircling Milky Way and the all-encompassing night or sky. Symbols of the human personality were also drawn.

The punishers sent by the invisible Chungichnish were depicted in abstract form and included the raven, the rattlesnake, the spider, the bear, the wolf, and the mountain lion. Each symbol was pointed out to the initiates, along with an exhortation to do the things that were proper, so that life would be happy and successful. There were no words for "right" and "wrong" in the Luiseño tongue, and their concept of morality was based on a belief in a system of inexorable cause and effect, so that if certain things were done, a good life would result.

Another ceremony for boys was the ant ordeal. The boys were laid on ant hills or put in a hole filled with ants; then more ants were shaken over them. After the torture was completed, the initiates gained dubious relief by having the stinging ants whipped off their bodies with nettles.

The other important ceremonies of the Luiseño were the mourning rites, which took place after the cremation of the body. There were at least six of these, including individual ceremonies; the tsuchanish, which commemorates all the deaths of the past year or years; and the eagle-killing ceremony, which was the annual commemoration of the group's dead chiefs.

The Luiseño had several dances which were only loosely connected with the ceremonies. One dance was the tatajuita, in which a single performer, dressed to resemble an eagle, with headdress and skirt of feathers and body painted with horizontal white bands, whirled rapidly. In the exciting and spectacular fire dance, the performers rushed up to the edges of the fire in waves, swiftly kicking the burning coals inward and stamping on the exposed embers with their bare feet.

Like most Mission Indians, the Luiseño accepted the Christian missionaries within a few years. The Mission San Luis Rey de Francia was established in 1798. As all the Spanish missions of California were founded between 1769 and 1823, the California Indians were the last in the United States to feel the influence of the white man.

Adoption of the mission way of life meant more than just worshipping the white man's God. The missionaries made the Indian neophytes build their brush houses around the mission church and abandon their wandering for the stationary life of the farmer. Although this life was very different from what they had been used to, many Indians were glad to embrace it because they saw how much more reliable the food supply could be if it was farmed. The Spanish taught them how to farm, introducing spades and hoes and showing them how to dig irrigation ditches. The missions were run as little self-contained communities until California and Mexico gained independence from Spain. Then the mission system broke down; and when the United States took possession of California after the Mexican War, chaos ensued. The Indians were frequently mistreated and their lands unjustly seized.

The Indians of many of the missions, such as San Diego,

Los Angeles, and Santa Barbara, have not remained close to their original homes because these areas have become populous urban centers. However, the San Luis Rey area is an exception, and today the Luiseño Indians still live in part of their ancient territory on the Pala Reservation. This reservation, and those of the other tribes, were set aside by the government between 1870 and 1907.

Today the Bureau of Indian Affairs of the United States government is responsible for the administration of the affairs of the Indians within the state of California. A bureau office at Sacramento handles most of the California reservations.

The "Indian problem" is a term that refers to the continuing exclusion of Indian people from the social and economic opportunities of American society. It is most evident in the low level of education most group members are able to acquire, the high rate of unemployment and low annual income among most groups, high infant mortality and disease rates, and the physically rundown nature of most Indian communities.

The Indian problem gets public attention from time to time. Because for most Indian groups—especially for those as small and as enmeshed in populous American complexes as the Mission Indians—very little of the indigenous culture remains, the solution seems to lie in more fully integrating the group members into the life of the region as a whole. We are witnessing a new spurt of effort in this direction as VISTA volunteers begin working on the reserves and as the antipoverty program starts to take effect.

The Diegueño way of life was substantially like that of the Luiseño, except that the former depended for their livelihood on the fish and mollusks they got from the sea. The Diegueño live along the coast in both Upper California and Baja California. Those who live in Upper California were known as Diegueño, or San Diegueño, from the Spanish mission at San Diego. These people speak one dialect, and their kinsmen in Baja California, known as Bajeño, speak another closely related dialect.

The Diegueño have the distinction of being the only California Indian tribe to bestow martyrdom on a Franciscan. San Diego, founded in 1769, was the first Upper California mission, and the Diegueño, unlike the other California Indians, were very hostile. They were a stubborn and proud people who clung to the tradi-

150

tions of their ancestors. The Spanish in turn had not perfected their methods of dealing firmly with the Indians. Within the first month after the mission was started it was plundered. A few years later, after moving the mission to its permanent site, the Spaniards were attacked in earnest. The Diegueño killed three Spaniards, including one priest.

In contrast to the mysticism of the Luiseno is the materialism of the Diegueño. In general their religious observances are the same, but the Chungishnich elements are absent from the Diegueño. The contrast in their sand paintings is illuminating. Whereas the Luiseño use abstract symbols, the Diegueño painting is full of visible objects of the universe—the sun, the moon, the constellations—and simplified but literal animal pictures.

The Diegueño perform the dance that has come to be known on television and in the movies as the war dance, though it had nothing to do with war. The basic step is a hop forward with both feet, followed by a stride. To successive songs the performers would repeat this dance, moving counterclockwise in a circle.

# THE TLINGIT

The Indians of the Pacific coastal region stretching from southern Alaska to northern California have developed several distinctive cultural phenomena. These range from totem poles to their own special brand of conspicuous consumption, of which the most spectacular example is the ostentatious destruction of one's property.

The region is an area of considerable linguistic diversity, but the cultural traits of the various peoples are fairly homogeneous. Among the larger groups are the Tlingit of the Alaska panhandle and the nearby Canadian lands, and the Kwakiutl of the central coast of British Columbia.

These Indians, whose population has been estimated as once having totaled ten thousand in fifty communities, were fortunate in having at their disposal a bountiful sea and abundant woodlands. The plentiful supply of fish—especially salmon—as well as shellfish and sea mammals, could readily be obtained from the nearby oceans and rivers. For much of the year the Indians spent relatively little time on finding this food, and they had a variety of methods of catching it. Fish were taken in traps and nets, as well as with harpoons, spears, rakes, and many kinds of hooks. Sea mammals were hunted from seagoing wooden canoes. The sea diet was supplemented with roots, berries, and bulbs gathered by the women. Deer, elk, mountain goats, and other land animals added variety to the diet. They were caught with snares and traps and hunted with bow and arrow.

The Indians developed techniques for drying and smoking meat and fish, as well as for extracting fish oil. This enabled them to accumulate large stores of food for the many lavish feasts they staged during the winter months.

In addition to the abundance of food, there was a readily accessible and seemingly inexhaustible supply of wood for shelter and utensils of all sorts. The Indians usually did not fell the trees, but let floods and storms knock them down; then the men went to work on them with carpentry tools made of stone, shell or bone.

A combination of leisure time, abundant materials, and talent made it possible for these people to develop woodworking to a high craft. Special features of Northwest woodworking were the bending of boards by steaming, and the joining and mending of wood by sewing it with spruce roots or other material. Wood was used to create objects of all kinds—tiny figurines and sixty-foot dugout canoes, storage boxes and eating utensils, ceremonial masks, rattles, and staffs, as well as grave monuments and totem poles.

Very little Northwest art was representational; rather it was highly stylized and conventional. Animal drawings had anatomical distortions, or the artist depicted only a significant portion, such as a claw, a leg, or the internal organs. The bear was represented by its claws, and the hawk by its curved beak.

Besides the artistic endeavors of a few of its members, the community devoted a great amount of time to the ceremonies and entertaining that were indispensable to their elaborate religious and social institutions. There was little feeling of tribal unity; the chief social and political unit was the village, a single row of rectangular wooden houses built near the beach in a sheltered area. Several families might live in one house, arranged by rank, with the noblest farthest from the door. Heraldic designs painted on the front of the house, as well as a totem pole planted in front, proclaimed the origin and status of the occupants.

If there was no tribal sense, there was a clan organization among villages speaking the same language. The Tlingit traced their descent through the female line, whereas the Kwakiutl reckoned descent through the father, although elements of double descent linked families in scattered villages together in a complex way among most of these groups.

The great social consideration of the Northwest Indians was rank, which depended not on family and ancestry but on wealth and property. Thus, except for the slaves who could never rise above their caste, the society was quite mobile, enabling one to advance up the social scale through marriage or the accumulation of property. The result was much scrambling about for social position, which expressed itself in ostentatious display of goods and property, as well as in conspicuous distribution of them. Since there was no true currency, although some shells had a fixed value, wealth was always measured by the possession of tangible property or the right to certain privileges, titles, names, dances, songs, or rituals. All forms of prestige tended to manifest themselves in public display.

A great way to shame a rival while enhancing one's own prestige was to invite him to a feast, and then dramatically give away or destroy some valuable property to show how little one had need of it.

Initially, the prestige-gathering ceremonies involved mainly the ostentatious distribution of food and goods to visiting parties from nearby communities; but as trade goods became more and more common throughout the early nineteenth century, their destruction as evidence of opulence became increasingly fashionable. A large canoe might be hacked to bits, or a hundred fine blankets would be heaped on the fire and then doused with valuable fish oil. The resulting smoke might choke the host, but the tears in the eyes of the rival would be from humiliation if he couldn't rival the show.

An important ceremony was the potlatch, which both earned wealth for the host and showed off his affluence and position. A potlatch might be held for various reasons, varying from group to group and including puberty rites and death commemorations. It involved a great feast at which the host lavishly distributed valuable property to all the assembled guests. The hitch was that the guests had to reciprocate at some future date—with interest of up to 100 percent.

The social hierarchy, beginning at the top, was arranged as

A TLINGIT CHIEF'S HOUSE IN ALASKA SHOWS THE HIGLY DEVELOPED WOOD WORK AND STYLIZED ARTWORK OF THE NORTHWEST. TOTEM POLES ILLUS TRATE MYTHS OR FAMILY AFFILIATIONS.

follows: Chiefs; kinsmen closely related to chiefs; poor relations and hangers-on of the nobility; a sort of middle class of free men, who had some valuable possessions; and a slave class, comprising war captives and Indians purchased from other tribes.

Among some tribes, including the Tlingit, the shamans rivaled the chiefs in power. Each shaman was believed to have a supernatural agent who helped him in curing the sick and foretelling events. The Northwest Indians had a rich mythology peopled with all sorts of nature deities, including fish, mammals, and birds. Many secret societies put on elaborate ceremonies that dramatize the stories of the spirits. These ceremonies take place during the winter, when the supernatural creatures are believed to dwell among mortals.

Until the 1880's, the main contact these Indians had with outside civilization was through fur traders, whalers, and occasional mission ships. Trading was well established by the end of the eighteenth century, and the stimulus it gave to this wealth-oriented society resulted in a great flurry of artistic creativity.

Though the roving presence of ship- and shore-based missionaries, the establishment of trading posts, and the more or less effective suppression of large-scale intervillage raiding were accomplished facts by the beginning of the last quarter of the nineteenth century, Tlingit culture and society remained relatively unchanged.

With the appearance of fish canneries and a market for fish during the 1880's and 1890's, the Tlingit, like many peoples of the northwest coast, could enter the cash economy—and the outer world—yet still retain many of their fundamental activities and the organization of their former life. In addition to fishing solely for subsistence, they caught fish for sale or credit to non-Indian buyers.

It was not until the period of the First World War, and immediately after, that direct, government-applied, restrictive controls were put on central parts of their culture. Because clergy and Indian Affairs branch administrators felt that the feasting tended to waste the Indians' resources, stringent laws were levied against the potlatch. Nevertheless, as the Tlingit are one of the groups most removed from the centers of provincial administration, these edicts have not had the sharp impact that they had among other coastal groups.

Slowly, and with many advances and much stagnation and regression, the Tlingit have moved into the marginal fringes of the white frontier economy, of fishing and lumbering and occasional wage employment that characterizes so much of the backwater regions of northern British Columbia.

156

# THE ESKIMOS

The main influence on the culture of the Eskimos has been the relentlessly cruel climate. Exposed to snow and ice for six to nine months out of the year, the Eskimos are necessarily of hardy stock. They inhabit a coastal area spreading from Greenland to Labrador, and are divided into six groups: the Western Eskimos from Alaska; the Mackenzie River Eskimos from Barter Island to Bathurst (few of these are left, for diseases brought by white settlers at the turn of the century have proved fatal to the Eskimos); the Eskimos of the Arctic Archipelago; the Caribou Eskimos from west of Hudson Bay; the Labrador Eskimos; and the Greenland Eskimos.

Despite a few differences in eating and dwelling habits, they are very closely related racially and culturally. Their language is highly inflected, and makes use of many suffixes, which when grouped together form different words with different meanings all from the same root.

The Eskimo, a member of the Mongoloid peoples, has a light brown skin and a broad, flat face with high cheek bones. His hair is coarse and black, though he has little body hair, and he stands about five feet three. He eats four to eight pounds of meat a day.

Although the origins of the Eskimos are as yet unknown, archeologists have been able to trace their development on the

North American continent back some two thousand years. There is evident relationship with Eskimoan and other Siberian aborigines of Northeast Asia.

Eskimos, as a general group, have two types of housing—permanent and semi-permanent homes. The permanent dwellings are sunk into the ground and have a two-foot-wide door. The actual entrance is larger, but it is cut into the earth on a slant so that cold air is kept out. For heat and light, the Eskimo uses a lamp that burns animal fat; the best fuel is seal blubber. If the house is overheated, a vent in the ceiling is unplugged, and fresh air circulates inside. Driftwood is scarce, so frequently bone is used as supports for the house. Bone pegs, fastened to the wall, serve as clothing racks.

The familiar igloos are the Eskimos' semi-permanent home (with the exception of the Canadian Eskimos, who use them permanently in winter). While out hunting, the Eskimo chops blocks out of hard-packed snow for a convenient shelter. So well trained are his eyes that he can chop out almost perfect pieces every time, without measuring them. The more time a hunter spends in an igloo, the better he makes it for the next man, because the fat-burning lamps melt the ice walls. When they refreeze, the cracks seal themselves. Usually a window is cut into the igloo. The window pane is made of a thin sheet of ice or a piece of animal gut. If a hunter plans to remain any length of time, he stretches skins on the walls for further insulation.

The igloo stays fairly warm. When inhabited by a group of four or five people it may be well above freezing inside while outside it is twenty or thirty degrees below zero. Once a solid coating of ice has been formed on the inner walls very little additional melting will take place, especially if there is skin and pelt insulation. Since animal fat produces little smoke when burned, no opening in the igloo is needed.

The women of the house usually remain indoors and sew leather. After an animal's hide has been removed, the women chew the skin to remove the remaining fat and soften the leather. This process makes it impervious to the cold and prevents it from cracking.

Eskimos wear several layers of clothing: an undershirt made of caribou or bird skins; a heavy coat of caribou, fur side out; and in especially bad weather, a waterproof overcoat made of animal gut. On their feet they wear sealskin mukluks, high moccasin boots, which are sewn tightly to make them waterproof. The hunter, in addition, wears goggles that look like miniature Venetian blinds. Made from thin slits of bone, they protect the eyes from the glare and prevent snow blindness.

The hunter travels lightly in winter, but must take a large supply of meat for his dogs. The sled dog, the only domesticated animal owned by the Eskimo, is strong and stocky, and a hard and willing worker. A dog team must be a unified group and respect the position of the head dog, otherwise they are difficult to manage.

As the hunter does not bring much food for himself, if it runs out and he has captured nothing, he sets traps. He freezes a piece of bent, flexible whalebone and puts it inside a small piece of fat. An animal swallows the fat, the fat thaws, and the bone sliver springs open, cutting through the animal's stomach. In another kind of trap, a knife is dipped in blood and stuck in the snow, blade exposed. The animal comes and licks the blade, thus slashing its tongue. This method is often used to kill marauding wolves.

For a change in diet, the hunter can eat birds. Taking the top block off the igloo, he puts pieces of meat around the hole. The birds flock about it. When a bird gets close to the hole the hunter grabs its legs and eats it raw.

Perhaps the major adaptation of the Eskimos, with their remarkably ingenious technological equipment, was to sea-mammal harpooning, with dependence on seals, walruses, and to some extent whales. Only a few inland Eskimo groups depended on land hunting.

The common sled is built of whale jawbone to hold the runners together. It is made in sections so that in going over cracks in the ice, it will ride more easily. The winters are so hard that often there is neither wood nor bone for making sleds. Taking pieces of walrus skin, the hunter dips them in water to make them more flexible. He then wraps them around salmon. When he has enough of them he puts them outside to freeze. Then from the salmon and walrus he ingeniously constructs a sled; when it thaws he eats it.

The word *Eskimo* means "one who eats raw meat." The Eskimos are not gourmets by European standards. Nothing is cooked, which is good, as they have very few vegetables for vitamins. Berries and greens, gathered in the short summer

159

months, are so rare that if a plant-eating animal is caught, its stomach's contents are eaten. Every part of the animal is consumed, including the blood.

In summer the best means of transportation is the one-man kayak. Resembling a canoe, it is made of skins stretched on bone or wood frames. When the person gets in, he hooks his jacket around the opening of the boat. If it tilts over, he flips himself up with his paddle or, if skillful enough, with the palm of his hand.

Eskimo family life is close, and no one has any more influence than the next of kin, except for the shaman, or medicine man. The Eskimos, like tribal peoples generally, raise their children gently and seldom punish them. Ridicule, disapproval, and unanimity among the group as to their moral codes and behavior seem sufficient to induce approved behavior in the children. Besides, the Eskimos have two specific reasons for not punishing their children: One is that on the average, children do not live very long; the other is that when a relative dies the child receives his name, which is thought to contain the dead man's soul.

No puberty rites exist. Girls come of age around fifteen, and have liberal sex before marriage. There are no wedding ceremonies, but trial marriages exist. Women usually have a number of children, and if any are born during a famine they may be killed. In fact suicide and mercy killing are commonplace. A husband thinks nothing of switching wives with a friend for a time. If a neighbor drops in, the husband gladly lends him his wife. The Eskimos are most hospitable, and there is no stigma attached to having "illegitimate" children.

The Eskimo religion is full of spirits and the supernatural. When a person dies it is thought he will go on to a better life, one without famine or hardship. The corpse is dressed in its best clothes, and moss is put in the nostrils to keep the spirit from escaping. It is then lifted out through the roof of the house and buried under a pile of rocks to keep the ghost from wandering around. Everything, the Eskimo believes, is possessed with a spirit. If a seal is killed, it is given a drink of water so when it goes to the land beyond it will tell of the hunter's kindness.

Presently there are about 35,000 Eskimos living in the Arctic. Their acculturation has proceeded at disparate rates and in rather different directions. In Canada, where close to half of the Eskimos live, they continued on in much their old way—hunting, fishing,

HE ESKIMO IS BELIEVED TO BE ONE OF THE LATEST MIGRANTS FROM ASIA
A THE BERING STRAIT. THIS GIRL, FROM LABRADOR, HAS THE MONGOLOID
YE FOLD, WHICH IS SELDOM SEEN IN OTHER AMERICAN INDIAN TRIBES.

and trapping—and knew little outside influence, except from the fur trader and missionary, until 1950. At that time the population was decreasing, and disease, famine, destitution, and declining fur and game animals had created extreme hardship. But through the first years of the 1950's the plight of the Canadian Eskimo became a cause célèbre, and a massive government relief and development policy was rapidly fashioned and instituted.

The basis of the policy was that hunting and trapping could no longer provide the minimal requirements acceptable to either the Eskimos or the Canadian government, therefore welfare and new wage employment should be funneled into Eskimo communities. By 1965 the hunting and trapping base had virtually disappeared. Almost every Eskimo family in Canada now lives in the new concentrated government-staffed villages that dot the Arctic shoreline.

The changes for the Alaskan Eskimo have been less dramatically sudden. The incorporation of wage and welfare economy and involvement with a frontier white society started two generations ago and continued at a steady pace. In addition, the population density of many Alaskan Eskimo communities, and the much higher proportion of other nonwhite peoples in the region, acted as a buffer against cataclysmic change. Publications in the Eskimo language, Eskimo community councils, and numerous elements of Eskimo culture have been preserved through adaptation to the new economic and political realities.

The atomic age presents a particular threat to the Alaskan Eskimo. Radiation surveys of seven Alaskan villages have shown that the Eskimos have far more radioactive cesium 137 in their bodies than the rest of the American population. Preliminary results indicate that the level of the radioactive substance is still rising, and radiation experts suggest it might become necessary to take measures to protect the Eskimo population. The report was presented to a Joint Congressional Atomic Energy subcommittee by the Atomic Energy Commission's Hanford Laboratories in Washington. Hanford scientists had gone to Alaska with a portable "whole-body counter" to measure the radioactivity in the bodies of Eskimos. The survey discovered that the Eskimos were receiving surprisingly high amounts of fallout radiation from atomic tests.

More than seven hundred Eskimos were examined by the

portable body counter. In the village of Anaktuvuk Pass, the average adult was found to have 450 nanocuries of cesium 137 in his body, and one individual had as much as 790 nanocuries. A nanocurie is a billionth of a curie; a curie is equal to the radiation from one gram of radium. The substance, which is chemically similar to potassium, accumulates in the muscles, where in sufficient quantity it can present a genetic hazard.

The reason for the unusually high concentration of cesium 137 in the Eskimos arises from the special food chain in the Arctic region. The lichens act as a "blotting paper" to pick up the radioactive fallout. Caribou thrive on the lichen, and the Eskimos in turn depend on the caribou for meat.

The only other inhabitants of the North American Arctic, the Aleuts, are a fast-vanishing people. They also adapted themselves to the specialized way of living demanded by the climate, but the tempering influence of the seawater gave them a more amenable climate that allows them more freedom in their way of life. The climate is essentially uniform the year round—cool, rainy, and foggy, with no sea ice and little snow. Consequently the Aleuts had no sleds and did no ice fishing. Instead they relied heavily on fish, especially salmon, as well as on plant products such as roots and berries, which are so scarce in the more land-bound, snow-covered areas of the Arctic.

As the people did not depend on seasonal changes to supply their food and other needs, they lived in permanent villages, in large sod and wood-plank communal dwellings that housed several families. Their clothing was designed to keep out the wet rather than the cold, and they always wore a transparent raincoat made of animal gut over their other clothes.

Today the life of the Aleuts has ben destroyed by the coming of the white man, mostly in the person of the Russian fur traders, who have exploited the area. Very few of the Aleut people are still alive, and none retain their old ways.

*Central America*

# THE AZTECS

Three indigenous, highly complex civilizations developed in the New World before the white man came: the Maya civilization of Guatemala, Honduras, and Yucatán had flowered before Columbus discovered America; both the Inca civilization of Peru and Bolivia and the Aztecs of the Central Valley of Mexico were at their height when the Spanish conquistadors encountered them.

When Hernando Cortez and his men reached the Valley of Mexico in 1519 they were amazed to see the massive Aztec capital, Tenochtitlán, looming ahead. Their discovery was soon to spell the doom of this mighty civilization. In a few short months this large urban center of some 100,000, with its towering stone temples and magnificent palaces, had been successfully besieged and burned. On the ruins of the largest temple, dedicated to the Aztec war god Huitzilopochtli, the Spaniards erected a Christian cathedral, and the site of the old Aztec capital was rebuilt as the Spanish capital, Mexico City. Thus European religion and culture began its reign on the ruins of the indigenous Indian civilization.

How long the Aztecs would have been able to retain their supremacy in the Valley of Mexico had the Spanish not invaded will forever remain a matter for speculation. What is known is that they built their mighty empire in only a couple of centuries. From 1325, when they established Tenochtitlán, until the Spanish conquest in 1519, they carried on relentless wars against all their neighbors. They ruled from the Atlantic to the Pacific in Central Mexico, and perhaps as far south as Guatemala and Nicaragua.

The Aztecs were not the first to develop a civilization in the Central Valley; agricultural tribes had already settled there several centuries before Christ. Their great religious center was built at Teotihuacán. Archeologists tell us that a great civilization flourished here from about the second to the tenth centuries after Christ. Then the area was occupied by Indians belonging to the Nahua group, the Toltecs, whose culture and artistry spread over much of Mexico, extending even into the Yucatán country of the Mayas. By the thirteenth century, however, they were replaced by another Nahua group, the Chichimecs.

At this time the Aztecs, also a Nahua group, had moved peacefully into the valley, coming from the north and northwest. In 1248 they asked for permission to settle in the valley and appear to have been little more than slaves to the other Nahuan tribes for a few years. In the early fourteenth century they made two settlements on islands in the lakes, on lands that were swampy and rejected by everyone else. One of their centers was at Tenochtitlán, which was to become their capital; the other was at Tlaltelolco.

Meanwhile the Aztecs had learned agricultural methods of growing corn from their Nahua masters. Agriculture was the basis of their life, and corn was their chief food. They practiced irrigation and chinampa farming: small artificial islands were built up with fertile soil in shallow water; these islands or chinampas were then intensively cultivated.

War, an essential part of Aztec civilization, was carried on for two reasons: Wars of conquest added land to their empire; and the Aztecs believed that their gods had decreed they should be masters of the world, so wars of aggression were needed to fulfill their destiny. In order to conquer their neighbors they had to remain apart from all other peoples, who must remain enemies until they were conquered and became subjects. For this reason, whenever a tribe became friendly with the Aztecs and a king's daughter was given to an Aztec prince in marriage, the priests would see to it that she was sacrificed to the gods so that hostilities would break out between the two groups once more. Eventually the other group would be conquered by the Aztecs.

According to an Indian account, one Coxcox (pheasant), the ruler of Culhuacán, gave the Aztecs land that was barren and full of rattlesnakes, expecting them to either starve or be killed. But the Aztecs liked snake meat. Then Coxcox offered to give the Aztecs their freedom if they took eight thousand prisoners. To his shocked amazement, the Aztecs presented him with several large bags filled with the severed ears of their prisoners, and thus won their freedom. Then the Aztecs asked Coxcox for his daughter, in order to pay her a special honor. They held a ceremony in a dimly lit temple, to which Coxcox came to make a ritual offering. When his eyes became accustomed to the darkness Coxcox received his third shock at the hands of the Aztecs: there before him danced a priest dressed in the skin of Coxcox' daughter.

War had still another important function: it provided a supply of prisoners who could be sacrificed to the gods. Human sacrifice was looked upon by the Aztecs as essential both to keep their gods happy and to keep them functioning. Gods, like humans, needed to be fed, and it was only the rich food of human blood and hearts that could sustain them. As in their mythology the god Quetzalcoatl had created the present race of man by sprinkling the bones of extinct races of men with his own blood, so it was necessary that the blood of men be offered back to the gods.

The constant need for sacrifices meant the Aztecs were always at war. Their tactic was close hand-to-hand combat so that the enemy could be taken alive. One of the men who has written on the Aztecs contends that they did much less killing than other conquerors because of their policy of taking prisoners. This seems unrealistic, for they extended their warfare beyond wars of conquest in order to take prisoners. These holy wars waged solely to get sacrificial victims were called wars of flowers. The Aztecs told the Spaniards that the reason they never completely subjugated one particular tribe was so they would always have a supply of prisoners from their steady warfare with them. At festivities marking the coronation of King Ahuizotl, the most warlike of Aztec leaders, it was estimated that no fewer than 20,000 prisoners were sacrificed.

To be a sacrificial victim was looked on by the Aztecs—and even by their neighbors—as the most noble way to die. Victims went to the highest form of paradise after death, even if they were not Aztec. A common form of human sacrifice was to have the victim mount the long stairway to the top of the Aztec temple, where he was spread-eagled on a stone slab in front of the altar

RIVERS ARE THE BEST ROADS THROUGH THE DENSE TROPICAL JUNGLES. THESE
CHOCO INDIANS POLE A DUGOUT CANOE IN THE DARIEN REGION OF PANAMA.

and held by four priests. A fifth priest would then make an incision in the man's chest, with an obsidian knife, and tear out his heart as an offering to the god. The body was then burned or thrown to wild beasts. Sometimes the flesh of victims was eaten at ceremonial feasts. Other methods of sacrifice included burning, flaying, decapitation, and shooting with arrows.

For one annual ceremony a young warrior was chosen from among the prisoners to impersonate the god Tezcatlipoca, the patron of princes, who presided over feasts and banquets. For a whole year the young man was dressed like the god, taught all the princely graces, and treated by everyone with the utmost ceremony and respect. Twenty days before the ceremonial feast he was was given four beautiful wives. On the day he was to die he was ceremoniously abandoned by his wives and court and had to ascend the long stairs to the sacrificial stone by himself. The

priests stripped him of his finery, laid him on the block, and tore out his heart. Then another youth was chosen for the next year. The Aztec moral behind this ceremony was, according to the Spanish historian Sahagún, "that those who enjoy wealth and pleasures in this life will end in poverty and in sorrow."

The Aztecs were brought up according to a strict stoic code that taught them to be morally upright and indifferent to pain. Children were taken from their families at the age of five or six and sent to boarding schools. The girls learned household arts and performed such duties in the temples as guarding the fires to see that they never went out. They had their heads shaved until they left school to be married. The boys of the nobility attended the *calmecac* schools. Here they received extensive training in religion, the arts, and the known sciences. These boys prepared for the

priesthood and other high positions. Whatever his occupation might be, a young man was also expected to be a warrior. Thus much of his training was designed to harden him to the privations of war. These schools were extremely strict and Spartan. The boys slept on the floor, purified themselves in outdoor ritual baths in all weather, and wore only loincloths the year round. They performed tasks for the upkeep of the temples and learned to perform all the personal sacrifices to the gods, including making balls of maguey spines dipped in their own blood.

The public school for boys was the *telpuchcalli*, or house of young men, where most of the youths were educated. Here the primary purpose was to prepare the boys to be warriors, although arts and crafts, history, and ordinary religious training were included. The discipline and curriculum at this school were not as rigorous as at the *calmecac*.

The strict, segregated upbringing of the young men and women did not allow for courtship, and marriages were usually arranged by the parents. For the wedding ceremony the young couple sat on a straw mat, and the skirts of their garments were knotted together as a symbol of their union. Then they ceremonially fed each other. The couple were expected to observe four days of fasting and penance while the wedding guests feasted and danced. At the end of the four-day period the marriage was consummated. The Aztecs were generally monogamous, although some rich nobles had many wives, each with her own household. Sexual fidelity was mandatory for women; men were allowed concubines.

Kingship among the Aztecs, though nominally elective, was in fact hereditary. There was a strong class organization, although one could raise oneself through accomplishment. The highest rank comprised the nobles, who were the priests and administrators of the empire. Next in status came the merchants, contrary to our conception of them as the bourgeoisie. Aztec merchants were renowned for their skill and traveled far and wide, penetrating as far south as Nicaragua and Guatemala. It was they who provided the maps and other information needed by the Aztec armies. Aztec merchants would go among distant peoples disguised as native inhabitants selling their wares. It has been said that Aztec conquest consisted of first sending merchants, then armies.

The common people, or plebeians, formed the mass of Aztec society. It was they and their serfs who did most of the farming.

THE VILLAGE OF SAN JORGE, GUATEMALA. RURAL AREAS SUCH AS THIS ACCOUNT FOR 63 PERCENT OF THE POPULATION OF CENTRAL AMERICA.

Although the nobles owned private estates, most of the land was held in common by the *calpullis* into which the cities were divided. The calpulli was a clanlike organization of families held together not by biological ties, but by the patronage of a common god. Although not conceived as such, they came to be territorial divisions of a city, and so were translated by the Spanish as barrios, or districts. Each calpulli owned lands outside the city that were divided among the members of the group.

The lowest class in Aztec society were the slaves, who were sold at the markets. People were often sold into slavery as punishment for a crime. Relatives of traitors also lost their liberty. Families in dire financial straits might sell a child into slavery. Occasionally slaves were sold for sacrifice.

The achievements of Aztec civilization were mixed. Primarily it was a neolithic civilization that used chipped and polished stone tools, although copper, bronze, and gold were used for craftsmen's tools and for ornaments. Like the other indigenous American civilizations, the Aztecs did not possess the wheel, but they had an efficient system of transportion over water via their lakes, which were connected naturally and by artificial canals. The Spaniards estimated that the Indians had some 200,000 watercraft at the beginning of the sixteenth century.

Like the Romans, the Aztecs had problems keeping their empire under control, and at the time of the conquest they were developing a practical method of collecting tribute and a complicated bureaucratic political system. The homes of the rich were comfortable and ornate, with elaborate furnishings and bathrooms. Moctezuma was able to greet Cortez and his men with all the royal elegance of a European monarch.

The Aztecs had two calendars. One, taken from earlier peoples of the valley, was based on a 260-day cycle; each day was named from a combination of one of the numerals 1 through 13 with one of twenty names of gods and holy objects. The other calendar, based on a solar year, comprised eighteen months of twenty days each, plus five additional days considered unlucky. The Aztecs were quite sophisticated in astronomical studies. They also used a written language consisting of complicated symbols, or ideographs.

The most highly developed and dominant element of Aztec civilization was their religion. The force and vigor of their painting and sculpture is a permanent monument to that religion,

MOST OF THE 800 INHABITANTS OF SAN JORGE ARE "LADINO-IZED" INDIANS, WHO HAVE ADOPTED THE LANGUAGE, RELIGION, AND CUSTOMS OF THE SPANIARDS. EVEN THEIR PHYSICAL APPEARANCE REFLECTS THE SYNTHESIS OF THE TWO CULTURES.

which both brought them to a civilized state and led them to perform such barbarous acts in its name. Whether or not they would have been able to escape the imaginatively and emotionally restricting elements of their priest-ridden society, if given more time to develop, will never be known.

At the time of the conquest the Aztecs and their subject peoples in the Central Valley of Mexico numbered about two million, mostly gathered in large urban centers. It is ironic that although the Spaniards, enlisting the help of their conquered neighbors, destroyed the Aztec civilization, they also did some things to immortalize it. They learned the Nahuatl tongue—similar to that spoken by the North American Shoshone—in order to communicate with the Indians, and consequently spread it around other areas of Mexico, converting it into a sort of lingua franca. They built their new capital on the site of the old Aztec capital. Even the name Mexico comes from the other name for the Aztecs, the Mexica. Today in Mexico about one million Indians speak Nahuatl.

Indians in Mexico are divided roughly into two groups. Those who live in rural areas still retain many of the ancient customs and beliefs of their ancestors. They are behind on modern technology and economics, usually speak no Spanish, and generally are racially pure. The other group is largely acculturated to Mexican modern society, and does not think of itself as Indian. In Mexico, as in the rest of Latin America, *Indio* is not primarily a term of racial designation, but rather one of cultural designation. An *Indio* is one who lives like an Indian—he is backward. To become truly a *mejicano*, one need only be fluent in Spanish, dress in modern Mexican fashion, and move away from established tribal territories. Hence, between 1940 and 1950 the Indian population decreased from 14.9 percent to 11.5 percent of the total, as more people learned Spanish and were otherwise "modernized."

In 1949 a decree of the Mexican Congress declared that the last Aztec emperor, Cuauhtemoc, "is the symbol of our nationality and therefore deserves the sincere devotion of the Mexican people." The actual culture of the real Indian is something else. The upper class in Mexico may pay lip service to the ideal of the Indian heritage, or may sincerely lament the lost glories of the the romantic Indian past, but he is nevertheless very proud of his Spanish or French ancestry. Still, it cannot be denied that Mexico's Indian past has made a prominent contribution to Mexican life today, especially in the fine arts.

174

# THE MAYAS

Deep in the dense jungles of Guatemala ruins of one of the great civilizations of pre-Columbian America are still being found. These magnificent stone structures erected by the Mayas range in clusters from the jungles of lowland Guatemala and British Honduras and highland Chiapas, Mexico, to the arid plans of Yucatán, Mexico. Mystery still pervades the silent stone temples, palaces, and courts, which never were lived in but served only as shrines to the gods of their builders. Stones are inscribed with a complicated hieroglyphic language whose messages remain largely undeciphered.

The Mayan civilization was dealt its death blow by the Spaniards in the early sixteenth century. At that time there was little left of the glory that had marked the height of its culture seven hundred to a thousand years earlier—the years when the Goths and Vandals were overrunning Central Europe and Charlemagne was molding the Holy Roman Empire. The Spaniards quickly reduced the Mayans to the status of laborers and servants, and they were largely ignored until the nineteenth century.

With the discovery of the ancient Chiapas city of Palenque by John Lloyd Stephens, the imaginations of others were sparked to carry on his work of exploration. Soon dozens of cities were discovered. Serving as guides and servants in the exploring parties were many of the Indians whose ancestors had built these awesome shrines. Information about the whereabouts of shrines came from other descendents, who gathered chicle, the chief ingredient of chewing gum. One group of Indians was found that had kept itself aloof from outside influences and retained a way of life remarkably like that of the ancient Mayas.

There is much to fascinate modern man in the accomplishments of the Mayas. Incredibly, they lacked many of the cultural acquisitions that were essential to the ancient civilizations of the

Old World—among them the use of metals, the plow, irrigation, beasts of burden, and the wheel. Yet they carved out a highly developed civilization that persisted for around 1,200 years. They cultivated at least twenty crops, and performed prodigious engineering feats. Furthermore, much of their territory was in one of the most uninhabitable jungles in the world. The theory that civilizations blossom in areas that are neither too easy nor too difficult to live in would seem to be refuted by the Mayas.

Their intellectual accomplishments are even more awesome, though unfortunately much has been lost to us. The Mayas developed the most complex system of writing in the New World— a system of hieroglyphics based predominantly on ideograms with some phonetic elements probably present. Unfortunately we have no Rosetta Stone to provide us with a key to its meanings.

Maya priest scholars set forth a mystic but chronologically precise calendar predicting the movement of heavenly bodies, and charted dates for rituals honoring the gods. We know much about them except what they said, which is the most profound enigma in American history.

In the sixteenth century a fanatical Franciscan monk, Bishop Diego de Landa, attempted to wipe out all trace of the native Mayan religion. He ordered the fine library of preconquest books and records burned because they were full of "pagan nonsense." He thus not only robbed future men of the greatest source of historical information and literature of the Mayas that existed; he also destroyed what might have provided a key to the written language. Bishop de Landa partially expiated his blunder by compiling an extensive history of Mayan civilization that provided future scholars with invaluable information. His work includes details on the glyphs that represent the days and months of the year, and thanks to his research, scholars are now able to determine the meaning of about a third of the Mayan hieroglyphs.

There are only three known records of the preconquest Mayas in existence today, and all are in European libraries. The best known of the three is the Dresden codex. (A codex is a piece of parchment, folded and enclosed between covers of leather or wood.) However, there is a great deal of Mayan literature from just after the conquest. In an effort to spread Christianity among the Mayas, Spanish monks taught them to read and write the

AN INDIAN VILLAGER, LOADED WITH HIS WARES, WALKS TO MARKET IN SAN JORGE.

Mayan language in Spanish script. Much of Mayan post-conquest life and history was thus recorded in the *Books of Chilam Balam* by Yucatán natives.

Although very little is known today of the levels the Mayas reached in literature and philosophy, what is known has inspired

comparison with the Athenians, with their city-state form of government and their philosophy of moderation.

Fortunately much more of the art work has been preserved than was the literature. Most art of preconquest Middle America is highly stylized and nonrepresentational. This is true of the Mayas, among whom it developed during the Classic era to its highest degree in the New World. Abstract art of high quality has been preserved in the sculpture and bas-relief work on the buildings and, along with hieroglyphs, on the stone columns, or stelae, recording passages of time. In addition, a splendid example of Mayan representational art has been discovered on the wall murals of three rooms in the ruins of Bonampak, in Chiapas. Here are depicted musicians, the judgment of captives, ceremonies, warfare, and processions in a vivid expressive style. All the figures are done in profile, as in Egyptian art.

The highest accomplishments of the Maya civilization were in the fields of mathematics and astronomy. Although they did not know that the moon circles the earth, and the earth the sun, the Mayas were able to predict quite accurately the occurrence of eclipses. They devised the ancient world's most nearly perfect calendar, made up of a series of "wheels" consisting of units of time, all of which turned independently of one another. The calendar had two years: one, the sacred year of 360 days; the other, the civil year of 365 days. Various gods literally bore each day on their backs through its appointed round.

The mystery of this sacred task performed by gods was central to Mayan religious beliefs. It was of the utmost importance that the god bearing each day be friendly toward the activities of man. The proper gods had to be placated at the right times, and activities had to be curtailed if an unfavorable god bore the day. For this reason the Mayas believed they must make no mistakes on their calendars. Mayan religion became tied to a rigid belief in astrology, and the complex calendar became the tool for ordering the complex activities taking place in the heavens. The eternal burdens borne by these gods also had a great mystic fascination for the Mayas. No other peoples on earth have ever been so taken with the mysteries of time and eternity. For this reason the Maya priests worked out their calendar for literally millions of years into the past. This might be compared to our working out on what days Easter would have occurred through some millions of years of past history.

HE SCALES AND MEAT ARE HUNG OUT OF DOORS AT THE BUTCHER'S SHOP N SAN JORGE. THE WOMEN IN THIS PICTURE WEAR INDIAN CLOTHES AND IGTAILS.

The Mayans would not have been able to work out their complex calculations if they had not had an advanced system of mathematics. In fact, theirs was the earliest civilization to employ the concept of the zero, essential to all but the simplest mathematics. The Hindus were the only other people in the ancient world to evolve this concept independently. The zero subsequently was adopted by the Arabs, and came to Europe in the Middle Ages by the way of the Moors.

The big riddle of Maya civilization is why it collapsed. Although the Mayan culture is said to have begun its formative period by about 500 B.C., the Classic era lasted from about A.D. 317 to 889. During this period the great cities of the Mayas were built. The first area of city-states to flourish was that of the northern highlands; included in it was the city of Teotihuacán. Later the lowlands took the lead, with great achievements in sculpture, hieroglyphics, building, astronomy, and arithmetic, as well as in pottery, figurine, and lapidary work. But starting about 800, the cities were abandoned, one by one, so that by 925 the old city shrines were all but unused. No one knows why this happened, but the best conjecture is that a wave of peasant revolts against the ruling classes of the nobility and the priesthood was responsible. In this case, the vast masses of people, who were barred from doing anything but working and providing occasional candidates for the sacrificial altar, finally came to feel that the religious duties performed for them by the priesthood were not sufficient to justify the people's servitude. It has also been suggested that the foreign influence of Mexican Indians—the Toltecs—who are known to have infiltrated parts of Yucatán at this period, may have helped to precipitate the breakdown in social structure and beliefs, a condition that could lead to revolt.

From about 925 to 975, only villages or groups of villages existed as political units. During this time the cities were used solely for occasional performances of simple rites or burial of minor chiefs.

Around 975 the influence of Mexico began to be felt strongly in Yucatán with the coming to power of the Mexican Itzá Indians, who established their capital at Chichén Itzá. Up to this time the Mayas had practiced human sacrifice in a very limited way. The Mexican invaders, however, brought with them the worship of Quetzalcoatl and other Mexican gods, who had to be supplied with

DRESSED AS SPANISH OFFICERS, MASKED INDIANS IN SOLOLA, GUATEMALA, PERFORM THE "DANCE OF THE CONQUEST."

human blood. From the Mexicans the Mayas now learned to wage war in order to obtain victims for their sacrifices. Chichén Itzá became a great military center at the cost of the priesthood. The art and sculpture of this period is inferior.

With the fall of Chichén Itzá in 1200, Maya groups again began to take control of the area, and there was something of a resurgence of their civilization. But the conditions had altered since the Classic era. Now, instead of city-states, there arose tyrannical empires. The city of Mayapán was the center of an empire in Yucatán, and Quiche set up an empire in the Guatemalan highlands. Mayan religion, language, and other elements of Mayan culture prevailed over the Mexican influences. Only the Mexican custom of warfare was retained. At this time many of the great ceremonial centers began to be used as real cities. In the century before the Spanish conquest, the empires of Mayapán and Quiche fell under internal revolts, so that when the Spanish arrived the Mayas were divided into small chieftainships, at perpetual war with one another.

Today there are two million or more Maya Indians living in Mexico, Guatemala, and British Honduras. They speak twenty to twenty-five languages of the Mayan family; some also speak Spanish. Large numbers of these people are living much the same as their peasant ancestors did when the Mayan civilization was at its height. They live in quiet villages, where they cultivate their fields, called *milpa*, which have been cleared from the jungle. They use the same primitive farming methods, and like their ancestors, they are forced to abandon their fields after a few years because they have not rotated the crops. The ancient ideals of temperance and live and let live are still practiced, but Christianity has supplanted the ancient gods.

Many of these Indians are of almost pure Mayan stock and resemble their ancestors quite closely. The men average about five feet four inches and are stocky. They have very broad round faces, with receding foreheads, small receding chins, large almond-shaped eyes, big noses, and drooping lower lips. They are said to have the broadest faces of any people in the world. In the old days the Mayas used to accentuate their sloping foreheads by tightly strapping an infant's head to a board, which produced a long, flat, receding forehead. In addition, the members of the nobility would decorate their bodies with extensive tattooing and

THIS GIRL FROM YUCATAN, MEXICO, HAS THE CHARACTERISTIC PROFILE C HER MAYAN ANCESTRY—RECEDING FOREHEAD AND CHIN, AND AN AQUILIN NOSE.

scarification. Teeth were often filed to points and were filled with jade, turquoise, or shell inlays. Oddly, it was considered beautiful to be crosseyed, and a mother would hang a small bead or piece of resin between her child's eyes in order to encourage this physical trait.

One strange group of Indians, living near the ruins of Palenque in the jungles of Chiapas, are the remnants of an old Maya tribe, the Lacandones. These Indians have assiduously avoided outside influences and have tried to keep up the old way of life, so they afford us a dramatic look into the Mayan past. Living, as they do, in jungles infested with malarial mosquitoes, the Lacandones are riddled with disease. As of 1959 their numbers had dwindled to 160, and they seem doomed to extinction. Men, women, and children wear their hair long and uncombed, giving a fearsome appearance to their faces, which bear uncanny resemblances to the death masks of their ancestors. Their language is

believed to be largely unchanged from that of the ancient Mayas. Ironically, the attempts of these people to keep the high cultural tradition of their ancestors intact has resulted in their having a low standard of living both culturally and economically. They visit the ruins of ancient ceremonial centers, where they burn copal resin and perform simple rites to the gods of their ancestors, but have no understanding of the finer points of the ancient religion.

The area of the old Mayan civilization has been a veritable gold mine for archeologists, revealing some strange and unexpected treasures. In 1945 a Mexican named Alberto Ruiz set out to explore the ruins of Palenque. He discovered in one of its temples a subterranean stairway that led to a crypt worthy of an Egyptian pharaoh, complete with treasures and the skeletons of servants who were sacrificed when the great man died. The body contained in the sarcophagus is believed to be that of a high priest.

At the end of the nineteenth century Edward Herbert Thompson, United States consul to Yucatán and a student of Mayan civilization, became fascinated by the tales he had heard about a great well, or cenote, that had been used for sacrifice. (Cenotes are underground pools sunk deep in limestone, and are the only sources of water on the dry northern portion of the Yucatán peninsula.) He felt sure these tales referred to a deep cenote at the outskirts of the great city of Chichén Itzá. Despite ridicule and opposition, Thompson succeeded in dredging the well, where he found the remains of much pottery, lapidary work, and other valuables, as well as the skeletons of dozens of sacrificial victims.

Starting in the 1850's and continuing well past the period of Thompson's excavations of the northern Maya ceremonial complexes, the Mexican government was involved in a sputtering war of conquest with the refugee groups of Indians throughout the Yucatán peninsula. Indeed, a Mexican general, Victoriano Huerta, who was to become the arch villain of modern Mexican mythology —for his overthrow of President Francisco Madero and his usurpation of power—gained his general's spurs by leading the last full-scale pacification campaign against the Indians of Yucatán in 1910.

In his classical work of the 1930's, anthropologist Robert Redfield describes a continuum of tribal to urban culture in

Yucatán. On the tribal end of the scale, he documents a small Indian community more or less hiding out in the jungles of southern Yucatán. This village was the remainder of a federation of Indian villages, brought together in a military confederation of Indian groups, which had staved off Mexican domination for three-quarters of a century.

These people believed that they had retained many of the gods and ways of their illustrious ancestors. They were highly respectful of the ruins left behind by the Mayas, and even sent a delegation to Thompson's excavations at Chichén Itzá in the hope that new alliances and the revitalization of the old centers would help them stave off the Mexican expansion. In fact the culture that these Indian groups were practicing at the time was a blend of some of the old religious forms and spirits and cosmology grafted onto a basic stock of militant Catholic organization.

# South America

# THE INCAS

One of the greatest empires of all history was that of the Incas. This largest of the Indian domains began as a military power about A.D. 1000 in the highlands of Peru. In 1100 the first Inca ruler recorded by history took the throne, and for the next four hundred years the Inca Empire expanded its territory and intensified its rule until the realm became known as the "four quarters of the world."

It must have seemed just that to the more than 3,500,000 Indians who made up the Inca nation. By 1500 it extended from Ecuador far south into what is now Argentina. At the height of its power it stretched 2,000 miles along the high plateaus of the Andes and the coastal plains of the Pacific Ocean, covering 380,000 square miles—an area as large as all the Atlantic seaboard states of North America.

But in spite of this vastness, the diverse Indian nations that constituted the empire were bound into a thoroughly organized and unified society. A state apparatus developed that included local, regional, and national administrators. These linked up with local community leaders in the provisioning of large-scale labor levies, of armies, and of various messengers and retainers at the different levels of the Inca state. One of the great virtues of the arrangement was that services never became so onerous for any sector of the population that they were unbearable; the labor services were drawn from a rotating pool of people, who were provisioned and whose home interests were looked after by their home communities.

An enormous and efficient bureaucracy ruled the empire, backed by powerful armies and supported even more strongly by the awe and reverence the people felt for the Saca Inca, the god-king of the empire.

Although there was complete regimentation, the people were the first consideration of the rulers. Great highways kept the farthest points of the empire together, advanced and beautiful cities flourished, huge reservoirs and aqueducts provided water for irrigation all year round. Agriculture, industry, and religion, with its rituals and festivals—everything in the life of the nation worked individually and together for the greatest possible good.

The Incas were a practical people whose morality taught them to keep their eyes on the affairs of the earth rather than on the stars. They worshipped the sun because it gave life to the earth, with which they and their society lived in complete harmony. As a people, they danced in unison with the rhythms of nature and enjoyed a peace and prosperity known by few nations in the course of history.

In 1531 the Spaniards came to the west coast of South America, and the Incas' harmonious pattern of political, social, and religious life was shattered forever. The great civilization crumbled, and the people were reduced to miserable slaves. There have been few stories to surpass that of the Spanish conquistadors' brutality against the Inca Indians. Those who were not among the thousands upon thousands massacred were tortured and then put to work in mines and on plantations providing luxuries for Europeans. They were totally suppressed, and a history of exploitation began that lasted through the Spanish rule in colonial times and still exists in many forms today.

Economically the descendents of the Incas are among the poorest people in the world. They still inhabit the highlands of Peru and Bolivia, living far above sea level amid the valleys and snow-capped peaks of the Andes mountains. It is only the true Indians who live here, either in lonely farming and herding communities or in small villages. The others, the half-castes and mixed bloods and pure Spaniards, inhabit the urban areas and make up the educated minority. Of the 3,800,000 souls in Peru and Bolivia, 50 percent are Indian, 35 percent are of mixed blood, and 15 percent are whites. It is the whites who dominate the country and exploit the Indians, who are the essential productive element of the economy. The latter are still despised and unwanted, even though they are in the majority in their own country.

Because of the history of tyranny and cruelty against them, the modern descendents of the Incas have become a taciturn and sullen people. Melancholy and resigned, they wander among the stones of their ancestors, keepers of a secret outsiders will never fathom—a secret of profound despair but also of hidden pride. Long ago these Indians developed a passive resistance that nothing can overcome. Much of their heritage, of course, is lost. Suppression, exploitation, and intermarriage have drastically changed the Indian's life. He keeps closest to his ancient ways in the remote plateaus and valleys of the Andes. Slowly as he comes to deal effectively with modern civilization, to wield political power (as he does now in Bolivia), will the full potential and variety of this hybrid Indian culture manifest itself.

The pure independent Indian civilization has passed its

zenith and has been in decline since the military defeat of the great Indian states. But it may yet play a role in partly shaping the cultures of the Andean region, as Indian populations enter the national society and members of the more urban sectors attempt to rediscover and re-establish a national heritage based at least partly on the culture of past Indian societies.

There are two major tribes (language groups) living now in Peru and Bolivia, the Quechua and the Aymara. Though these tribes inhabit different areas, speak different languages, and associate rarely, they are, in all important aspects, similar both in their character and their culture. The Aymara, who live on the vast barren pampas of Bolivia, are perhaps even more stoical than the Quechua of Peru. Because life is so uncertain on the Altiplano (the high plateau of the Peruvian Andes), their whole culture is caught up in divining and trying to control the future. In this the Quechua and the Aymara are very similar and can be discussed as a single people, for both are the children of grandeur and oppression.

AT AN ALTITUDE OF 12,500 FEET, LAKE TITICACA, PERU, IS THE HIGHEST LARGE NAVIGABLE LAKE IN THE WORLD. INDIAN FISHERMEN, DESCENDENTS OF THE INCAS, BUILD CANOELIKE BOATS OF TIGHTLY BOUND REEDS.

Two other tribes in the Andes region who can rightly call themselves Inca descendents are the Uru and the Chipaya, both of whose members speak basically the same language. The Uru inhabit the region of Lake Titicaca in Peru and rely mainly on the fishing done in the waters there. The Chipaya are a pastoral people who live in Bolivia. Because these two tribes are so remote and isolated they have remained closer to the Inca customs, but they are also so primitive and backward that this cannot be counted as a positive aspect.

To look at an Indian of the Andes today is to see an individual of medium stature with dark brown pigmentation, a large head, broad face, prominent cheekbones, a fleshy aquiline nose, and small almond eyes. His long-faced features are the same ones that stare out of ancient Inca works of art.

In the most isolated areas—or in communities that still strive to retain what they consider to be Indian ways—one still sees the elaborately woven and embroidered ponchos and shawls, the knitted stocking caps for men, and the local variant of sandals.

Indeed, regional or community distinctive dress is in itself a characteristic of Indian villages throughout much of the Andean area. But even in such items, the Indians have merely retained and slightly modified what were the forms of dress for common people in sixteenth-century Spain. One may generally say that where the mestizo and more acculturated Indian communities now use the tailored trousers and shirt and jacket, usually with some sort of poncho overgarment, that was so typical of the last century, the clothing that is now regarded as being Indian—simplified knickers, doubletlike vest, and highly colored poncho—is still Spanish in origin, but of a much earlier period.

Although his diet is poorly balanced and often insufficient, the Indian is capable of extraordinary physical endurance. His strength is not exceptional, but his stamina is astonishing. He has a high degree of physical insensibility, which renders him almost impervious to the effects of hunger, cold, exhaustion, and pain to an extent that is perhaps unequalled by any other people.

Agriculture is the staple of the Indian's culture. Without it he could not live. He worships the land, and when deprived of it he becomes disorientated, devoid of a place in the universe. His farming techniques are simple and traditional. Draft animals are not used; the most complicated tool is a primitive hand plow whose only concession to modernity is an iron blade. Apart from the cash and commercial crops grown by large and middle-sized landholders, and some small holdings used by Indians to acquire cash for store purchases, the indigenous complement of food crops is still the staple of Indian agriculture. These are primarily potatoes, quinoa and other local root crops, maize, and cotton, as well as coca, a luxury item. Quinine is either raised in plantation holdings on the eastern slopes of the Andes, or collected from unused lands; its importance on the world market has been all but eclipsed by the development of more effective, chemically generated drugs.

Too often the Indian does not extract very much for his labor. But he goes on with it as he always has, plowing by hand from sunrise to sundown, and observing the ancient agricultural rituals. Periodically he gives offerings of coca and liquor to the earth, but the meager blessings he receives in return are barely enough to keep him from starving.

In the higher altitudes of the Andes, where farming is im-

THE RELIGION OF THE INCA DESCENDENTS IS A CONFUSED MIXTURE OF ROMAN CATHOLICISM AND THE SUN WORSHIP OF THEIR ANCESTORS. SPIRITS, GOOD AND BAD, INHABIT EVERYTHING FROM ROCKS TO PIECES OF THREAD.

possible, herding is the chief means of subsistence for the Indian. The famous llama, which is the main tended animal, serves as the chief source of communication, trade, and transport. Hunting and fishing, except as it is practiced by the Uru tribe, play a very small part in the Indian's life.

Of the manufacturing industries, weaving holds the top position. Literally everyone weaves among the Indians—men and women, the young and the very old. Every spare moment seems to be taken up with some kind of weaving. It is as if the people are trying to express with their brilliantly colored fabrics and baskets a mute protest against the bleakness of their life and environment.

Also important among the Indians is trade and market day. The marketplace is a very ancient institution among these tribes, deriving directly from the Inca culture. It is like walking into the past to wander through the market on a busy day and watch the women bartering sacks of potatoes for corn or coca.

The descendents of the Incas have a set social life, living out their entire lives on a few square miles of earth. They usually reside in very small farming communities or villages, and the community itself is the basis of their social life. Each one is like a

separate world; one village rarely communicates with another, except for trade purposes.

Gradually through the centuries, because outsiders have brought them so much trouble, the Indian has developed a great fear and distrust of the stranger. He clings fanatically to his own familiar group, the one into which he was born. If one member of the community happens to lose his land, then every other member feels the grief and loss as his own. Outside marriage is viewed with disfavor; marriage within one's group is met with complete approval. The family, of course, is more closely knit than the community, offering as it does the greatest security against the alien and the unknown.

Courtship is usually the high point of the Indian's life; everything afterward is downhill. During these declining years the only excitement the Indian finds is in the occasional fiestas, into which he throws himself with a frightening violence. Music, which is probably the happiest element of the Indian's life, is a vital feature of the fiestas. Playing on instruments that have come down directly from the Incas, the Indians dance for hours in frenzied delirium. Liquor and quinine taken as a narcotic are indulged in excessively.

Liquor and narcotics are used daily by almost every adult Indian. Many outsiders feel that these two elements have done more than any other thing to undermine the Indian's life. But they were originally resorted to only as an escape from an intolerable condition.

Political organization, such as it is, does not play nearly as vital a part in the Indian's life as does religion. Religion is the greatest constant in tribal existence. This is strange, considering that the religion itself is not particularly well organized by our standards. It is a confused mixture of Christian and pagan rites. Beneath the superficial observance of Christianity, the ancient pagan beliefs of the Incas still persist in the hearts of their descendents. The modern Indian worships the sun as it was worshipped hundreds of years ago. They persist in the belief that it is the center of the universe and the giver of all life. Next come the earth and the moon. After these are countless small deities and spirits.

Spirits, good and bad, inhabit almost everything in the Indian's mind. Objects all the way from rocks to pieces of thread

OLK DANCING AT THE ANCIENT INCA FORTRESS SACSAHUAMAN, OUTSIDE UZCO. THE WALLS, BUILT WITHOUT THE USE OF IRON OR THE WHEEL, ARE ,800 FEET LONG. THE LARGEST STONES WEIGH 200 TONS.

HIGH IN THE MOUNTAINS OF PERU, MACHU PICCHU WAS THE LAST HOLDOUT OF THE INCA EMPIRE FROM THE SPANIARDS. THE CITY WAS THOUGHT TO BE LEGENDARY UNTIL ITS DISCOVERY IN 1911 BY THE AMERICAN EXPLORER HIRAM BINGHAM.

have their own special spirit. The Indian's religion divides his world into a simple dualism of good and bad, black and white, and his whole effort is spent in trying to avoid the constant evils of his life by believing in a Christian God, in an animate sun, and in all the innumerable good spirits that are there around him somewhere in his bitter world.

Infancy, education, adulthood, old age—all are bleak prospects for today's Inca Indian. Throughout his life he remains hemmed in from all sides. He is taught there is no weapon with which he can defend himself. Only recently have outsiders begun to consider the Indian's age-old problem. When the Spaniards came in the sixteenth century the Inca Indian was left in a void between a past forever dead and a future as yet unborn. That future is still waiting for its emergence.

T FESTIVAL TIME INDIANS FORGET THE POVERTY AND DRUDGERY OF THEIR VERYDAY LIVES. [TOP] INDIANS OF CUZCO, THE INCA CAPITAL OF PERU, PLAY ONCH-SHELL TRUMPETS. [BOTTOM] MASKED DANCERS IN BOLIVIA.

# THE JIVAROS

The South American Jivaros are world-famous for one product that they have provided for the international market: shrunken human heads. Although the sale of shrunken heads, or tsantas, as the Indians call them, has been illegal for some time, they are still smuggled out of Ecuador and Peru. Lately, however, many buyers have found that the shrunken human heads they bought at high prices are in reality monkey heads.

The Jivaro culture is dwindling today. There are essentially two reasons for this, both of which are connected with the white man. First, their numbers are decreasing because of both the white man's diseases and his firearms; the latter have increased the efficiency of the Jivaros' wars of extermination. Second, some groups have come under the influence of missionaries or other emissaries of white civilization, and this has considerably altered their orientation to their way of life. Their culture is based to a large extent on warfare, and the heads which are obtained from the enemy become not only war trophies, but also powerful religious fetishes. The Jivaros are, therefore, much less able to adapt their way of life to European civilization than are other more peaceful groups whose ideals do not differ so radically from the white man's.

However, there are still many Jivaros, or Jibaros, as they are called in Spanish, who today live deep in the Amazon rain forests of southeastern Ecuador and northern Peru, often in areas that the white man has not yet penetrated. Their total population is estimated to be fifteen to twenty thousand. They are divided into five separate groups, generally antagonistic toward each other. Customs and institutions vary slightly among the different groups. Only once have all the tribes been known to unite, and that was in a general insurrection against the Spaniards in 1599, at which time they succeeded in massacring most of the whites who had settled in several prosperous little towns in their midst. Ever since, foreigners have been extremely cautious in their dealings with them.

All aspects of Jivaro life are geared to the exigencies of warfare. They do not live in villages but in large isolated communal houses called *heas*, which accommodate several families of near relatives. The *hea* is strategically placed, either on a high hill or on the bank of a river bend, so that enemies will have difficulty approaching undetected. The houses are walled with strong chonta tree poles; for further protection, many of the houses have an extra wall of poles. Small rooms, each accommodating one warrior, are built along the inside walls; they are completely closed except for one small hole to the outside through which the defender may thrust his gun or spear. Thus the warrior can still keep on fighting even if the house is overrun by the enemy.

The surrounding area of community fields of manioc and bananas are also protected by high chonta pole fences so the enemy cannot approach the *hea* through the fields. Traps are set up around the house if an enemy attack is expected. One trap, known as the hole of death, consists of a man-sized pit dug in the ground and camouflaged with brush and sticks. Pointed chonta poles at the bottom of the pit impale anyone unlucky enough to fall in. Warriors hide near the holes to speedily dispatch the helpless victims.

As most of the attacks take place at night, the Jivaros use another ingenious trap, which was devised in ancient times. A series of pointed chonta sticks are fixed on a bowlike formation of stretched lianas anchored to a tree. Attached to the contraption is another liana, which is stretched along the ground. When an enemy steps on this he triggers the device, which releases the chontawood spears, as a bow does an arrow. Even if none of them hit their mark, the commotion will alert the household. Since the advent of firearms in Jivaro country another trap has been employed that is even more effective both as a weapon and as a warning. A black string is stretched between two trees across the path at chest level. Attached to one end is a cocked rifle that goes off when the string is touched.

As soon as an attack is detected, drum signals are sent out to warn the neighboring houses and call on them for aid. The would-be attackers, realizing their presence is known, will often retreat without attacking. In Jivaro warfare, stealth and treachery are the preferred tactics, though the Indians are capable of fighting with great bravery and fearlessness when forced into the open.

Jivaro youths are taught to be brave warriors at an early age and always to defend the honor of their family. This means that any wrong done to them must be avenged. The idea of retaliation leads to the two kinds of killing in which they engage. However, it is the intragroup blood feud that adheres most closely to the retaliatory justice of an eye for an eye, whereas the intertribal wars of extermination are more likely to be based on ancient jealousies and suspicions.

A blood feud may have a number of causes. For example, A's pigs trample B's fields. Soon afterward, A's wife dies of an ailment, which is attributed to the avenging sorcery of B. In retaliation, B's father is set upon and murdered by a group of A's relatives a few weeks later. With this murder the feud is in full swing and may perpetuate itself until all the adult members of one of the families are dead. However, the two families may become tired of the bloodletting and will mutually consent to quit, often by formal treaty.

Adultery or seduction often triggers a blood feud. Jivaro women have a relatively high place in their society, and the men are very jealous of their wives. A woman believed guilty of adultery may be savagely beaten by her husband, often to the point of death. This will bring retaliation by the wife's relatives. But if the woman is believed to be an innocent victim of rape, then the husband will feel honor bound to murder her attacker.

Any sort of death is likely to provoke a feud. And as the Jivaro does not recognize natural causes, death is always attributed to supernatural causes, which may be induced by a sorcerer. Sorcery is considered a powerful weapon, and therefore every great warrior is skilled in it, especially if he is the war chief of his tribe. There are also professional sorcerers, who are under constant suspicion and are themselves frequently murdered. The sorcerer who fails to cure a patient will be killed if he does not run away.

The Jivaros do distinguish between the evil caused by witchcraft and that caused by disease. Included among the former are ailments that produce violent swelling or pain in localized parts of the body, such as colic and rheumatism. Ailments classed as diseases are mostly those that have been imported by the white man; their chief symptom is fever, and they include dysentery and smallpox. If the evil that results in a death was unintended, such as that caused by carrying a disease to a house, then blood revenge is not required. But the wrongdoer must pay a material compensation to the bereaved family.

Material compensation is sometimes paid in cases where a wrong done a long while ago must be avenged. For example, a man may be murdered who has no adult, able-bodied male relatives to avenge his death. His sons, if he has any, will be responsible for this task when they are grown. However, the matter may cool down in the intervening years, and a gift of pigs may settle the feud.

Blood revenge is not exacted if a murder is committed within a family, for the idea of honor that motivates revenge is considered a family affair.

The fierce wars of extermination carried on between tribes may continue for a long time, though the original cause is long forgotten. Animosities are often sustained by the practice of witchcraft, or *tunchi*, between rival chiefs. Intertribal wars are never conducted for territorial conquest; on the contrary, the lands of the enemy are considered fearful and disgusting. Besides, the limitless jungles of the Jivaro country make any fight over land meaningless.

One of the Jivaro tribes, the Canelos, has been especially hated and menaced by its neighbors because its members espouse Christianity. The other Indians deeply resent the Canelos' accepting the beliefs of the white man and making themselves dependent on him. Ironically, though professing Christianity, the Canelos have a reputation among the Jivaros as powerful and clever practicers of the ancient witchcraft.

The object of the intertribal wars is the complete extinction of the opposing tribe. When an enemy *hea* is attacked, all members of the household are massacred, if possible, except for the attractive young women, who are taken as concubines. Sometimes young children will also be spared and carried off to be brought up as members of the conquering tribe.

The famous shrunken heads are obtained from persons slain in these intertribal wars. Old people's heads are considered especially valuable because of the strength and wisdom that an old person is assumed to have attained simply by having survived so long.

Preparations for an attack on an enemy tribe are elaborate. The war party is led by the war chief, who is the only kind of chief that the individualistic Jivaros recognize. Although this office is hereditary, no man is chosen unless he has the necessary experience, which includes the taking of at least one head. Preceding the attack, the warriors conduct special ceremonies, including a series of stylized dialogues, songs, and dances. Then the war party leaves home and travels, often for many days, through the forests to its destination.

For the attack, which is generally planned for just before dawn, the warriors don special ornaments, including ear tubes several inches long, which they believe will give them supernatural powers. The uncovered portions of their bodies are painted black; this is to distinguish them from their enemies and, more important, to make them resemble demons. Their demonic appearance will terrify their enemies, as well as impart to the attackers some of the demons' supernatural strength.

The Jivaro attacker strives for two things when he kills his enemies. First, he wants the head, which will give him increased prestige and power, both natural and supernatural. Second, he strives to mutilate and bloody the enemy dead as much as possible, for then the soul of the dead man will be struck with fear and will quickly depart without haunting the killer.

Sometimes it is impossible for a warrior to sever the head of his fallen enemy, because the body will be rescued by the victim's relatives. But the man who succeeds in capturing a head will usually celebrate with an elaborate victory feast, which is the outstanding ritual of Jivaro religious life. The warrior will become known as the "lord of the head." These elaborate ceremonies, which culminate in a great feast two or three years after the killing, serve two functions: The earlier ceremonies are mostly to protect the warrior from the soul of his dead enemy. In the later rituals the emphasis is on developing the magical properties of the head, which serve to make it a valuable fetish.

During the early ceremonies the head is prepared and shrunk. This process takes several weeks and is begun while the war party is still en route home. First, a long cut is made down the back of the head; then the scalp and skin of the face are skillfully drawn from the skull. The skull and the fleshy parts are thrown away, and the skin is placed in boiling water. This frees it from microbes, makes it contract slightly, and gives it more consistency. The skin is allowed to cool and then a ring of vine is placed about the head and gradually tightened. Meanwhile, the slit down the back of the head has been sewed up.

The next step seems to have no practical function. Three small heated stones are placed in the head, which is then shaken. The actual reduction of the head is accomplished by filling it repeatedly half full with hot sand. As the sand is shaken about in the head, the remaining flesh is burned away while the scalp grows thinner and smaller. After each treatment with sand the inside of the head is scraped with a knife. The head is carefully molded as the shrinking progresses, so that the features are retained. When the reduction is complete, the head is about one-fourth its original size—about as big as an orange. All through the shrinking process the hair has been carefully preserved. When the head is finished, small chonta pins, painted red, are passed through the lips and intertwined with red cotton thread. This is meant to magically control the enemy's soul and to paralyze his curses. The head is also dyed black with charcoal.

The heads of certain animals also are made into trophies. Although monkey heads are most important for the tourist trade, it is the head of the sloth that the Jivaro considers most valuable. According to Jivaro myth, all creatures were originally Jivaro men in primitive times. Later on, many men were transformed into animals. But the origins of the sloth may still be readily distinguished because it closely resembles an old man. Sloths, then, are considered to be Jivaros, and are therefore enemies whose heads are almost as valuable as other enemy Jivaros'.

The Jivaro areas were laid open to punitive expeditions by both the Ecuadorian and Peruvian armies during the late 1930's and early 1940's. Indeed, Indians living in the areas considered unpacified at that time were fair game for official and unofficial hunting parties of local and national whites, much like the white man's scalping raids in the United States during the last century.

Probably more important than this, in the last two decades increased population throughout the coastal and upland regions of both Peru and Ecuador has impelled larger numbers of traders and colonists to push out into uninhabited (except by Indians) jungle lands. Actual alienation of lands and new disease contacts, along with increasing opportunities of parttime employment, have brought new acculturative pressures on the Jivaro, as in other Indian areas, with the Indian groups taking on a marginal culture of the frontier settlers.

# THE CAMAYURÁ

The village is a dozen mud huts gathered in a circle in the midst of a rough clearing. Pass over it in a plane and you probably wouldn't see it. A stranger approaching it on foot would be likely to miss it as he worked his way around the thick, all but impenetrable second-growth jungle surrounding it on three sides. Only from the river, which is the village's fourth boundary, is it exposed to view.

Even then memory is no guide, for the Indians who live in the village are nomads. The area remembered from a previous trip is likely to have been stripped of its huts and scrubby fields of manioc, and given over to the tangled growth of the rain forest. But the stranger whose interest is the welfare of the Indians will be grateful for their elusiveness; it is their main protection against the rapidly expanding civilization of modern Brazil, a civilization that threatens to swallow them whole.

This is the country of the Rio Xingú, a major waterway that rises in the sandstone plateaus of Brazil and flows northward to the mighty Amazon, passing through the rain forests of the Mato Grosso—and past the small scattered villages where handfuls of primitive Indians still cling proudly to the ways of their forebears.

This is no land for the weak of heart. The jungle is an area

WOMEN OF THE UPPER XINGU, BRAZIL, POUNDING MANIOC IN A WOODEN MORTAR. AFTER IT HAS BEEN PASSED THROUGH A SIEVE THE FLOUR IS USED FOR MAKING BREAD.

A FISHERMAN FIRES A BARBED ARROW FROM THE BOW OF A DUGOUT CANOE ON THE UPPER XINGU. THE LENGTH OF THE ARROW PROVIDES STABILITY UNDER WATER.

MANIOC AND FISH ARE THE DIETARY STAPLES IN THE UPPER XINGU REGION. THESE PIECES OF MANIOC CAKES, WHICH HAVE BEEN GRILLED ON A CLAY GRIDDLE, ARE SPREAD WITH A FISH PASTE.

of colossal beauty and menacing silences. An incredible variety of forest trees, no two alike, soar upward a hundred feet or more, coming together at their peaks to form a green canopy that shuts out the sky and provides a home for birds, monkeys, and an occasional giant sloth. The sparse soil between the buttressed tree trunks is left to the insects and snakes. It is a land in which one must either conquer nature or make an uneasy peace with her. The latter course is the one chosen by the Indians.

In the very heart of this world is the Upper Xingú basin, a land in which seasons are tolled not by changes in temperature but by changes in precipitation. The basin is crisscrossed by rivers—the tributaries of the Xingú—which are easily navigated by canoes and plentifully stocked with many forms of fish. These characteristics explain why the Indians of the Mato Grosso cluster in this area. The isolation of the area, once maintained naturally, is now aided by the Brazilian government, which has called a halt to the search for gold and diamonds that a few years ago threatened to flood the territory with miners. Thus the Indians have managed to keep a fingertip hold on their way of life.

Nevertheless, the control of the Brazilian Agency for Indian Protection and that of other agencies is most effective for foreigners or outsiders entering the area. There is therefore the problem of the surrounding Indian groups largely acculturated to the values and life styles of a rough and tumble frontier world. These people, as well as the Brazilian colonists, who themselves have adapted to the largely uncontrolled and rather personal life that exists on the margins of a modern state, move back and forth with only little inconvenience and limitation of national laws.

The Indian population was never great, and like the Indians who once inhabited North America, they occupy a potentially rich land that must some day support many times their number. In short, they are doomed, and their disappearance is already well under way. The several language groups that inhabit the basin number about a thousand individuals; and contact with the modern world, even in the form of missionaries, journalists, and anthropologists, continues to take its toll.

Brazil's government has belatedly but effectively taken steps to protect the Indians. Admission to the Xingú territory is now controlled by permit, and permits are scarce. They are issued mostly to anthropologists, whose aim is to study the life of the

AN INDIAN MOTHER AND CHILD BATHING IN THE UPPER XINGU RIVER. THE TRIBES OF THIS REGION ARE FOND OF THE WATER AND ARE USUALLY QUITE CLEAN.

Indians, and whose interest is in keeping that life intact. Anthropologist Kalervo Oberg was one of the fortunate few to gain a permit to study the Xingú tribes. Working with the Smithsonian Institution, he entered the area in the late 1940's and emerged some months later with a report that is still the main source of our knowledge about the Indians. While studying all four of the language groups in the area—the Carib, the Arawak, the Tupi, and the Trumai—Oberg concentrated intensively on a single village, that of the Camayurá, one of the two Tupi-speaking groups in the area.

The Camaruyá village comprises a hundred or so people, who live in mud huts thatched with dried grass. The buildings, each of which houses a dozen or more Indians, are domed ellipsoids set in a circle around a clearing that serves as the village social center, market, factory, and dance hall. The circle measures about a hundred yards in diameter and is the bull's-eye of a dartboard of larger circles: the encircling fields, only half-cleared of the forest brush, which cluster about the village's perimeter; the circle of thick second-growth forest, which encloses the fields like an in-

verted moat; and finally the more easily traveled main forest, which seems to rush away to infinity. Only to the south is the pattern broken. There the fields give way to a grassy, sloping clearing that leads down to the river, some two hundred yards distant.

The grass thatching of the rude huts is the most prominent man-made feature of the village. Up to two feet thick, it provides shelter from the constant drizzle of the rainy season and the fierce noonday sun of the dry season. The ever-present danger to the huts is fire; a spark will set them instantly ablaze. But the Indians have few possessions to lose, and a new hut can be constructed in short order, with the entire village pitching in to help. Because the quality of the soil is poor, the Indians are forced to pursue a seminomadic existence, moving their village every two or three years; so the huts need not be designed for permanence.

Inside, the huts are dark and shadowy. Windows are either unknown or considered unnecessary, and the small doors admit little of the bright sunlight. The fires, kept going constantly by the women, cast flickering eerie images upon the drab walls, revealing the meager furnishings: hammocks, strung from the walls to a supporting central pole; personal belongings—bows and arrows, baskets, gourds, small pottery—stored neatly near the hammocks; the larger pots and baskets, kept near the center of the hut, for the use of all.

The huts of the Camayurá provide a fascinating variation in communal living. The people who inhabit any single hut represent segments of two larger extended families. The core of a household group consists of a group of brothers whose wives are often sisters. Typically a hut will house a man, his wife, his children, similar families of brothers and first cousins, and a tribal elder of uncertain blood relationship. The varieties and complications of this arrangement are best left to the anthropologists; suffice it to say that each house group lives and works as a unit, sharing a common field and canoe, cooking in the same pots, hunting and fishing with the same weapons.

In many ways the Camayurá are typical of all the Xingú tribes. They are semiagricultural; what crops they can coax from the harsh soil they supplement with fish and occasionally with small game taken in the forest with primitive bows and arrows or poison-tipped darts. The village, like all Indian villages in the

XINGU INDIANS CONSTRUCTING A FISH DAM BETWEEN POLES PLANTED IN THE RIVER. FISH ARE PLENTIFUL IN THE XINGU AND ITS TRIBUTARIES.

Amazon valley, is semipermanent because of the poor soil of the rain forest.

That the jungle soil should be lacking in fertility seems strange, accustomed as we are to think of the jungle in terms of richness of life. In fact, it is the very richness of plant life in the rain forest that makes the soil poor. Because weather conditions are extremely favorable to plant life, almost all of the soil's natural minerals are busy keeping the great trees alive. The fertility of the soil is soon exhausted. When this happens the Indians, with a minimum of fuss, simply pack up and move to a new area, which is quickly cleared by burning and emplanted with a new circle of huts.

Fear and hardship are the most poignant common denominators of the lives of these people. Malnutrition and starvation are omnipresent shadows upon the horizon, like the clouds of the rainy season that may bring to the parched land too little rain— or too much. Disease is common, and the jungle, even to these people who in a more romantic period were called Children of Nature, is filled with hidden terrors.

The Indians live in dread of a host of unnatural and supernatural menaces that form the core of their religion. The spirits that infest the Camayurá world are called the *mama'é*. These spirits, according to Camayurá belief, are responsible for what goes on in the world, including such things as animal and plant growth, life and death, accidents that may befall a man, the change of the seasons, and the state of the river.

Most of the other tribes in the region have in their religion a parallel set of spirits, called *mopit* by the Aueti, *olé* by the Trumai, and *papataím* by the Waurá. The spirits are said to live in the woods and in the air, and the shaman, or high priest, gains his power by his ability to control them. Sometimes shamans of two or more tribes will work together to influence the spirits of each group for a special project of some kind. Each man has his own *mama'é*, which Indians described to Oberg as little men with white hair and long black beards. Other spirits take on the form of the animal or plant they infest, or else are represented by abstract symbols.

But it would be wrong to see only the discomforts and fears of the tribal way of life; it would be unjust to dismiss the idea of Children of Nature altogether. For mixed in with the hardships

HUTS ON THE UPPER XINGU ARE INHABITED BY SEVERAL RELATED FAMILIES. HAMMOCKS ARE SLUNG FROM THE OUTSIDE WALLS TO A CENTRAL POLE. THE DOMED ROOFS ARE THATCHED WITH THICK LAYERS OF GRASS TO KEEP OUT THE RAIN.

of everyday life are rare joys, joys at once simple and sublime: the joy of a successful fishing expedition; the universal joys of marriage and newborn children; the joy of the feasts that are celebrated for every conceivable reason.

Perhaps it is the hardship that invokes the extraordinary closeness of the tribe and the easy willingness to fully accept any stranger who is not clearly an enemy. "We were accepted as brothers," Oberg reported of his arrival at the Camayurá village. His small expedition found the Indians more than willing to share their food and their quarters, expecting in return only the openness that makes possible the primitive communism that is the economic base of tribal life.

The sense of community is one of the strongest factors in the lives of these Indians. So strong is it that the lines of authority and hierarchy, which all cultures establish to serve as the glue of the society, are barely needed and so have become ill-defined. Atop the rude power pyramid in the Camayurá village sits the *morerekuat*, the chief, who combines in his person both temporal and spiritual authority. As well as being political leader of the tribe, he is also the group's shaman. (In many other tribes the

functions are distinct.) His power over the people derives, Oberg suggests, from the worship of the sun, called *kuat* in the Camayurá language. The Camaruyá probably believe the *morerekuat* is the descendent of the sun or its representative spirit.

Nevertheless, the role of the *morerekuat* in the Camayurá village is mostly an honorary one. His hut is indistinguishable from the other buildings, and he expects and receives few special privileges. Though his advice is often sought out, much of the everyday business of the tribe is guided by *ad hoc* leaders chosen by the subgroup tackling any particular task. Hunting and fishing parties, as well as war expeditions, are generally carried out by the young warriors of the village, who choose a leader among themselves. Significantly, it is when a *morerekuat* dies that his special rank is signaled by elaborate ceremony. His major functions include representing the village before strangers or on trading expeditions, and leading social and religious ceremonies.

In most of the tribes Oberg studied, the line of succession to the chiefdom is uncertain. Sometimes, as in the case of the Umotina tribe, the son of the chief succeeds him, subject to approval of the village elders. The Nambicuara, on the other hand, seem to choose a man for his abilities and virtues—physical prowess ranking first among them. The Bacairi have a sort of vice-chief called *itaida*, usually a young man who may or may not be the son of the reigning chief (*pima*), but who succeeds him when the chief dies. The Camayurá follow a hereditary succession, allowing the eldest son of the chief to take over the office.

Certain functions, particularly house building and ritual, are performed by the tribe as a whole. Most routine tasks, however, are the province of the house group, and usually it is the oldest male in the hut who is the voice of authority in everyday matters. This, of course, will vary from tribe to tribe. Warlike groups will of necessity have strong tribal leaders, whereas peaceable people like the Camayurá will find little need for them.

Oberg observed a division of labor, common among the various Xingú peoples, based on sex. Male and female functions in society are clearly marked out, with the latter usually doing the larger share of the work. Though the men are responsible for clearing new fields and planting the manioc and feed grains that make up the Indian diet, it is the women who perform the daily agricultural functions. Men build houses, make weapons and

214

canoes, fish and hunt, and assist in harvesting the crops. Despite these chores, they are apt to have more free time than the women, who, besides caring for the fields, must cook the food, fetch the water, weave the baskets, take care of the children, and remain half awake at night in order to tend the fire.

Like wives the world over, a Camayurá woman's work is never done. Once the fields have been planted they must be kept free from the choking weeds and underbrush, which spring up fast in this tropical land. After the crops are in, their preparation is tedious and time consuming. The staple crop of the Camayurá is the manioc tuber, of which the two principal varieties in South America are bitter and sweet. The Camayurá grow only the bitter variety, which has an advantage over the sweet in that it produces a flour that may be stored. But it has one considerable drawback: The plant contains a dangerous concentration of prussic acid, a deadly cyanide compound. Hence it must be carefully processed. The manioc tubers must be peeled, grated, pulped, and pressed over a large sieve (*tuavi*), made of bamboo and cotton twine, to remove the poisonous juice. Usually three women work together at this job. The resulting mass is then rolled into balls, dried for several days in the sun, and finally ground into meal from which the pancakelike *menyu* is made. Sweet potatoes, maize, tobacco, cotton, and various fruits are also grown by the Camayurá. Beans, strangely, are not part of the Camayurá diet, but are grown by neighboring tribes such as the Nambicuara.

Fish is second only to manioc in the diet of the Camayurá, and indeed in the diets of almost all the Xingú tribes. The importance of fish to the Indians cannot be overestimated; the large number of taboos and customs surrounding the act of fishing is just one indication of this. Happily, the waters of the Upper Xingú and its tributary the Kuluene are stocked with an inexhaustible supply and variety of fish. Oberg reported that a hook and line left in the water for one minute bagged a fish.

Several methods of catching fish are used by the Camayurá, the most successful and common being the use of poison from the timbo plant. Dams and various kinds of traps are set. Along the shore a number of hunters with bows and arrows wait for the poison to take effect while others sit in canoes on the water. The poison drives the fish to the surface, where they are shot with arrows, caught in the traps, or grabbed barehanded.

215

Hunting plays a less significant role among most of the Xingú tribes, its importance varying according to the disposition of the tribal warriors and the effectiveness of the tribe's weapons. What hunting is done is seldom for the purpose of obtaining food. More typically, a jaguar is brought down for its skin, fangs, claws, and bones; birds are sought for their plumage.

Religion occupies most primitive tribes to a degree not easily conceivable to the modern mind. Almost every workaday task has its taboos and rtiuals, which the Indians take with complete seriousness. An incident related by Oberg is typical. The Camayurá believe that sexual intercourse on the night before a fishing expedition will limit the catch. During one such expedition the *morerekuat* said that the men should hand over their bows and arrows to the boys because the men had had intercourse, and the fishing was not good. This was done, and the boys actually seemed to catch more fish.

While religious beliefs and myths vary from group to group, there are certain constants. Each tribe has its own myth that explains the origin of both the tribe and the human race. The Umotina, for example, say that one day some ripe figs fell from a tree. From these sprang a man named Aipuku, a woman named Brabela, and three other human beings. The story goes on to explain the creation of the different races (who sprang from sores in Aipuku's legs), the origin of maize, and so on.

In general, the Indians completely anthropomorphize nature, endowing such things as plants, rocks, and winds with spirits, whose attitudes toward human beings can range from totally benevolent to totally malevolent. It is to placate these spirits that taboos and rituals are followed. The shaman of the tribe gains his unique distinction from the belief that he has extraordinary powers over the spirits. The Camayurá believe this power was given to the first shaman by a bird, a yellow-breasted flycatcher, and the knowledge has been passed down through the generations.

Most of the ritual in Indian life springs from the belief in these spirits. Each ritual—and all the ceremonial objects such as flutes, rattles, and masks involved in the ritual—has a special and often quite sophisticated significance in the lives of the Indians. In fact, once the hypothesis of the *mama'é* is accepted, the rest of the Indian religion usually follows in a perfectly rational and intelligent manner. For example, if you believe that spirits con-

216

trol the growth of crops, it makes good sense to keep these spirits in good humor with the proper ceremony. And the ceremony itself, once understood, makes equally good sense: the beating of drums and gourds represents the thunder that will bring the needed rain; the swaying of the dancers is symbolic of the growing crops.

The Indians are at least somewhat aware that their rituals are more representative than literal. The Indians of the Xingú, like primitive peoples everywhere, have suffered from the naïveté of civilized man. There is more subtlety in the religion and customs of the Indians than meets the eye; and in this subtlety, a great deal more humanity exists than is generally recognized.

*Australia*

# THE ARUNTA

The Arunta, along with the similar tribes that inhabit the desolate wastes of central Australia, are among the most primitive people on earth—so primitive, in fact, that some anthropologists considered them throwbacks, relics of the Neanderthal cavemen who preceded the true Homo sapiens in Europe. This, however, is not true. Nor, as has sometimes been suggested, are the Arunta "archaic white," a lower evolutionary form of the Caucasian. But it is a measure of the uniqueness of the natives of Australia that such theories have been advanced to explain their very existence.

Today we know that the Arunta belong to a distinct race called the Australoid, which includes, along with the other native Australians, such diverse peoples as the pre-Dravidians of India and the Sakais of the Malay Peninsula, as well as groups found in New Guinea, Java, and the Celebes. In each of these cases the Australoids are indeed relic groups, remnants of earlier and more primitive societies that were pushed into the most remote regions by later Mongoloid or Caucasian settlers, and in every case the Australoids remain the most backward group of the region, their culture approximating that of the Stone Age people of Europe.

It is uncertain when the Australoids first came to Australia. Most anthropologists now believe that they migrated during the last ice age, ten or twenty thousand years ago, and then were cut off from their native New Guinea when the ice caps melted and the Pacific inundated the lowlands that had formed a land bridge between New Guinea and the Australian continent. However, a few scientists still hold that Australia was populated by peoples moving across the sea, as were the Polynesian islands.

In any case, it is quite certain that Arunta society, until the advent of the European, changed little over the thousands of years. Australia is a continent where time stood still, and evolution reached a dead end. The kangaroo, which in so many ways is the apt symbol of Australia, is among the least developed of mammals; it carries its young in a pouch from a very early stage in their growth because it has only a rudimentary placenta. The platypus, too, is a relic of some ancient natural experiment: though furry and warmblooded, it lays eggs and has webbed feet. In fact, all the mammals of Australia are marsupials, the most primitive of all mammals. The same isolation that cut.the fauna of Australia from the mainstream of development and evolution could not fail to affect the Arunta.

The Arunta (sometimes called the Aranda) are lean, small-boned, chocolate-colored people, averaging under five and a half feet. They have a certain look of fierceness, accentuated by deep-set dark brown eyes under prominent brows that are covered thickly with hair, a natural protection from the strong sun. Their noses are broad, which, combined with their dark skin, gives them a superficial resemblance to Negroids, but their lips are thin, almost Caucasoid. Their hair is dark, usually abundant and wavy or curly, and their jaws are prognathous and very strong. Although malnutrition—a condition brought about by the disappearance of game as a result of the encroachments of civilization —has left many present-day Arunta potbellied, in their natural state they have the strong chest, arms, and thighs of a long-distance runner. For them a trek of one hundred miles on foot is common.

Largely as a result of their isolation the Arunta never developed the arts we associate with so-called primitive peoples—pottery, weaving, basketry, the use of metals, agriculture, and the domestication of animals. And though the Arunta are hunters, they did not develop the bow and arrow on their own. Their weapons are boomerangs, as well as spears thrown with the aid of a spear-thrower, a lever that has the effect of extending the

221

A YOUNG WARRIOR OF THE AUSTRALIAN "OUTBACK." WITH BROWN SKIN, BROAD NOSES, THIN LIPS, AND HEAVY EYEBROW RIDGES, THE ABORIGINES OF AUSTRALOID STOCK ARE DISTINCT FROM ANY OF THE WORLD'S MAJOR RACES.

CLINGING TO THEIR STONE AGE CULTURE, THE ABORIGINES LIVE WITHOUT AGRICULTURE, METAL TOOLS, OR DOMESTIC ANIMALS. THEY HUNT WITH PRIMITIVE WOODEN SPEARS AND BOOMERANGS.

thrower's arm, substantially improving the toss. The Arunta kill enough game at one time to last only a few days. Their entire way of life is geared to movement; they are probably the least encumbered nomads on earth.

An Arunta man's entire store of possessions weighs about twenty-one pounds; a woman's, only twelve. They would have little use for the large stores of meat taken, for example, by African antelope or elephant hunters. The aborigine lives by his knowledge of where game and water are likely to be found at any particular time. The game herds follow shifting supplies of water, flocking about each new waterhole; the aborigine follows.

Game meat is eaten raw or roasted. The women search for seeds, roots, fungus, bird and reptile eggs, snails, and ants to supplement the diet. The principal game hunted by the men are the kangaroo, the wallaby, and the emu. The Arunta dress up to look like emus to excite the bird's curiosity. Drugs are used in hunting other game. Upon arriving at a waterhole, the Arunta drink their fill, and then spread a vegetable drug over the surface of the water. They then wait for the inevitable—provided, of course, they have not made the mistake of wandering into an area devoid of game. The kangaroo seems to be especially appreciated for its fat, which is usually eaten raw soon after the animal is killed. The emu, though valued for its meat, is also highly prized for its plumage, along with its strong leg tendons, which are used as cords.

Among the meager possessions of the Arunta are quartz tools, obtained from neighboring tribes, and string bags, which serve many of the functions of the nonexistent pottery. For clothing, the women wear small pubic aprons. Men sometimes wear a similar apron; but they often go naked, except perhaps for a belt of human hair from which weapons are hung, leaving the hunter's hands free. Both sexes wear nose bones. On ceremonial occasions the Arunta paint their bodies with red ochre. Their bodies are often heavily scarred, and some of the scars are deliberate.

Arunta shelters are dome-shaped, made of a frame of stakes and twigs, and thatched with grass. At night a constant fire is maintained, but it cannot drive away the chill of the desert, where the temperature may fall to the 20's. Yet the Arunta sleep uncovered and naked.

But even though the technology of the Arunta is the world's

ALTHOUGH THEY NEVER LEARNED TO WEAVE BASKETS OR MAKE POTTERY, THE ABORIGINES HAVE LEFT SOME POLYCHROMATIC PAINTINGS ON CAVE WALLS IN THE NORTHERN TERRITORY. THEIR ARTWORK IS REMARKABLE FOR ITS ANATOMICAL ACCURACY.

most primitive, their social patterns are extremely complex. Each Arunta group is divided into two moieties, or kinship groups. A person from one moiety must marry a person belonging to the other moiety; a boy belongs to his father's moiety and must marry a girl belonging to the moiety of his mother. This rule originated in incest taboos, and is designed to ensure that incest does not occur. The Arunta have little understanding of the biological nature of fatherhood. They believe that pregnancy is due to a spirit and not—at least not directly—to sexual intercourse. After all, they reason, some women never have children.

The moieties, which are divided into sections and subsections, thus further limiting the choice of a marriage partner, are the bedrock of all Arunta social patterns. The terms of address of the kinship system are extended to all members of the moiety, and kin terms or nicknames are the common form of address. A person's real name is kept secret, for it is a sacred name and may be whispered only on the most solemn occasions. This name is chosen by the elders of the clan and the child's natural father.

The political system is not so highly structured. There are no official tribal leaders (although the Europeans at one time used to choose "chiefs" to deal with), and when decisions must be made the old men of the tribe are consulted. Like so many groups,

the Arunta equate experience with wisdom. The elders may advise on justice, but justice usually is a family concern; for serious offenses such as murder, strict retribution—an eye for an eye, a tooth for a tooth—is demanded. Other than this, fighting is rare, and there is nothing resembling organized warfare.

As with the majority of primitive peoples, religion plays a great part in the life of the Arunta. Each clan or moiety is regarded as descended from a plant or animal, which is the group's totem (or one of its totems). These totems inhabit the surrounding territory, along with the spirits of the dead Arunta. Even if an Arunta leaves his territory, his home is always considered to be where his totem dwells; he may never adopt another tribe's totem.

Sacred stones called churingas are kept in the secret totemic center, generally some sort of cave or cranny. The stones are flat and oval and are painted with white and brown designs, mainly concentric circles. These designs represent emu tracks and camping places of the totem hero. Some of the churingas, made of wood and pierced with holes, are actually bull-roarers, a term used by anthropologists for certain objects found among primitive peoples in many areas; when swung about on the end of a string, the bull-roarers produce a pulsating droning sound, intended to terrify the uninitiated. Women and children are forbidden to approach the totemic centers.

The Arunta believe birth to be connected with the churinga. When a girl reaches puberty she marries a man to whom she may have been betrothed before her birth. When she becomes pregnant she tells her husband where she was when she first felt the baby stir. He goes to the tribal elders to find out what totemic ancestor is buried closest to that spot, and this totem is then the father of the child. If twins are born they are killed, because multiple births are considered unnatural and thus dangerous.

The elders make a churinga for a newborn child from a stone taken from the totem center area, and it takes its place among the other sacred objects. Then the sacred name is given the child, a name his mother will never know, for it will only be spoken during men's ceremonies.

Until puberty, all children stay with their mothers. Puberty rites are performed on both boys and girls, but the male rites are more extensive and much more of an ordeal than are those for the female.

The first of these is designed to impress the youth with his new responsibilities as a full member of the tribe. The boy is thrown up into the air while one of his elders shouts an admonition such as: "I'll teach you to give me food." Each time the boy comes down the same elder hits him with a stick. This is done repeatedly. The emphasis in this lesson seems to be on the all-important Arunta virtues of sharing and of obeying one's elders and showing them respect. Women have a part in these ceremonies, dancing in a circle around the participants, waving their hands as the boys are tossed upward. At the end of this ceremony, the boys are painted with ochre and their noses are pierced.

The second rite takes place after the novice reaches puberty. The women, as well as other divisions of the tribe, may not attend this ceremony. Only a few youths at a time undergo the ordeal, which goes on for ten days. The boys are seized and dragged off to a specially prepared and cleared rectangular area, which is surrounded by brush and low ridges of earth. The first part of the ceremony is concerned mostly with re-enactments of tribal history and mythology for the edification of the youths. The re-enactments are interrupted by sudden attacks upon the initiates. These apparently serve to traumatize them; that is, to reinforce the important lessons of the ritual by associating them in the boys' minds with some striking physical experience. In effect, the Arunta make sure this will be a ceremony the youths will never forget. At one point, a number of men fall heavily upon the initiate, who is lying on the ground; at another, two men cut veins in their arms and sprinkle blood on the initiates.

Then follows the circumcision, which is done with a stone knife. The blood is preserved and brought to the women's camp, where some of the boy's female relatives (but not his mother) smear the blood over their breasts and foreheads. A younger brother of the initiate is given the excised foreskin to eat, in the belief that it will help him grow tall and strong.

Another ordeal that occurs around this time is the custom of scalp biting. The mature men will surround a candidate and bite his scalp until it bleeds. One reason given for this is that it makes the hair grow. This seems so trivial to the writer, however, that the custom probably has some other, deeper meaning, as yet unknown.

The initiate is given a whole month to recover from his emotional and physical wounds before he is forced to submit to the most painful ordeal of all: subincision. The penis is slit along most of its length, usually laying open most of the urethral canal as well. Although this is both extremely painful and dangerous, most of the initiates recover and live to submit the next generation to the same cruel rites. So drastic is this operation that the affected parts never quite return to normal, and the men must squat to urinate.

The final phase of the initiation period lasts four months and culminates in the fire ceremony, *engwura*. This is a public rite that attracts Arunta from distant camps. It is a time of dancing, singing, and rejoicing. Yet it, too, is not without its ordeals. Before the fire ceremony the initiates are ceremonially bled from the arm. During the ceremony itself they lie down on green boughs laid on a fire and have burning grass and sticks thrown on them by the women, or else they kneel on the coals of a small fire. The ceremony ends in a sex orgy, as do some of the other public ceremonies of the Arunta. Most of the ordinary incest laws are ignored, but the basic rules prohibiting father-daughter, mother-son, and brother-sister incest are maintained.

In contrast to the long, arduous initiation given the boys, the girls' rites are short and simple. At puberty a girl is visited by her betrothed, who ceremonially rubs her breasts with fat and ochre "to make them grow." No other significant initiation rites take place until a day or two before the girl's marriage. Then the future husband turns the girl over to certain kinsmen of his, who take her off to the bush and rupture her hymen with a stone knife. The men are then free to have intercourse with her, a sort of *jus primae noctis* (in medieval Europe, the right of a feudal lord to a female vassal on her wedding night). This right is sometimes extended for a short while after the couple are joined, which is effected by the bride's mother, who places the girl's arm in the man's hand.

The culture we have been describing can hardly be said to exist in untouched form any longer. As always, the encroachment of technological civilization has taken its toll. The Arunta, along with the other Australian aboriginal tribes, are disappearing. Of the thousands that existed when the first white settlers pushed into Arunta land, about four hundred remain, and these are mostly old people, clinging stubbornly to their traditional ways. Their children have disappeared into the cities, and although revivalist cults

A SUCCESSFUL HUNT IS CELEBRATED BY A CORROBOREE, WHICH MAY LAST FROM A FEW DAYS TO A FEW WEEKS. THESE DANCERS, IN CEREMONIAL PAINT, ARE IMITATING THE ACTIONS OF ANIMALS.

spring up sporadically in attempts to regain the Arunta cultural heritage, it is quite clear that the Arunta way of life, even the Arunta people themselves, will soon be extinct. It is worthwhile to examine how Arunta life was destroyed.

The history of first contacts between European civilization and the aboriginal culture of Australia is one of almost unbroken conflict and bloodshed. The earliest recorded landings, in fact, ended usually with battles between sailors and natives. When the Dutch ship *Duyfken* landed in 1606, a pitched fight took place in which nine Dutch sailors were wounded with spears, and an uncounted number of natives were shot. This seemed to set the pattern for the next two and a half centuries.

The first permanent white settlers of Australia were convicts that the British government, under Pitt, was anxious to deport. Along with the convicts came guards, who were hardly more law-abiding than their charges; and the early days of the Australian settlements are marked with violence, directed particularly against the aborigines, who were being pushed off their land. The

Arunta and their fellows, being rather docile and ill-prepared to defend themselves, suffered considerably. An incurious people, well-adapted to their own particular way of life but static and unable to change, the Arunta could not adapt to the way of life that the Europeans attempted to impose, as could certain of the peoples of Africa, for example. And since the Arunta way of life was so spectacularly different from the European, so apparently primitive to people who did not properly understand it, the Europeans often considered the natives to be little better than animals.

Even when the intentions of the government were benign, the aborigines often suffered at the hands of men who pushed into the unexplored areas of Australia; for pioneers, the government and the law are far away. Though British officials in London wrote humane laws dealing with the aborigines, in the back country of the continent massacre after massacre took place. And because the aborigines had no tribal chiefs, did not recognize the alien conception of land ownership and so could not comprehend the property rights that were the basis of the European culture, even enlightened attempts to deal with them were bound to fail.

As early as the beginning of the nineteenth century, missionaries were being sent from England to educate and convert the aborigines. Missions dotted the Australian backwoods by the end of that century. But invariably the missionaries sowed confusion and conflict. The elders scorned the missionaries, and the youths who attended the missionary classes and services were cut off from the sacred churinga. Generational conflicts arose. As Marie Reay, in *Aboriginal Man in Australia*, noted:

When an Aboriginal must repudiate all tribal obligations and customs to become a Christian, conflict must develop . . . between the old men who are unwilling to relinquish their traditions and the younger people for whom the adoption of new ways offers more rewards. When the children grew to adulthood . . . they regarded themselves as superior to the "wild blackfellows" who had been their forebears, but they found they could not achieve status among people of purely European descent. They grew up culturally barren. . . .

Disease, too, played a role. The settlers introduced new strains of viruses into the continent, viruses to which they had some immunity, but which readily attacked the aborigines. For many years epidemics spread through the aboriginal settlements, killing off the population. But perhaps most important of all was the loss of traditional hunting land. Not only was the game destroyed by the settlers (the wanton slaughter of the kangaroo by the white man perhaps ranks second only to the annihilation of the buffalo on the American plains), but the aborigines were forced off their land—land that had special religious significance, for it was the land of the churinga. Even if a new area had game aplenty, the heritage and tradition so necessary to the morale, and ultimately to the existence of the people, was gone.

Experience has shown that the aborigine, like other subject peoples, can embrace and come to understand modern civilization only if the door to this new world—which in Australia is almost entirely a white world—is opened to them all the way, not just a crack. The past two generations have seen a resurgence of revival movements in Australia. These have not taken place among the very small fraction of full-blooded aborigines, who still live their old nomadic life; rather, they have arisen among "detribalized" aborigines, who have gathered around cattle stations, towns, and mines. These people speak their own languages, at least among themselves, and maintain many of their social customs and religion. However, many of these partially acculturated groups have been strongly impressed with Christianity, and in several areas have formed their own churches, largely independent of white missionary influence. They have even organized religious conventions, somewhat resembling the old American revival meetings.

The effect of these revivals in religion, language, and social ceremony is to give the aborigines a feeling of solidarity in the face of the frustrations involved in trying to live with white society. By and by the aborigines come to realize that the white way of life is not necessarily preferable to their traditions, and that even as they begin to enjoy more of the benefits of civilization, even as they become educated and progress economically and politically, they need not say good-bye to all aspects of their old way of life.

*Oceania*

# THE YAPESE

When one thinks of the South Seas, the islands of Polynesia are likely to come first to mind. But there are many other island groups scattered throughout the vastness of the South Pacific, as any veteran of the Pacific campaigns of World War II well remembers. These are called Micronesia, or "land of the small islands"; and at the western tip of one of the larger groups, the Carolines, is the Yap Island group. Situated about five hundred miles southwest of Guam, the Yap group comprises four islands and ten small islets that form an encircling band around a central lagoon nineteen miles in diameter.

The Caroline Islands have had a hectic political history during the last two centuries. The Carolines were discovered and annexed by Spain during the 1790's, but in 1885, a German gunboat landed on Yap and claimed the islands for Germany. Pope Leo XIII sustained Spain's claim in the ensuing dispute, and Germany withdrew. However, after the Spanish-American War, Spain was forced to sell all the islands of Micronesia to Germany. The islands were in turn seized by the Japanese in 1914 and the League of Nations mandate turned them over to Japan after World War I.

Under the Japanese, Yap was the headquarters of an administrative district; it had three government schools, as well as

234

Roman Catholic missions. Meanwhile the United States and Japan were engaged in still another dispute over the little island because of its importance as a transpacific cable station. In the resulting treaty the United States secured cable and radio rights free from Japanese control or censorship. During World War II the United States captured the islands of Micronesia. In 1947 the area was designated a trust territory of the UN, with the United States as trustee; since that time the United States has administered the islands. The population of Yap has stabilized itself at about 5,800 (1961) after decreasing sharply during the 1920's and 1930's.

The Yapese are small of stature and build, with medium brown skin and wavy hair. They are of a racial and linguistic stock distinct from that of the other Caroline islanders and are believed to be the descendents of an ancient Malay race that conquered Yap's aboriginal inhabitants. Archeologists have begun to study the numerous prehistoric stone relics found on Yap and other islands of the Carolines, but have not yet determined much about their origins.

To the Yapese, who inhabit a lush tropical island built on Pacific volcanic mountain peaks, the coconut is an important source of food and drink. The milk of the young coconut is drunk, and the meat is grated, mixed with water to form a paste, and eaten with fish. Grated coconut has become an important item for trade with Europe and America, and the sun-dried shredded meat, called copra, is an ingredient of many fine soaps. Breadfruit, bananas, taro, and yams are also important foodstuffs.

In the rocky crannies along the coasts is an abundance of squid, crab, and shellfish. Fishing is the chief activity of the Yapese men, who take to the open sea for such fish as bonito, and fish in the lagoons at night by torchlight. Poison is also used to catch fish. First they are herded into cave pools or small lagoons at high tide; then the pools are contaminated with poisonous plants that drug the fish and make them float to the surface, where they are easily netted. The drug does not make them inedible.

During the fishing season the fishermen must not set foot in their houses, but must stay at the community bachelor house, or *failu*. They must have no contact whatsoever with any women, except for the mistress, or *mispil*, of the failu. While staying at the failu they cannot join in the evening songs and dances of the other men.

The Yapese live in rectangular houses constructed of timbers from coconut palms, which are securely lashed together with coconut-fiber rope. The structures are practically all roof, with long steep thatched gables reaching almost to the platform on which they are built. This platform, made of slabs of limestone rock, stands a few feet above the ground. The interiors of the houses are quite dark and gloomy. There is no furniture, but the houses are filled with mats woven of banana and coconut fiber.

The houses are scattered in small groups about the island, with little regard for the ancient districts that used to separate the often hostile and warring tribes. The groups of houses do not have a highly developed village organization, but the failu serves as a community gathering place and council house for the men; it is strictly taboo for the village women. The long narrow house is built communally by a group of unmarried young men, who then leave their parents' homes and live in the failu until they take wives.

It is the custom for the men of the failu to choose for their mispil a young, attractive, and unmarried girl who lives in another village. When she is chosen, a group of the men set out in a spirit of high adventure to carry her off from her father's house. The girl is usually pleased to be installed in her new position, because she will be well treated and will not have to work in the taro fields as do the other women and girls. Although the women in the failu's village shun her, she is held in high esteem by all the men, as well as by her family and former neighbors. Her position is one of honor because it attests to her beauty and desirability. When she becomes pregnant one of the men of the failu marries her, and the young couple take their place as ordinary members of the community.

The former mispil retains one sign of her old position throughout her lifetime: her arm and leg tattoos. Mispils are the only women who undergo tattooing, although the men, especially in former days, were frequently heavily tattooed all over their bodies. Tattooing is done with a sliver of bird bone dipped in carbon made from charred coconut husks and driven into the skin with a blow. The process is very slow and painful.

There is another class of people who never wear these

NATIVE DANCERS ON YAP, A TINY ISLAND GROUP IN THE WESTERN CAROLINES. THE YAPESE RETAIN THEIR NATIVE CULTURE DESPITE CENTURIES OF COLONIAL RULE UNDER SPAIN, GERMANY, JAPAN, AND THE UNITED STATES. YAP IS NOW PART OF THE UNITED NATIONS TRUST TERRITORY OF THE PACIFIC.

ornamental tattoos. They are the members of the old Pimlingai tribe, who are treated as communal slaves by the rest of the islanders. At some time they were probably subjugated in war, but no one knows why they have remained slaves.

The Yapese have no custom of handing down tribal lore and history by word of mouth, as the Polynesians do. Instead, their knowledge of their society usually goes back no further than the memory of its oldest living inhabitant. The Yapese do, however, have a few myths connected with their religion.

The religious faith of the Yap islanders has been a source of concern to the successive administrators of the island. Roman Catholic missionaries, active since the days of the Spanish, have succeeded in converting about half the inhabitants. Most of the other half have retained their ancient beliefs, though a few have espoused the Shintoism or Buddhism advocated by the Japanese.

Yapese religion, like the rest of their society, is not highly organized. The islanders practice a kind of ancestor worship, but have no set ritual ceremonies. They employ the services of a *mash-mash*, or witch doctor, but there is no priest class.

Chewing betel is a popular habit among the islanders, especially the young men. The chewing quid is prepared by putting a slice of areca palm nut and some lime in a pepper leaf. The result is a mild narcotic that colors the saliva red.

The Yapese use what is probably the most unusual currency found anywhere in the world. Their chief instruments of barter are thick unwieldly stone discs, called fei, ranging from six inches to twelve feet in diameter. The stones' value, established long ago by a shrewd tradesman, is maintained by the fact that these stone discs can be obtained only in the Palau Islands, more than three hundred miles away. The money is made from a high grade of calcite, which must be fine, close-grained, and white to have the greatest value. Thus the worth of a fei is measured not only by its diameter but also by its quality. The fei have been transported to Yap across the open seas aboard frail outrigger canoes. The stone disc has a hole in the middle in which a pole is inserted to enable it to be carried. Even so, the stones are difficult to move, and theft is practically unheard of. A man generally keeps his fei in his house so that it will remain smooth and white. If his wealth increases, however, it will soon outgrow the house and must be kept in the front yard. Outside, it will become gray and rough, but the owner has only to chip off the outside coat and polish the stone.

There is another reason why stealing another's fei is impractical. One does not need to physically possess a fei in order to own it. Instead, when a man buys a fei from a neighbor, the heavy disc may remain in the neighbor's yard forever, but the fact of the exchange is established with the people, and the buyer is known to possess the wealth that is still to be seen in his neighbor's yard. The new owner may in turn barter, with the stone remaining in his neighbor's yard, and actually sell it without ever having to move it.

The story is told of a man who bought a very large fei from a village far away. It was necessary to transport the stone by water, and en route a bad storm came up. The men in the canoe knew they would drown if they did not get rid of the heavy

EUROPEAN MISSIONARIES HAVE CONVERTED ABOUT HALF THE YAPESE TO ROMAN CATHOLICISM. HERE A GROUP OF NATIVES, IN TRADITIONAL DRESS, ATTEND MASS IN A JESUIT MISSION.

weight, so they dumped it overboard. Arriving home, they told their story, and it was agreed that the buyer still owned the fei, as he had obtained it in barter and had lost its physical possession through no fault of his or of his men's. For generations the reputed wealth of his family was based on the possession of the stone, which lay at the bottom of the sea.

Once, under German administration, the Yapese damaged a road that the Germans were building. The Germans wanted to levy a fine on the natives in order to prevent further damage, but the former had no use for stone discs and the latter possessed no marks. Finally someone came up with a solution. The Germans went around with black paint and marked the stone discs with "X's", which signified that the government now owned them. The effect was remarkable: The distraught natives immediately went out and repaired the road, after which the officials removed the black marks on the stones. The natives then celebrated their regained wealth with a large feast.

Though Yapese society is not highly organized, it has been fairly durable and unchanging in the face of all sorts of disruptive activities carried on by white men. How long it will last is difficult to determine.

# THE SAMOANS
# AND TAHITIANS

The legendary lure of the South Seas has been a recurrent theme in European and American literature, music, and art. The Polynesian islands that make up Tahiti and Samoa have received the most attention. Several writers and artists have found a refuge from civilization in these islands, notably Paul Gauguin, Rupert Brooke, and Robert Louis Stevenson. It has been said that the real reason for the mutiny of the *Bounty* was not Captain Bligh's cruelty, but the crew's desire to return to their Tahitian girl friends. Those who have managed to resist the call to Polynesia may wonder if it is really as good as it sounds.

As to climate, Samoa and Tahiti could hardly be more of a paradise. The temperature during the day is in the 80's, and at night it averages in the 60's and 70's. There are few storms, and the rainfall is spread evenly throughout the year. The landscape of green mountains and blue lagoons, especially spectacular in Tahiti, is hard to match. Even the animal life seems designed for man's comfort, there being few snakes and fewer houseflies. The only unpleasant animal is the giant coconut crab, which scurries over the beaches and up the palms, destroying the young coconuts.

Beyond these natural beauties, it is the tales of the beautiful Polynesian women and their sexual freedom that seem to have engaged the imaginations of bored and jaded Western men seeking another Eden. These accounts have been working their way back to Europe and America since Captain Cook discovered the islands in 1769. The beauty of the Polynesian women, and the men as well, has been unchanging in the ensuing years. Tall, graceful, and well-built, with light brown skin and straight dark hair, these people are among the most physically attractive in the world. To the Westerner, the Polynesian's broad, flat nose is the least attractive feature, but to the islander it is especially beautiful.

The customs of these people have undergone some changes in the years between the white man's first appearance and today. Correspondingly, the attitudes of the men who have gone there have changed from the delight of the early sailors to the pity and shock of the missionaries and the perplexity of the modern administrators.

The exact origins of the Polynesians, which seem to be essentially the same throughout the Polynesian islands, remain a mystery. It is known that the islands were formerly inhabited by aborigines with Negroid and Mongoloid affinities. In Tahiti these people were known as the *manahune*, or plebeians, because they were reduced to serfdom by later conquerors. The manahune had a fairly civilized culture with well-developed agriculture, craftsmanship, art, and religion. The people who conquered them are known as *hui arii*, which means "dynasty of kings." These people, who arrived in Tahiti around A.D. 600, had a highly developed culture with complex political institutions, court etiquette, dynastic traditions, costumed dances, and drama. They seem to have centered their operations in Tahiti, spreading their influence and power gradually to the surrounding islands.

There have been many theories as to where these highly civilized conquerors came from. One school maintains they came from the West, and some evidence exists that seems to indicate they sailed from the western coast of the Americas. It has been suggested that an Indian tribe (now extinct) of Southern California spoke a language related to the Polynesian tongues. Such American Indian cultural traits as the cultivation of the sweet potato, the ceremonial and ornamental use of feathers, and the cult of human sacrifice, which is practiced by some Polynesians, provide further evidence. That they may have set out from the west coast of Peru is supported by the journey of the raft *Kon-Tiki*, in 1947, which was carried to Polynesia from Peru by the tidal currents.

Most scholars, however, believe that these people came from the East, from India or southern Asia. There is much linguistic evidence to connect the Polynesians with the western coast of India. In addition, there is a remarkable similarity in the construction of the long narrow boats they both use. If this theory is true, the Polynesian also contain a Caucasoid strain.

The race has also been linked to the ancestors of the Japanese. The evidence so far is largely linguistic. According to a recent, widely accepted classification, Japanese is part of the "Malayo-Polynesian" family of languages, a far-flung group found as far west as Madagascar.

Before the days of the white man there were many similarities and some differences between the cultures of Samoa and Tahiti. The natives of both island groups engaged in fishing and growing taro, yams, and sweet potatoes, as well as bananas and breadfruit. The coconut palm, although used, was not so important as a food as is generally believed. The women spent much of their time weaving the elegant, ceremonial fiber mats that served as the clothing of brides and as gifts for honored dignitaries.

The Polynesians are excellent builders of houses and canoes. Possessing no nails, they skillfully bind together the planks with fiber ropes. Their rectangular low-roofed houses are sturdy and attractive. The boats are able to hold up to one hundred men, and can withstand the force of the open seas for long periods. The Polynesians, because of their spectacular journeys of exploration and settlement, have been called the Norsemen of the Pacific. The territory that they covered—which forms a huge triangle bounded by Hawaii, New Zealand, and Easter Island—is four times as large as Europe.

Social distinctions were rigid in Tahiti and Samoa. However, Samoa had the more democratic society, as the tribal chiefs were elected. There were many levels of leadership that the men strove for, fulfilling certain duties and taking part in ceremonies. In Samoa there was also a special group known as the "talking chiefs." Their duty was to speak for the real chiefs at special functions, using the formal language reserved for such occasions. The chiefs were considered too dignified to stoop to any sort of

242

communication with ordinary people. These chiefs also had life and death authority over their subjects.

The sexual mores of the Samoans were based on social position. Most of the people were allowed great freedom, both before and after marriage, without inciting social censure. There was scandal only if the man's social position was inferior to the woman's.

In each village there was one girl who had to retain her virginity until marriage. Attractive and socially poised, she was called the *taupo* and was usually the eldest unmarried daughter of the chief; but if the chief had no suitable daughters, the taupo would be chosen from another high-ranking family. The taupo had to pass a brutal test of virginity before her wedding, in front of as many as one thousand wedding guests. She was led naked before the assembly and seated crosslegged, facing the chief. Then, as the guests waited breathlessly, the chief would thrust his two forefingers into the girl's vulva. When the blood began to trickle down her thighs, the crowd would let out a cheer, for the honor of both the tribe and the chief was assured. If, however, the girl failed to pass the test, her brothers or near relatives would rush forth and immediately club her to death.

The taupo had other duties besides guarding her chastity. She was the official hostess for the village and in charge of preparing the kava at important ceremonies. Kava-drinking is to a Samoan meeting what pipe-smoking was to North American Indian gatherings. Kava is prepared from a kind of pepper root, which is chewed to a pulp by a group of young strong-jawed people. The pulp is spit into a bowl and mixed with a little cold water. The taupo mixed the drink, following a set ritual, and periodically tested it.

The taupo also took a prominent part in the young people's dances and was expected to be especially impressive at these events.

If life was rigid with regard to the social duties and limitations of the taupo, it was not so for other girls. The problem of children born out of wedlock was easily solved, since it carried no social stigma for mother or child. If a birth was not wanted, abortion would commonly be induced by violent massage. Furthermore, infanticide was an accepted practice.

Religion was not a highly organized institution in Samoa;

there were ceremonies to be observed, but there was no priest class. In Tahiti, however, the religious life was more highly organized, and there was a priest class made up of members of the aristocratic *hui arii.*

Also in Tahiti, chieftainships were hereditary, and the social structure was much more rigid than in Samoa. There were two definite classes who were said to be of different "blood." The ruling aristocracy treated the commoners like serfs. In Tahiti there was also an intermediate class that enjoyed more privileges than the commoners, though lacking the luxuries of the aristocracy.

The sexual mores of the Tahitians were perhaps freer than those of the Samoans, and there was no counterpart of the virginity test of the Samoan taupo. In both Samoa and Tahiti when an occasional young man found himself rejected by the girls he might become *moetotolu,* or sleep-crawler. At night the *moetotolu* would sneak into a girl's home, usually when she was expecting her lover, and take the girl by surprise. Sometimes she would submit because she would not want to cause a disturbance in the household. But if she did call for help, the whole house would go running after the man, who, if caught, would receive a thrashing and suffer the general scorn and contempt of the whole village.

When European sailors started visiting the islands they were duly impressed with the beauty and hospitality of the natives. The sailors were quick to take advantage of the prevailing sexual freedom, but they introduced a new note of debauchery. The natives soon learned that the women could earn trinkets for their favors; the result was prostitution. This European influence was felt much more heavily in Tahiti than in Samoa, since the latter had a stricter moral code and a tighter social organization that resisted European domination.

Veneral disease was inevitable, and soon most of the natives were infected. These and other diseases rapidly carried off a considerable number of the native population. In addition, many of the women became sterile. Thus it looked as if the native populations might become extinct. However, in 1795 a new and radically different European influence invaded the Polynesian islands. In that year the London Missionary Society arrived in Tahiti. The Polynesians were at first astonished to see such a somber, continent group of white men. But within a few decades the Pro-

ALTHOUGH INTERMARRIAGE IS INCREASINGLY COMMON, THE SAMOANS AR
THE MOST RACIALLY PURE OF THE POLYNESIAN TRIBES. THE WOMAN IN TH
PICTURE IS PERFORMING THE KAVA CEREMONY BY SQUEEZING KAVA ROO
IN A WOODEN BOWL.

testant missionaries, plus the Roman Catholics who arrived soon afterward, had succeeded in nominally converting all the Samoans and Tahitians to Christianity.

The missionaries may have offset the debauchery of the sailors but they had little success in changing the sexual mores of the natives, for the Polynesians have none of the Western attitudes of guilt and shame connected with sex, nor do they share the West's ideas of romantic love. For example, in Samoa today only the unmarried girls who live in the missionary houses remain chaste, and frequently they will leave the house to lead the freer life of the village.

A further European influence descended on the Polynesians when European colonialism reached Polynesia. Tahiti, formerly called Otaheite, was held by the British during part of the nineteenth century. However, in 1842 while the Tahitian queen was away her ministers ceded the island to France. It has remained a French protectorate ever since. The French have been reasonable, lenient administrators, levying few taxes, but doing little to

retain the native customs of the island. The islanders enjoy full French citizenship.

The Tahitian ruler at the time, Queen Pomare IV, was one of the most colorful monarchs of the nineteenth century. She enjoyed a great vogue in European circles, and was regarded as the Queen Victoria of the South Seas. However, her long string of lovers belied her similarity to the English monarch. She was the daughter of King Pomare II and one of his two sisters, with whom he lived simultaneously. Pomare II, who kept telling the missionaries that he loved Christ like his own brother, so long as they kept him supplied with brandy, died of drink in 1824. His only son, who succeeded him, was sickly and soon died. In 1827, in an unprecedented move for a woman, Queen Pomare came to the throne. During her long reign of fifty years much of the Europeanization of her island took place.

Today in Tahiti the old-fashioned outrigger canoes used by the natives for fishing are about the only truly Polynesian products left. Both clothing and housing have been Europeanized and especially Frenchified. A visitor to Papeete, the capital and main town of the island, sees European night spots, dancing, and clothing all being enthusiastically adopted by the Polynesians. There has been considerable racial mixing on the island, and there are few full-blooded Polynesians left. The only group to remain aloof from the racial and cultural mixing are the Chinese settlers, whose numbers have increased sharply in the past decades to the extent that Chinese has become the third language of the island, after Tahitian and French. The 1956 population of Tahiti was 44,247, with Papeete having a population of 17,288.

Samoa is actually an archipelago about 350 miles long comprising fourteen islands with a total area of 1209 square miles. The 1961 population of the entire group was 134,478. Samoa is divided into Western Samoa and American Samoa. The latter is an unincorporated territory of the United States; Western Samoa, which had been under the administration of New Zealand from 1920 through 1961, has been an independent sovereign state as of January 1962. Before 1920 it was a German protectorate.

It is still possible to speak of a native Samoan culture in a way that is not possible with Tahiti. Despite considerable racial mixing, the Samoans are the most racially pure Polynesians remaining in the South Seas. Today, although many of the young people are moving to town, away from the villages and the traditional social structure, the native way of life is still fairly evident. Many of the old rules have been relaxed. In the old days, for example, there was a strict taboo against any social mixing between relatives (whether by blood or marriage) of opposite sexes who were close in age, once they had reached puberty. Most families no longer observe this taboo, but it is still considered vulgar to make any sort of off-color remark or reference to sex in the presence of a sibling.

In former times the Samoans, like most other Polynesians, learned by heart the long detailed genealogies of their families and tribes. Today this practice is being replaced by family record books.

The Polynesians enjoyed a highly developed culture for years before the white man arrived. Now this way of life has been to a large degree obliterated in a few centuries. However, though the customs are changing and the race is becoming mingled with others, the spirit of the people still pervades the islands, easily conquering all would-be invaders.

# THE ARAPESH

The Arapesh peoples are found in the western part of the Trust Territory of New Guinea administered by Australia. They live in the coastal zone on the beach, in the mountains, and on the plains lying toward the interior of the mountains.

The mountain Arapesh are a mild people who think there is no evil in men, and who live in such trust and affection with each other that they are totally unequipped to handle aggressive, ego-centric personalities when they appear. The gentle, motherly mountain wife is no match for the fiery, aggressive Arapesh plains-woman who occasionally runs away to the mountains and wins a mountain husband away from her weaker rival.

The mountain Arapesh prefer to do such tasks as gardening, house-building, and hunting in groups rather than singly or in husband-and-wife pairs. Farming is difficult for these people, who live in an area generally unsuited to agriculture. It is a land of swift-falling streams, steep ravines, and thick tangled brush forest. Most of the gardens are made on steep hillsides, which are approached with difficulty on narrow, slippery paths. The gardens are practically impossible to fence off as protection against the maraudings of wild pigs.

The division of labor between the sexes is a marked feature of the mountain Arapesh culture. The men are the food gatherers,

248

and as such they do the hunting and the cultivation of the taro and banana gardens. The role of the woman is to produce children and to care for the home, although she may help in certain stages of banana growing.

The man's and woman's roles merge for a time during the bearing of children. When a woman discovers she is pregnant, she and her husband must have frequent intercourse for the first few weeks, during which time the husband is thought to mold the seed inside the mother until it is perfect. From that time on, during the pregnancy and even after the birth, sexual intercourse is forbidden, and the woman must be tranquil so that the perfectly formed seed may expand undisturbed in her womb. All sexual intercourse during this early stage of pregnancy is called work, because it serves the specific purpose of making the baby. All other sex not devoted strictly to making babies is called play.

When the birth occurs the husband does not stay with his wife. He awaits the news elsewhere, and by saying "Wash it" or "Don't wash it," signifies whether the child shall be allowed to live or left to die on a palm frond, unwashed. Boy babies are more apt to be kept, because they remain with their families and are a comfort to their parents in old age. Because of the husband's exacting "work" in the forming of the baby, the verb "to bear" (the baby) is applied to the husband, as well as to the wife.

After the birth the husband performs a ritual that marks his return to the man's role. The height of this ceremony is the man's capture of a ritual "eel," actually a large white ring placed at the bottom of a pool of water. In Arapesh culture, the eel is connected symbolically with the phallus, and is the special taboo of adolescent boys. Hence, the ceremony seems to symbolize the father's resumption of a more strictly masculine nature, after his close association with feminine functions.

Arapesh marriage is based on comfort and affection, rather than on passion. Children are betrothed at an early age and they live together in the boy's village until they are old enough to have sexual relations and live as man and wife. The girl is frequently only five or six when betrothed, whereas the boy is several years older. The girl learns to regard her betrothed as an affectionate older brother, and ideally the protective attitude of the husband toward his gentle wife holds throughout their life together. Both are taught not to have sex relations before they are grown, as it is believed to stunt the growth of the boy and to prevent the falling of the girls' breasts, which is regarded as an essential feature of beauty. Thus promiscuity is rare before marriage.

Extramarital relations are also fairly rare, because sexual relations are looked upon as potentially harmful to the function of the man, who only dares subject himself to this danger within the familiar and friendly protection of marriage. Young men are cautioned to stay away from strange women and to sleep only in the houses of female relatives when away on trips, lest they be seduced. Relations with a strange woman would surely impair their food-gathering magic. Indeed, the very presence of a highly sexed and aggressive woman in a village is believed dangerous because her female sexual nature will interfere with the male magic that makes the yam crop grow.

The food-producing activities of the men are exacting and

difficult. In addition to the problems of tilling rocky, sloping
gardens, the men complicate things by their insistence on community gardening. Instead of each man having his own garden, a
man has a part interest in several gardens, which he tills with
various combinations of other men. Each man has a garden
where he is the host and in each of the other gardens he tills he is
a guest. The security that this system offers in cases where some
gardens are ruined by failure or destruction is more than offset by
the difficulties that arise from trying to coordinate tilling operations.

Although the Arapesh live together in permanent villages,
during the growing season each family lives in a makeshift
thatched hut in the garden of the current host. These garden plots
and homes are scattered over the mountainside. Considerable
time is consumed in shouting directions and in traveling from one

THE WORLD'S SECOND LARGEST ISLAND, NEW GUINEA HAS A NATIVE POPULA-
TION OF MORE THAN A MILLION PEOPLE. AT LEFT IS A GROUP OF DANCERS
FROM THE HIGHLANDS.

plot to another so that the various groups can till each garden en masse.

Warfare is all but unknown among these friendly and co-operative people. The freedom with which young children and women wander alone in the bush is evidence of their lack of fear of headhunters and raiding parties. Living in a hard physical environment, the mountain Arapesh have developed a culture that is notable for its softness and lack of aggressivenes.

In recent times the entire Arapesh region has been heavily recruited for contract labor on the various coastal plantations. Indeed, going off to work on plantations both before marriage and during the early married years has become almost as established an institution in this New Guinea region as in South Africa.

The important difference is that only a small number of colonists and a relatively restricted amount of land has been alienated; the traditional subsistence farming can continue, although under the increasing pressure of population growth.

# THE MANUS

The Admiralty Islands are situated off the northeastern coast of New Guinea and form part of the New Guinea Trust Territory administered by Australia. During the last generation an exciting drama has taken place in this remote spot where a few thousand people have struggled to adapt themselves from a savage Stone Age tribe to a modern machine-age society.

Similar struggles are going on all over the world, from the barren tundras of Siberia to the jungles of the Amazon. Everywhere the problem is basically the same: How can a human society accomplish the evolution of several thousand years in a few decades? It is inevitable that in this rapid changeover many of the beliefs and customs of primitive societies must be lost. But attempts must be made to retain what is most important in these societies—their cultural and racial identities.

On the Admiralties live a tribe who have made perhaps the most drastic changes in the shortest time of any primitive peoples. A unique opportunity to observe the details of their whirlwind transition was furnished by the studies of Margaret Mead and Reo Fortune, conducted in 1928–1929. Dr. Mead recorded her observations of the Manus, a people numbering approximately two thousand, in her book *Growing Up in New Guinea,* now a classic in social anthropology. Dr. Fortune produced a detailed account of

WORKMEN CLEAR THE DENSE FORESTS FOR THE CONSTRUCTION OF A ROAD BETWEEN KLAMONO AND SORONG, NEW GUINEA. ECONOMIC PROGRESS WILL DEPEND ON DEVELOPING SUCH NATURAL RESOURCES AS THE OIL DEPOSITS IN THE WESTERN PART OF THE ISLAND.

the functioning of religion in Manus society. In 1953 Dr. Mead returned to the Admiralties to observe these same people again, recording the experience in her book *New Lives for Old.*

The Manus inhabit the largest of the Admiralty Islands, called Manus, and several small islets near it. Dr. Mead focused her study on the village of Peri, one of the twelve Manus villages on the southeast coast.

In 1929, the typical Manus, like those in Peri, dwelt in crude thatched huts built on high poles over the lagoon, and lived by fishing and trading. Children spent their days romping in the water; at an age when youngsters of more modern societies are given toy boats to float in the bathtub, Manus children were given canoes to paddle about in. To supplement their supplies of fish and shellfish, the Manus traded shrewdly with their inland and island neighbors for coconut oil and the starchy diet staples sago and taro, together with such luxury items as betel nuts, carved beads, and lime gourds and sticks. As entrepreneurs they reigned supreme on the island's south coast.

They were still ready to fight to settle arguments. The older men could remember when they spent their youthful energies on war expeditions against their neighbors, often selling war captives to neighboring cannibals, or bringing home captive women to serve as brutally used prostitutes until they either died of exhaustion or were sent home worn and haggard, though sometimes handsomely rewarded for their services.

These warring practices had been outlawed by the European administrators of the island, first the Germans and later the Australians. Instead the young men went away for from three to five years to work for the Europeans as indentured laborers, giving them a few years of adventure before they returned home to take up the responsibilites of marriage and communal life.

The responsibilities and pressures in this primitive society were indeed great. Marriage was a lifetime of conflict and bickering, with no feeling of companionship or tenderness.

The young couple, often betrothed before puberty, had never laid eyes on each other. On the contrary, the very name of the betrothed was taboo to the young boy or girl, and each was taught to hide in shame and embarrassment if members of the betrothed's clan should appear in the village. As betrothals were made between members of nearby villages, such harrowing encounters were likely to be frequent.

Throughout married life the loyalties of husband and wife were to their clans rather than to each other. Thus marriage could never equal the comfort and warmth of a brother-sister relationship. The arrival of children worsened conditions between the parents, for they fought over the attentions of each child. Meanwhile the young children grew up oblivious to the restrictions of adult society, indulged by the adults, and enjoying their high position.

The Manus woman could never attain much status as a mother, for her children belonged more to her husband and his clan than to her. However, she could gain stature as a medium at the eerie séances at which the ghosts of dead relatives seemed to come whistling down through the darkness. She also had the opportunity to develop into a clever businesswoman, as the Manus system called for much of the trade to be done separately by man and wife—often in competition with each other—with their respective clans.

Sex did not bring a married couple closer, for it was looked upon as a violent shameful act performed in the darkness of night. Girls were taught by their mothers that sex was painful until the first child was born, and unpleasant thereafter. Husbands and wives regarded each other's bodies with shame, and sex play was taboo between man and wife. Such activity was restricted to cousins. When asked if her husband ever touched her breasts, an indignant Manus woman might reply that of course he didn't, that the privilege was reserved for her male cousins.

That confidences were not exchanged between the sexes is illustrated by the astonishing fact that Manus men did not know that their women menstruated. When told that this was the way with women, they shrugged and said that Manus women were different. Likewise, a wife never told her husband when she became pregnant. He was generally the last in the village to know.

Weddings were primarily economic undertakings. Large advance payments of shell money and dog's teeth were made by the boy's clan. At the time of the ceremony the girl's family had to match these payments in pigs and coconut oil.

For her wedding the bride wore a fantastic costume. Her hair was dyed red; her face, arms, and back were painted orange. Bands of dog's teeth were wrapped around her forehead, arms, and breasts; a girdle of dog's teeth held up two heavy shell aprons. Hidden in the arm bands were bits of foreign items such as knives, forks, and spoons, combs and mirrors, or porcelain pipes—objects that were never used except for wedding ceremonies. Long pieces of cloth trailed from the arm bands, as well as bird of paradise feathers. Tiny feather combs were arranged in her dog's-tooth crown. Her earlobes were weighted down with clusters of dog's teeth. As a crowning touch, an 18-inch pendant of shell, bone, and dog's teeth hung from her nose.

Stooped under the weight of this load, the bride was carried in a canoe to her prospective husband's house, where his female relatives stripped her of her finery like a flock of vultures. She spent the night in the hut with her future female in-laws, and the next day she was carried home and dressed again. This time she was carried in a large canoe containing a carved bed. During the day's festivities she remained veiled in the canoe while speeches were made and property distributed. Little girls of three and four would strut about in their first grass skirts, unmindful that they too would some day sit laden with shell and bone in a canoe.

To the accompaniment of drums, the men performed their dances of ceremonial insult, which dared the opposing clan to match their exploits. For the dance, the men replaced their usual loin cloth with a white sea shell as a phallic covering. The object of the rapid leg and body movements was to make the penis swing about wildly from side to side and up and down. At the sidelines naked little boys of four and five were trying to master the difficult technique of swinging nonerect penises about. Boys of ten and twelve gathered in groups to practice, with phallic coverings made of nut shells.

Spiritual life among the Manus revolved around the police functions of the guardian spirit of the male head of the household, usually the spirit of his own father. This spirit, called Sir Ghost, punished with sickness and misfortune those members of his clan who did not observe all the sexual restrictions and complex taboos. Infractions against these rules could be remedied only by public confession.

Within thirty years, many elements of this culture disappeared. The Manus today wear Western clothes; they have moved their homes to dry land and pattern them after army barracks; they are building schools, clinics, churches, and other public facilities.

The great impetus for change resulted from the influx of

troops to the islands during World War II. For a time the Admiralties were occupied by Japan; then the Allies gained control. As many as one million American servicemen lived on these islands —whose native population was a mere fourteen thousand.

The Manus were fascinated by American machines and gadgets. Having been taught from birth to respect property and to learn to do things efficiently, they were naturally impressed by American know-how. They were also impressed by the Americans' attitude toward them, treating them as individuals and not as a separate caste; previous white men had addressed them as "boy." They learned that a respect for property could be combined with a respect for human life, as when the great resources of a United States military hospital were set in action to save a life. The Manus, who valued property so highly, had never thought that it could be used to help people, as well as to prove superiority by providing ostentatious show.

After the war the Admiralty Islands returned to the administration of Australia, but it was obvious that things would never be as they were before. The young men were unwilling to serve as workers for a few years and then return to the village. Before the war most of the Manus had been converted to Roman Catholicism, but now they became restive with the missions. For a time right after the war a version of the Cargo cult, called the Noise, swept through the islands. Along with this essentially hysterical and destructive nativistic cult there developed another movement aimed toward growth and responsibility known as the New Way, or the Paliau Movement.

Its leader, a man named Paliau, a native of the island of Baluan, was not a Manus, but his main strength lay with them since they were the strongest tribe in the area. Gradually Paliau and his followers overcame the opposition of the Australian administrators, who came to see they were a responsible group. The New Way soon won over most of the Catholic converts, although a few still stayed with the missionaries. Paliau's objectives were to bring the good things of the white man to the Manus—democratic government, universal suffrage, schools, clinics, money, and individual and community sense of responsibility. Thus the New Way differed from the Cargo cults, which sought to bring in the white man's wealth and property, but otherwise expel his influence.

Now the young Manus boy goes to school each day instead of going off to be an indentured laborer. The people have learned to speak Neo-Melanesian, a sort of pidgin Manus–English, which is now spoken by all the Melanesians. Their new church is based on Christianity while still retaining elements of the old religion.

Throughout Manus history, from the days of the Sir Ghosts to the time of Roman Catholicism to the present church of the New Way, heavy emphasis has been laid on the confession of sins. This emphasis is still strong today, with confession necessary to alleviate anger—the emotion that warps men's lives—and cure the sins that are thought to cause community deaths.

Whereas in the old days death was believed due to the magic performed by a Sir Ghost as payment for an unconfessed sin, to-day it is believed that sin can directly cause death. A new strain has been put on marriage, for it is now believed that all child deaths are due to the unconfessed sins of the parents. Marriage has improved little, but the children still have an easy time of it.

The old avoidance taboos have vanished, as have the phallic dances and the shell and dog's-tooth costumes. Young people now choose their own mates. From watching American movies the Manus saw that American marriages seemed happy because the partners displayed a great deal of public affection. Manus husbands thereupon ordered their wives to act affectionate, but this has not changed the basic attitude toward sex and marriage.

The same energy and resourcefulness that made the Manus the most prosperous of the tribes in their area a generation ago are now turning them into a twentieth-century people. Today they are attempting to organize their dwellings, work, political setup, and income so as to parallel European-administered towns.

Some of the elements they have chosen to adopt from the West, and the emphasis they have put on certain things, are not what we would expect. This stands as a tribute to the ability of a society to retain its identity by adapting from another culture only those things that fulfill its own needs.

# THE DOBU

Perhaps no area in the world has received so much anthropological investigation of its native peoples as has the South Pacific. And here among the dozens of peoples who have evolved interesting cultures of wide diversity perhaps none are more bizarre than the Melanesian Dobu. These Negroid, bushy-haired people have evolved a culture where suspicion and deceit are the prime factors of human relationship. They spend their lives being persecuted by in-laws, trying to steal their neighbors' yam crops by magic, and never trusting their wives in the presence of another man—with good reason.

These fascinating, emphatically nasty people live on an island of volcanic ash just off the eastern tip of New Guinea. Dobu is part of the D'Entrecasteaux Islands, which are administered by Australia as part of the Territory of Papua. To the north lie the Trobriands, made famous by the writings of pioneer social anthropologist Bronislaw Malinowski. The Dobu people have also been studied by Ruth Benedict and Dr. Reo Fortune.

The Dobu have been declining in numbers since the white men came to their islands. Many of them have been separated from their culture by being recruited as indentured laborers. They are good workers who do not rebel against the scantiness of the rations given them, because the Dobu are used to half starving in their native villages.

But their reputation among their island neighbors is not so pleasant. They are considered to be dangerous and treacherous savages, with diabolic magical powers. Up until the white man intervened, early in the twentieth century, the Dobu were cannibals, whereas few of the neighboring tribes shared this custom.

The Dobu have a complicated social organization based on competition between matrilineal groups; they have no chieftainship, as do their neighbors and the Trobriand islanders, and most other Melanesians. The largest social unit is a district of between four and twenty villages. Each district wages warfare against every other Dobuan district. Until the white man took control, a Dobu rarely ventured into an alien locality except to raid and kill. But it is not to be thought that the people within a district can look to each other for comfort and support. Nothing could be further from the truth. Indeed, death and robbery, either by witchcraft or, less commonly, by physical act, are to be expected from a neighbor. There is only one group to whom a Dobu can turn for assistance and that is his mother's family, who live and work together in their own village and are eventually buried together in the common burial ground in the center of the village.

It is not surprising that marriage is not a very happy state for a Dobu, for he must marry someone outside this trusted mother's line, "mother's milk," or *susu*, as it is called. The married couple spend alternate years in the villages of each other's susus. While among a spouse's susu the mate is constantly tormented by in-laws, who work him or her unmercifully. Furthermore, the man or woman in the other's village is constantly tormented by jealousy, for although one may not marry a member of one's susu, it is an accepted practice to have extramarital relations with them. The only thing that makes it bearable for the neglected spouse is that the next year he can get even. The children are immune from this hatred until they grow up, at which time they are no longer allowed free access to their father's village. If the father dies, the young children immediately stop going to the father's susu. If the mother dies, after a certain period of mourning the father and the children may no longer speak to each other, and the children are brought up by the mother's susu.

Even the marriage itself is contracted in hostility, with the mother of the girl bodily blocking the door so that the young man, who has spent the night with the girl, may not escape. From the time that the Dobu boy and girl reach puberty, and sometimes even before, they are accustomed to free sexual intercourse with adolescents of other households. The young men spend their nights with the unmarried girls, and they remain unattached by spreading their favors widely and leaving the house long before daylight. Eventually the young man tires of his roaming, and settles down to a steady companion; he grows more and more careless about leaving in the morning, until he is finally caught. During the time that he is betrothed he will have to work in the taro and yam gardens of his own mother's family and that of his prospective wife. The wedding ceremony, like other Dobu events, is a sullen gathering ending with the couple's receiving food prepared by their new mothers-in-law.

The Dobu, who are promiscuous all their lives, are convinced that a man and woman never meet alone without sexual intent. For this reason a woman never goes abroad without being chaperoned, because otherwise, if she encounters a man, she would be seduced. Sexual prowess is considered extremely important, and a wife is taught that the best way to keep her husband is to keep him as exhausted as possible. Yet, despite this emphasis on sex, the Dobu are as prudish as the Puritans of early New England. Members of the same sex will never uncover in front of each other, nor does anyone allow himself to be observed when attending to bodily functions. The great volume of promiscuous sex activity is conducted in the utmost secrecy, and if an unmarried girl should bear a child, it is considered a shameful disgrace. Abortion by means of massage or emetic herbs is common. Dr. Malinowski was thus deceived by the prudish Dobu, who assured him that their women were chaste.

Magic holds a uniquely important place among the Dobu. They believe that everything is brought about by it, including sexual desire, disease, death, and the growing of crops. Magical incantations are guarded with great secrecy and are handed down from generation to generation. When the Dobu trade with the Trobrianders, it is the Dobu men who own magic charms who can strike the best bargains.

Only by magic can one's yams be persuaded to remain in his own garden. They believe that at night the tubers travel freely underground while the plants stay in place above ground. The yams return to their home only during midmorning. Therefore cultivation and harvesting are never done during the early morning hours. Magic is used to call one's yams back home from the gardens of others where they have been lured. At the same time, a man attempts to persuade the traveling yams of others to remain in his garden, so a large harvest is an unmistakable sign of skullduggery rather than of good cultivation. Everyone keeps the volume of his harvest a close secret so he will not be bombarded by the retaliatory magic of his neighbors with smaller harvests.

Magic is suspected when a sickness or death occurs. The prime suspect is the spouse of the afflicted one, for who has more opportunity for treachery? If a man is thought near death, he and his wife immediately go to his village so that the surviving wife will be in the power of her husband's susu if she is believed guilty of his death.

The women are feared as witches. A witch carries out her evil intent by flying abroad at night in spirit while her body sleeps at her husband's side. Her special power is that of extracting the spirit from her victim, after which he wilts and soon dies. The men are sorcerers, empowered with the ability to cause death and disease by casting spells on the personal leavings—food, excreta, saliva—of a victim. Certain people are known to possess the ability to cause certain diseases. Therefore, when someone becomes ill with such a disease, the only solution is to seek out the sorcerer who caused it and persuade him with gifts and favors to lift the spell and save the life of the stricken one.

Poisoning is common. It is considered superfluous to cast a magic spell when poison is employed. A man is apt to poison someone whom he suspects of having cast a spell on him. Because of the fear of poisoning, a person outside his own susu will never accept food unless the donor first eats some.

These scheming people, who consider an honest and affectionate man a doddering fool, scarcely conform to the popular image of the inhabitants of the South Sea paradise. And yet they are a facet of the astonishing variety of peoples who exist throughout the world. As Ruth Benedict has pointed out, given all the possible variants on the basic human elements of society, the number of possible combinations that may result is infinite. Each of these combinations is a unique, living society made up of unique human beings.

# *Epilogue*

As they spread throughout the world, the civilizations that rightly or wrongly felt they had reached the height of development—Christianity, Islamism, Buddhism, and, in a different sense, the technological civilization that is now bringing them together—all became tinged with "primitive" ways of life, "primitive" thinking and "primitive" behavior. Without their realizing it, the "primitive" ways have been transforming the higher civilizations from within. For the so-called primitive or archaic peoples do not simply vanish into a vacuum; most are incorporated with greater or lesser speed into the civilization surrounding them. At the same time, the latter takes on a more universal character. Thus primitive people, far from diminishing in importance, concern us more with each passing day.

But as we have seen, relentless pressures spell the demise of our primitive peoples: on the one hand there are the spectacular technological advances that have breached the natural barriers protecting the tribes; on the other, there is the equally spectacular population growth that now threatens mankind with overcrowding, driving him deeper and deeper into areas of the world that were once the exclusive province of the primitive cultures.

On his forays into remote places, civilized man has brought with him the civilized diseases against which a primitive's body may have no defense. The tragic fate of the Urubu, an Indian tribe from northeastern Brazil, is typical of many others. In 1950, only a few years after they were discovered, they contracted the measles. Within a few days, out of the population of 750 there were 160 deaths. An eyewitness has left this stark description:

We found the first village abandoned. All the inhabitants had fled, convinced that if they ran far away they would escape the sickness which they believed was a spirit attacking the villages.

We discovered them in the forest, halted in their flight. Exhausted and shivering with fever in the rain, nearly all of them had fallen victim to the disease. Intestinal and pulmonary complications had so weakened them that they no longer had strength to seek food.

Even water was lacking, and they were dying as much from hunger and thirst as from the disease. The children were crawling about on the forest floor trying to keep the fires alight in the rain and hoping to keep warm. The men lay burning and paralyzed by fever; the women indifferently thrust away their babes seeking the breast.

In addition to infectious diseases, vitamin and other nutritional deficiencies are also a serious problem imposed by encroaching civilization. Motor-vascular disorders, eye lesions, and dental decay, unknown to primitive man when he lived according to his ancient ways, make their appearance when he is confined to villages and forced to accept drastic changes in his diet, particularly modern processed foods. Then even the old and tried traditional remedies, such as charcoal dressings for severe burns, prove useless. Simple diseases to which tribesmen have long been accustomed become extraordinarily virulent.

The near or total annihilation of primitive peoples is also traceable to other, less direct—but no less related—causes, such as the collapse of the social structure or pattern of living. The Kaingang of São Paulo lived by a series of strict social rules. The inhabitants of each village were divided into two groups, on the principle that the men from the first group could marry only women from the second group and vice versa.

When their population diminished, the foundation permitting their survival collapsed. Under the rigid system of the Kaingang, it was no longer possible for every man to find a wife, and many had no choice but celibacy unless they resigned themselves to mating within their own group, which to them was incest; even then their marriage had to be childless. In such cases a whole population can disappear within a few years.

Research must be speeded up to take advantage of the little time that remains to gather information about these vanishing islands of humanity. Such information is vital, for, unlike the natural sciences, the sciences of man cannot originate their own experimentation.

Every type of society, of belief or institution, every way of life, constitutes a ready-made experiment whose preparation has taken thousands of years and as such is irreplaceable. When a community disappears, a door closes forever, locking away knowledge that is unique.

As the remaining time for research grows shorter, as primitive man is to a greater and greater extent absorbed into the mainstream of civilization, the anthopologist finds himself facing a sensitive and difficult problem: the need to dispel the distrust and resentment of research colleagues from societies he formerly studied.

To help dispel these ill feelings, Dr. Claude Lévi-Strauss has proposed that research should henceforth no longer be "one way only"; that, for example, in exchange for continued freedom to investigate, Europeans and Americans should invite African anthropologists and sociologists to come and study their cultures in the same way that Europeans and Americans have studied the Africans.

We have not yet conjured up a civilization where all men—no matter what corner of the globe they inhabit; no matter what their way of life, education, or professional activities; no matter what their age, beliefs, sympathies, or aversions—are, to the very roots of their consciousness, totally intelligible to all other men. So long as the ways of thinking or acting of some men perplex other men, it will be rewarding to meditate upon the differences.

# PHOTOGRAPH CREDITS

# INDEX

(For photographs see list on pages xi-xiii.)

267